WORLDS TOGETHER, WORLDS APART

VOLUME 1

A Companion Reader

WORLDS TOGETHER, WORLDS APART

VOLUME 1

A Companion Reader

EDITED BY

ELIZABETH POLLARD
CLIFFORD ROSENBERG

W · W · NORTON & COMPANY
NEW YORK · LONDON

W. W. Norton & Company has been independent since its founding in 1923, when William Warder Norton and Mary D. Herter Norton first published lectures delivered at the People's Institute, the adult education division of New York City's Cooper Union. The firm soon expanded its program beyond the Institute, publishing books by celebrated academics from America and abroad. By midcentury, the two major pillars of Norton's publishing program—trade books and college texts—were firmly established. In the 1950s, the Norton family transferred control of the company to its employees, and today—with a staff of four hundred and a comparable number of trade, college, and professional titles published each year—W. W. Norton & Company stands as the largest and oldest publishing house owned wholly by its employees.

Book design and composition by Westchester Publishing Services
Production managers: Andy Ensor and Linda Prather

ISBN: 978-0-393-93777-0 (v. 1)—ISBN: 978-0-393-93778-7 (v. 2)

W. W. Norton & Company, Inc., 500 Fifth Avenue, New York, NY 10110
    wwnorton.com

W. W. Norton & Company Ltd., Castle House, 75/76 Wells Street,
London W1T 3QT

1 2 3 4 5 6 7 8 9 0

ABOUT THE EDITORS

ELIZABETH POLLARD (Ph.D. University of Pennsylvania) is associate professor at San Diego State University and a historian of the ancient world, in particular of Roman and Greek civilizations. Her research on witchcraft accusations against women in the Roman Empire and Roman-Indian trade employs the methodologies of history, religious studies, classics, and women's studies. She was named SDSU Senate Distinguished Professor for Teaching Excellence in 2013. Her pedagogical interests include the effectiveness of web-based technology and world history in teaching, learning, and writing about ancient history. She teaches the world history survey regularly, and serves on the Executive Council of the World History Association.

CLIFFORD ROSENBERG (Ph.D. Princeton University) is associate professor of European history at City College and the Graduate Center, CUNY. He specializes in the history of modern France and its empire and is the author of *Policing Paris: The Origins of Modern Immigration Control Between the Wars*. He is currently studying the spread of tuberculosis between France and Algeria since the mid-nineteenth century.

For Brad, Amelia, and Jack
—*EAP*

For Kim and Henry
—*CR*

CONTENTS

CHAPTER 5 | WORLDS TURNED INSIDE OUT, 1000–350 BCE

CHAPTER 6 | SHRINKING THE AFRO-EURASIAN WORLD, 350–100 BCE

Chapter 10 | Becoming "The World," 1000–1300 CE

Casebook | Mobilizing for War in the Age of the Mongols

CHAPTER 11 | CRISES AND RECOVERY IN AFRO-EURASIA, 1300S–1500S

PREFACE

Worlds Together, Worlds Apart sets the standard for instructors who want to teach a globally integrated world history survey course. Each chapter of the text—of both the Full and Concise editions—revolves around significant world historical moments, situated within a clear thematic and chronological framework. The text explores the forces that brought major regions and cultural traditions into dialogue with one another; bringing some together while isolating others, bringing worlds together and giving rise to new forms of inequality at the same time.

In creating *Worlds Together, Worlds Apart, Concise* (2015), we intensified world-historical themes and balanced the global coverage that explained and illustrated those themes, all the while streamlining the prose and heightening the narrative. We also wished to provide written and visual sources that advanced our goals of thematic clarity, global coverage, and compelling storytelling. The "Competing Perspectives" and "Interpreting Visual Evidence" features we developed for each chapter of the Concise edition were the result of those efforts. These features offered multiple perspectives on a central issue highlighted in a given chapter's narrative: for instance, Chapter 1, which is focused on "becoming human" and where to begin the story of world history, includes various creation narratives; Chapter 6, with its emphasis on the early silk roads (350 BCE–100 CE), offers for analysis images of coinage from across the Eurasian landmass; Chapter 10, "Becoming 'The World,' 1000–1300," balances the literary accounts of world travelers and the visual evidence of contemporary mapmakers; Chapter 13, "Worlds Entangled, 1600–1750," provides a range of narratives and statistics on the Atlantic slave trade and images of material objects used by elites in various settings around the world with wealth from the slave trade; while Chapter 20, "The Three-World Order, 1940–1975," includes propaganda posters from World War II that show how belligerents on all sides mobilized consent and demonized enemies and contrasts them with texts from leading anti-colonial nationalists who challenged the resulting Cold War order. This new edition of *Worlds Together, Worlds Apart: A Companion Reader* has given us the opportunity to go into greater depth and to provide longer selections for instructors who want to explore themes more extensively.

The preface to the first edition of *Worlds Together, Worlds Apart: A Companion Reader* (2011), compiled by Kenneth L. Pomeranz (University of Chicago, formerly at UC–Irvine), James B. Given (UC–Irvine), and Laura J. Mitchell (UC–Irvine), laid out a number of principles that guided their choice of sources. These principles included avoiding the "obvious" text when another text might make the case more effectively, incorporating visual sources when possible, seeking out non-elite evidence that illustrates how themes play out in different places, and selecting sources that are particularly teachable and varied in genre. In revising the *Companion Reader* to create this second edition, we retained these exemplary principles. At the same time, we endeavored to bring the selections in the reader more in line with the themes, and in some instances the periodization, of both the Full and Concise editions of the text. While the primary sources have been selected with a particular eye to supporting *Worlds Together, Worlds Apart*, they can also be deployed on their own as resources for exploring with students the many significant themes central to understanding global history.

To that end, Volume 1 of the newly revised reader contains eighty-one sources, thirty-four of which are new to this second edition. As with the first edition, the new sources are introduced with headnotes that contextualize genre, authorship, and themes. Guiding questions follow each source in order to help students analyze their world historical significance in a way that complements the themes traced in *Worlds Together, Worlds Apart*. In lieu of a separate casebook on women, new sources that bring women and/or gender to the forefront have been incorporated throughout Volume 1.

Examples include new sources on Hadza grandmothering as a model for understanding *Homo erectus* resource-gathering and childcare (Chapter 1), a letter detailing the struggles among the female members of a drought-stricken household in 2000 BCE-Egypt (Casebook 1), Homer's catalog of ships that sailed to Troy ca. 1200 BCE, which gives a glimpse of gendered stereotypes in Mycenaean and Archaic Greece (Chapter 3), Livy's reporting of Cato's anxiety about women's participation in political debates as the negative consequence of Hellenism's influence in Rome of the second century BCE (Chapter 6), and Ouyang Xui's description of the career of the Tang-period eunuch Zhang Chengye (Chapter 9). Replacing the casebook on women is a collection of sources that explores the relationship between humans and the environment in the second millennium BCE. The interactions between humans and the environment is a recurring theme highlighted throughout the Concise edition, and is particularly striking around 2000 BCE, when significant environmental changes appear to have adversely affected—and in at least one case, brought to an abrupt downfall—civilization in each of the major river basin civilizations of Afro-Eurasia, from Egypt to Mesopotamia to the Indus Valley and beyond to East Asia. Other notable additions to this revised second edition of Volume 1 include: Donald Johanson's account of his 1974 discovery of the *Australopithecus afarensis* remains later nicknamed "Lucy" in Chapter 1; selections from the Amarna Letters that elucidate the diplomatic relationships among Egyptian, Babylonian, and Hittite leaders in the late 14th century BCE, in Chapter 3; a pairing of the Jewish and Neo-Assyrian accounts of Sennacherib's siege of Jerusalem around 700 BCE that offer competing contemporary reporting of the same event, in Chapter 4; Roman and Han pay records from the first century CE, in Chapter 7; and an excerpt from *Njal's Saga* to illustrate Icelandic migrations around 1000 CE, in Chapter 9. Beyond the broader incorporation of women and gender and the introduction of the new casebook, in some instances sources were retained but moved to a different chapter where there is a better fit with the themes and chronology. Examples include: moving the Sermons and the Teachings of the Buddha from Chapter 6 to Chapter 5, to fit the overarching theme—new religions and philosophies in the first millennium BCE —of the reader and the corresponding chapter in the Full and Concise editions; shifting Ashoka's edicts from Chapter 5 to Chapter 6, for better chronological and thematic fit, namely the spread of Buddhism along the silk roads; and placing Pliny's the Elder's description of the Seres in Chapter 7, which lays the groundwork for both transregional and comparative study of the Roman Empire and the Han Dynasty.

Changes to Volume 2 of the *Companion Reader* also work to bring the reader into closer alignment with the Full and Concise editions by amplifying central themes. Notable examples include gender, with new documents on the Mughal harem in Chapter 12; on gender and justice from an eighteenth-century Chinese county magistrate in Chapter 14; and on Margaret Sanger's views on race and birth control in Chapter 19. The environment receives additional coverage with a selection from Rachel Carson's *Silent Spring* in Chapter 20 and Pope Francis' recent encyclical *Laudato Si'* in Chapter 21. Other additions include official records from the Ming Shi-lu (明實錄) on one of Zheng He's voyages, in Chapter 11; the notebooks of Thomas Thistlewood, on the brutality of Caribbean sugar plantations, in Chapter 13; an account of the Boxer Rebellion by a Chinese Christian in Chapter 18; and an original translation of an essay by the French demographer Alfred Sauvy, in which he coined the term Third World, in Chapter 20.

In sum, the overriding goal throughout has been to offer a range of different kinds of sources, from the famous to the obscure, from the elite to the ordinary, to capture as many different kinds of perspectives as possible and to give students experience working with different kinds of texts. We hope these sources will enrich classroom discussions and provide the basis for building analytical skills that enable students to see the world from a wide variety of perspectives. By engaging seriously with this material, by confronting multiple perspectives and points of view, students will learn about the past and ultimately come away with a new appreciation of the complexity of the world around them today.

Elizabeth Ann Pollard, San Diego, CA
Clifford Rosenberg, New York, NY

Acknowledgments

We would like to thank the Irvine team that prepared the first edition, Alan Karras for his thoughtful feedback and suggestions, and our students for shaping this volume and teaching us what works best in the classroom. We are grateful to Jon Durbin, Travis Carr, and Elizabeth Trammell at W. W. Norton for their advice and efforts tracking down rights to sometimes obscure materials.

WORLDS TOGETHER, WORLDS APART

VOLUME 1

A Companion Reader

Chapter 1

BECOMING HUMAN

Finding Lucy (3.2 million years ago and 1974)

The past 125 years have seen numerous groundbreaking paleoanthropological finds that have supplied vital new pieces to the emerging puzzle
of human evolution. Eugene Dubois brought to light the nearly
2-million-year-old "Java Man" (*Homo erectus*) in Indonesia in 1891. Java
Man was remarkable for its big brain, upright walking (bipedalism),
mastery of fire, wide-ranging food consumption and extensive migration.
Raymond Dart discovered the 3.3- to 2.1-million-year-old fossil of the
"Taung child" (*Australopithecus africanus*) in southern Africa in 1924.
This human ancestor, the first to be found in Africa and whose molars
had only just begun to show, was a three-year-old child who may have
died from an attack by a bird of prey, as evidenced in part by peck marks
around the eye sockets of the skull. Mary Leakey found the 2.3- to
1.2-million-year-old remains of "Dear Boy" (*Paranthropus boisei*) in the
east African Olduvai Gorge in 1959. This species' thickly enameled teeth
and strong jaw suggest it could eat tough-to-chew foods like nuts and
roots, a feature that may have allowed Dear Boy to get through times
when more easily consumed food sources were scarce. Tim White's team
unearthed the 4.4-million-year-old "Ardi" (*Ardipithecus ramidus*) in
Middle Awash, Ethiopia, in 1994. The pelvis, hands, and feet of this
nearly 4-foot, 110-pound female have prompted arguments that she was
comfortable moving through the trees using both her hands and feet,
as well as walking with two feet on the ground.

Despite the intrigue of these finds, arguably no other set of hominid
remains found before or after is as renowned as "Lucy" (*Australopithecus
afarensis*). The 3.2-million-year-old fossil hominid captured the world's
imagination almost as soon as she was discovered in 1974 by Donald
Johanson. In the following passage, Johanson recalls the thrill of

discovery, the "friendly rivalry" amongst paleoanthropologists, and the contentious initial presentation of his classification of Lucy as a new hominid species.

Whenever I tell the story, I am instantly transported back to the thrilling moment when I first saw [Lucy] thirty-four years ago on the sandy slopes of Hadar in Ethiopia's Afar region. I can feel the searing noonday sun beating down on my shoulders, the beads of sweat on my forehead, the dryness of my mouth—and then the shock of seeing a small fragment of bone lying inconspicuously on the ground. Most dedicated fossil hunters spend the majority of their lives in the field without finding anything remarkable, and there I was, a thirty-one-year-old newly-minted Ph.D., staring at my childhood dream at my feet.

Sunday, November 24, 1974, began, as it usually does for me in the field, at dawn. I had slept well in my tent, with the glittering stars visible through the small screen that kept out the mosquitoes, and as sunrise announced a brilliant new day, I got up and went to the dining tent for a cup of thick, black Ethiopian coffee. Listening to the morning sounds of camp life, I planned with some disinclination the day's activities: catching up on correspondence, fossil cataloging, and a million other tasks that had been set aside to accommodate a visit from anthropologists Richard and Mary Leakey. I looked up as Tom Gray, my grad student, appeared.

"I'm plotting the fossil localities on the Hadar map," he said. "Can you show me Afar Locality 162, where the pig skull was found last year?"

"I have a ton of paperwork and am not sure I want to leave camp today."

"Can you do the paperwork later?"

SOURCE: Donald C. Johanson and Kate Wong, *Lucy's Legacy: The Quest for Human Origins* (New York: Harmony Books, 2009), pp. 3–21. [Editorial insertions appear in square brackets—*Ed.*]

"Even if I start it now I'll be doing it later," I grumbled. But something inside—a gut sense that I had learned to heed—said I should put the paperwork aside and head to the outcrops with Tom.

A couple of geologists joined us in one of our old, dilapidated Land Rovers, and in a cloud of dust we headed out to the field. I sat in the passenger seat enjoying the passing landscape peppered with animal fossils . . . Tom put the Land Rover through its paces, and as we picked up speed in the sandy washes, my mind switched gears into fossil-finding mode . . . Tom and I threaded our way along smaller and smaller gullies.

"Somewhere around here," I said. "Pull over." Then I laughed as it occurred to me that in the remote desert you don't have to pull over, you just stop driving. We got out and spent a few minutes locating the cairn that had been left to mark the pig skull's locality, a little plateau of clay and silt sediments bordered by harder layers of sandstone. A year earlier, a geologist had been out on a mapping mission and the plateau was obvious on the aerial photographs we had toted along; otherwise we might have overlooked it. After carefully piercing a pinhole into the aerial photo to mark the spot and labeling it "162" on the reverse side, we lingered. I was reluctant to return to camp and my paperwork. Even though the area was known to be fossil poor, we decided to look around while we were there. But after two hours of hunting all we had to show were some unremarkable fossil antelope and horse teeth, a bit of a pig skull, and a fragment of monkey jaw.

"I've had it. When do we head back?" Tom said.

"Right now." With my gaze still glued to the ground, I cut across the midportion of the plateau toward the Land Rover. Then a glint caught my eye, and when I turned my head I saw a two-inch-long, light brownish gray fossil fragment shaped like a wrench, which my knowledge of osteology told me instantly was part of an elbow. I knelt and picked it up for closer inspection. As I examined it, an image clicked into my brain and a subconscious template announced hominid. . . . The only other thing it could have been was monkey, but it lacked the telltale flare on the back that characterizes monkey elbows. Without a doubt, this was the elbow end of a hominid ulna, the larger of the two bones in the forearm. Raising my eyes, I scanned the immediate surroundings and spotted other bone fragments of similar color—a piece of thighbone, rib fragments, segments of the backbone, and, most important, a shard of skull vault.

"Tom, look!" I showed him the ulna, then pointed at the fragments. Like me, he dropped to a crouch. With his jaw hanging open, he picked up a chunk of mandible that he wordlessly held out for me to see. "Hominid!" I gushed. "All hominid!" Our excitement mounted as we examined every splinter of bone. "I don't believe this! Do you believe this?" we shouted over and over. Drenched in sweat, we hugged each other and whooped like madmen.

"I'm going to bring the ulna to camp," I said. "We'll come back for the others." I wanted to mark the exact location of each bone fragment scattered on the landscape, but there were too many pieces and time was short.

"Good idea. Don't lose it," Tom joked, as I carefully wrapped the ulna in my bandanna. I decided to take a fragment of lower jaw, too, for good measure. I marked the exact spots where the bones had lain, scribbled a few words in my field notebook, and then got back into the Land Rover.

* * *

Tom announced our arrival [at camp] by honking the horn, and as we pulled to a stop our inquisitive teammates surrounded the car.

I jumped out of the Land Rover and everyone followed me to the work area, where a large tent fly protected our plywood worktables. Still in a state of semi-disbelief, I sat and unpacked the precious remains. Reassured that they were in fact real, I sighed with relief.

Everyone leaned over to see the tiny fragments of arm and jaw. The questions came fast and furious. Is there more? Where'd you find it? How did you find it? And then there was a stunned silence as the import of what we'd found sunk in. It hit me that if I had walked just a few more paces and looked to my left rather than my right, the bones would still be there on the slope. And in the ever-changing landscape of the Afar, a single desert thunderstorm could have washed them off the plateau, over a cliff and into oblivion, forever.

*　*　*

We celebrated the discovery with a delicious dinner of roasted goat and panfried potatoes washed down with a case of Bati beer my students had somehow managed to smuggle into camp. Conversation became less animated and more technical, focusing on morphology and size. I felt from the beginning that the fossils belonged to a single individual because there was no duplication of parts in the remains we collected; the pieces all had the same proportions and exhibited the same fossilization color. I further argued that the skeleton was a female specimen of *Australopithecus*—a primitive human forebear—because of the small size of the bones relative to those of other australopithecines. All australopithecines were sexually dimorphic; which is to say males and females exhibited physical differences beyond those pertaining to the sex organs. So if the lightly built ulna we discovered were from a male, then a female would have to be unbelievably tiny.

While we were all talking, *Sgt. Pepper's Lonely Hearts Club Band* was playing on a small Sony tape deck. When "Lucy in the Sky with Diamonds" came on, my girlfriend Pamela Alderman, who had come to spend some time in the field with me, said, "Why don't you call her Lucy?" I smiled politely at the suggestion, but I didn't like it because I thought it was frivolous to refer to such an important find simply as Lucy. Nicknaming hominid fossils was not unheard of, however. Mary and Louis Leakey, giants in the field of paleoanthropology, dubbed a flattened hominid skull found in Tanzania's Olduvai Gorge "Twiggy," and a specimen their son Jonathan found received the moniker "Jonny's Child." But most of the scientists I knew wouldn't give their fossils a cute name based on a song by the Beatles. The next morning, however, everyone wanted to know if we were going to the Lucy site. Someone asked how tall Lucy was. Another inquired how old I thought Lucy was when she died. As I sat there eating my breakfast of peanut butter and jelly on toast, I conceded that the name Lucy had a better ring to it than A.L. 288, the locality number that had been assigned to the site.

At my request, the government representative from the Antiquities Administration who had escorted our expedition sent word to the director general of the Ministry of Culture, Bekele Negussie. He arrived a few days later with some of his colleagues. While I answered their questions, I resisted referring to our australopithecine as Lucy because I was uncomfortable about an Ethiopian fossil bearing an English name. When the team returned that afternoon from the site bursting with news of more Lucy fragments, additional information about Lucy, endless speculations about Lucy, my discomfort grew. After dinner Bekele and I sat outside the dining tent looking up at a brilliant starlit sky. I talked about the implications of the discovery, how it might impact prevailing theories about hominid evolution. And we discussed arrangements for a press announcement in Addis Ababa in December.

He listened in silence, then regarded me very seriously and said, "You know, she is an Ethiopian. She needs an Ethiopian name."

"Yes!" I agreed, relieved. "What do you suggest?"

"Dinkinesh is the perfect name for her."

I mentally inventoried my Amharic vocabulary, which was just enough to shop for basics, greet people, ask directions, and, most important, order a cup of the best coffee in the world. The word *Dinkinesh* wasn't there. "What does it mean?"

With a broad smile, as if he were naming his own child, he answered. "Dinkinesh means 'you are marvelous.'"

He was right, it was the perfect name. Of course, today most of the world, including nearly every Ethiopian I have spoken to, calls her Lucy. And Lucy is the name that has appeared in crossword puzzles, on *Jeopardy!,* in cartoons, and on African Red Bush Tazo tea bags. In Ethiopia she has lent her name to numerous coffee shops, a rock band, a typing school, a fruit juice bar, and a political magazine. There is even an annual Lucy Cup soccer competition in Addis Ababa. Once, while driving through the town of Kombolcha on the way back to Addis after a field season, years after the discovery, I spotted a small sign that said LUSSY BAR. I brought the car to a screeching halt and my colleagues and I went in to have a beer. When we asked the proprietress how the place got its name, she explained in a solemn voice that many years ago a young American found a skeleton named Lucy in the Afar region, and that she took great pride in naming her bar after the fossil that proved Ethiopia's status as the original homeland to all people. With a grin, I told her I was the American who had found Lucy. She shrieked in delight and insisted that we have our picture taken together to mount on the wall. I sent the photo to her, and for all I know, it hangs there still. But sometimes I still think of Lucy as Dinkinesh, because she truly is marvelous.

At the end of the 1974 field season, Lucy, painstakingly wrapped and packed in a cardboard box, made the day-and-a-half journey from Hadar to the National Museum of Ethiopia in Addis Ababa. Lucy was expected, and when my colleagues and I pulled up to the museum in my Land Rover, the director, Mamo Tessema, and his curatorial staff greeted us warmly. The cardboard box, a temporary home for Lucy, was whisked off and locked in a carefully guarded room.

Over the next few days I worked with Woldesenbet, the no-nononsense collections manager, to officially tally every fragment and formally catalog Lucy as part of the National Museum of Ethiopia's collections. The entire Ministry of Culture was abuzz with the news that she was now in Addis Ababa, and Bekele and the minister made preparations for her official coming-out party, a public announce-ment at the ministry. A throng of scientists, antiquities people, min-istry officials, university faculty, and journalists jammed the room that had been specially prepared by the ministry. Resplendent on a black cloth, Lucy was an instant hit. Everyone in the room jostled to catch a glimpse of her bones.

The press conference was intense, and Bekele had to finally call a stop to the questions. Three million two hundred thousand years after her death her image would grace the front page of newspapers all over the world. Not exactly an overnight success, I thought. In a way, we had both arrived, Lucy and I. Her path to that press con-ference was quite different from mine, to be sure. But the reason we were there together was because we had met in the right place at the right time.

*   *   *

Friendly rivalry is at times a good thing because it motivates us all to work a little harder, a little longer, and take chances we otherwise might not take. Chief among my rivals was Richard Leakey, son of Louis and Mary, who had made some spectacular finds at Lake Turkana in Kenya, including a specimen known as 1470, then considered the earliest evidence of *Homo.* Tall and lanky with sunbleached hair and boyish good looks, Richard exuded authority and confidence. We'd met several times, and the previous year I'd brought the fossil knee to Nairobi so that his team at the National Museums of Kenya could make a cast of it. He graciously allowed me to see their hominid fossil collection, including specimens that hadn't been published yet or even announced. Honored to be a member of the "inner circle" of scholars who were granted such access, I felt it was now my turn to return that favor, so I invited Richard; his wife, Meave; and his mother, Mary, to Hadar. A licensed pilot, he flew to Ethiopia in his own plane and landed at our hastily cleared airstrip, dubbed Hadar International Airport. In addition to Meave and Mary, Richard brought his brother-in-law, a paleontologist named John Harris. As they walked Hadar's astonishingly fossil-rich hillsides, I enjoyed watching their dumbstruck expressions, thinking that was how I must have looked to Maurice [Maurice Taieb, French geologist working in the Afar region] when I first came here.

Over dinner we debated the fossil identification of the new hominid jaws that Alemayehu [Alemayehu Asfaw, researcher at the Ethiopian Ministry of Culture] had found. Richard favored classifying the larger one as part of a member of our own genus, *Homo,* whereas I thought it belonged to a male australopithecine. We weren't just arguing about the jaws, though. Richard believed that the 1470 skull was 3 million years old. But like many other experts in the field, I suspected that the geological dating was wrong because the animal fossils found along with it, particularly the pigs, were identical to those from the Omo that were dated at about 2 million years. Although we disagreed, I was thrilled to be exchanging ideas with some of the giants in the field. The stimulating conversation, which included students and other Hadar team members, left everyone excited but exhausted.

On Saturday we drove Richard and his group out to the airstrip, helped them load up, and waved good-bye as they took off for the flight back to Kenya. The following day I found Lucy.

During the 1974 field season at Hadar, Ethiopia's emperor, Haile Selassie, was overthrown by the Derg, a violent military junta who capitalized on Selassie's decreasing popularity following a poorly managed famine in the very region where we were working. I was deeply concerned about how this turn of events would impact our future plans to work at Hadar. Sure enough, when we returned in 1975, the political atmosphere had changed from calm to violence and fear. With increased funding from both the United States and France, the IARE (International Afar Research Expedition) team had grown to include more students and more specialists in paleontology and geology. I had always been concerned about medical issues in the field—dysentery, malaria, snake bites, appendicitis— so I was pleased when Mike Bush, a young, softspoken medical doctor with a passion for archaeology, expressed interest in joining my expedition. Not only was Mike a great guy to have in camp, as well as a competent physician, he also turned out to be a keen-eyed and avid surveyor. Late in the morning on November 2, Mike's dedication paid off. I was in the middle of a conversation with David Brill, a *National Geographic* photographer, when Mike interrupted us to say that he had found what he thought might be some hominid teeth. David, a tall, skinny guy from Wisconsin, was excited because after hounding me for days, this might just be the photo op he had been pushing for—a hominid find. We followed Mike back to the spot.

"Right there," Mike said, pointing. I crouched, squinted, and was amazed to see two gray teeth embedded almost invisibly in gray stone. How had he managed to spot them? "Upper premolars," he added.

I grinned, looking up at David. "Here's the hominid I promised you."

* * *

Hoping for a noteworthy discovery, Maurice had persuaded a French film crew to spend most of the field season with us. One of them had positioned herself upslope from us near a little bush, and suddenly she called down to me, *"Quels sont ceux-ci?"* She was holding up a couple of fossils, and as I approached her, much to my astonishment, I could see that one was a heel bone and the other a femur, both unmistakably hominid.

"Could this be another skeleton?" I yelled, and everyone scrambled up the steep hillside. It turned out to be a mother lode of hominid fossils: During the rest of that season and the next, location A.L. 333 furnished more than two hundred fossils, including a partial baby skull, portions of an articulated foot, some articulated hand bones, most of an adult male brain case, parts of faces, and numerous mandible fragments. Together these represented, in our best estimate, at least thirteen individuals—nine adults and four children or infants. From the title of my 1976 *National Geographic* article, the 333 collection was dubbed "the First Family."

Maurice speculated after careful inspection of the geological strata that the fossil-bearing layer was the result of a single geological event such as a flash flood; a snapshot of a group of hominids who lived, died, and were buried together. Unlike the usual discoveries of single specimens, the 333 assemblage offered unprecedented insight into the anatomy not only of a single species but of individuals who had actually known one another millions of years ago. Again, I marveled at the circumstances that had led to the discovery. Had I turned down Mike's request to join our expedition, the well-concealed teeth might not have been found, and A.L. 333 could have gone unnoticed.

By 1977 Ethiopia was under the ruthless leadership of Mengistu Haile Mariam, and it was too dangerous to conduct fieldwork. I was now the curator of physical anthropology at the Cleveland Museum of Natural History, and the major part of my job was to oversee the study of the unmatched hominid harvest from Hadar. The process involved cleaning the stone matrix from each piece of bone in order to obtain a clear picture of its surface anatomy, taking color and black-and-white record photos, molding and casting each specimen, as well as describing each fragment in meticulous detail for publication. All of this had to be accomplished by 1980, when the fossils would be returned to the National Museum of Ethiopia for safekeeping.

I assembled a team—consulting experts, researchers, students, and colleagues—to systematically undertake a comprehensive study of the Hadar collection.

* * *

While we were working on detailed descriptions of the bones in early June 1977, I was unexpectedly invited to present an evaluation of the Hadar hominids at a Nobel Symposium in Sweden. Convened by the Royal Swedish Academy of Sciences to address the "Current Argument on Early Man," the symposium commemorated the two hundredth anniversary of the death of the Swedish botanist Carolus Linnaeus, whose taxonomy (the practice of describing, classifying, and assigning Latinized binomial names to all biological organisms, living or extinct, for placement in a hierarchical system) is still the basis of modern classification. I could think of no occasion more fitting than a Nobel Symposium to present our results. My parents had emigrated from Sweden in the early 1900s, and I felt honored to deliver a paper in the country of my ancestors. I knew that some of paleoanthropology's most accomplished scholars would be in the audience listening carefully for speculative claims or factual errors.

* * *

Richard Leakey opened the conference [in May 1978] with a relatively short talk on his work at Lake Turkana in Kenya, describing the many hominid discoveries found there. Then it was my turn to walk to the podium. With my stomach in knots, I presented my paper, "Early African Hominid Phylogenesis: A Re-evaluation," describing the Hadar hominid collection and delivering evidence that they represented the same species as fossils found at Laetoli, in Tanzania, by Richard's mother, Mary. I made my case that all of the fossils bore more primitive anatomical features than any other known hominid species. And then I announced that these hominids belonged to a new species: *Australopithecus afarensis*. As I listened to my words reverberating through the small auditorium, I thought about the sixteen-year-old who dreamed of finding the missing link: He was now standing, dressed in a three-piece suit, before the most distinguished audience on the planet, publicly pronouncing Lucy's scientific name for the first time. It was a provocative thing to do. Many researchers thought that the fossils were simply east African versions of *A. africanus*.

From the sound of people shuffling in their seats and a few audible aspirations I could sense the immediate skepticism. My mouth went dry and I took a sip of water. In my next slide I showed a redrawing of the human family tree and elaborated on the major implications of the new species for understanding the shape of that tree. I was fully aware that most of the assembled favored placing Dart's Taung baby, *A. africanus*, at the base of the tree, the common ancestor to all later hominids, including modern humans. But I boldly maintained that it was now time to relegate *A. africanus* to an extinct side branch of human evolution, and to position *A. afarensis* as the trunk of the tree, the last common ancestor to all post-3-million-year-old hominids. Dead silence. I took another sip of water, the lights came on, and Carl Gustaf Bernhard, the moderator, called for questions. Not a single hand went up. The silence was broken when the moderator suggested that we break for high tea.

During the remaining days of the symposium I continued to argue the main points of my paper, but most of the guests were unconvinced. How could I be sure that all the Hadar hominids were of a single species, they wondered. Based upon what evidence did I put Hadar and Laetoli fossils in the same species? I knew that my colleagues and I faced months of work, possibly years, before our conclusions were accepted and Lucy could assume her proper position on the human family tree.

Questions

1. Johanson recollects the serendipity of his find: "It hit me that if I had walked just a few more paces and looked to my left rather than my right, the bones would still be there on the slope. And in the ever-

changing landscape of the Afar, a single desert thunderstorm could have washed them off the plateau, over a cliff and into oblivion, forever." What does Johanson's chance discovery of Lucy, described more fully in the extended passage, suggest about the challenges inherent in collecting the evidence for human evolution?

2. How do paleoanthropologists, like Johanson, the Leakeys, and Tim White, gather their evidence and construct their arguments?

3. As compared with Java Man, the Taung child, Dear Boy, and Ardi, why do you think Lucy holds such a prominent place in the story of human evolution?

New Skulls and a "Bushy" Human Family Tree (7 million years ago and 2002)

On July 11, 2002, reports about the Toumai skull found in Central Africa and published that day by French anthropologist Michel Brunet in the journal *Nature* grabbed headlines. "Fossil Unearthed in Africa Pushes Back Human Origins" (John Noble Wilford, *New York Times*) and "Skull Alters Notions of Human Origins" (Tim Friend, *USA Today*) were emblazoned on the front pages of newspapers. The find, taxonomically classified as *Sahelanthropus tchadensis*, stunned the world of paleoanthropology and beyond because of its age (nearly 7 million years old), its location (in Chad, not in eastern or southern Africa where other major finds, like Taung child, Dear Boy, and Lucy, had been located), and its mix of chimp-like and hominid features. The Toumai skull was chimp-like in size, but had the smaller teeth, with thicker enamel, that one would expect of a human ancestor. Similarly surprising was the argument by researchers that the spinal column of Toumai went into the base of the cranium at an angle that would suggest *Sahelanthropus tchadensis* walked upright.

What was most groundbreaking about the find, however, was that it forced anthropologists to fundamentally rethink the hominid family tree. The following article from *USA Today* (July 11, 2002), the day the Toumai skull story was published, offers insight into how stunned prominent paleoanthropologists were by *Sahelanthropus tchadensis* and how they were beginning to come to grips with what the find meant for the picture of human evolution. One of those scholars, Ian Tattersall, who was quoted in the 2002 article as saying, "We've got it all wrong," has since sketched out a new "tentative hominid family tree," also included here.

The discovery of yet another human ancestor—this one the oldest so far at 6 million to 7 million years—will have paleontologists rushing back to the drawing board to design yet another human family tree. . . .

Over the past few decades, the evolutionary family tree has morphed from an oak with a nice straight trunk and neat branches into something more like an unmanicured hedge. The new discovery by Michel Brunet and colleagues from nearly a dozen different institutions will make the tree of human origins even more confusing, experts say.

Where different ancestors are placed on the tree is a matter of contentious debate among scientific camps. Lines between various hominids—human ancestors—have been drawn and redrawn with each new addition to the human family bush.

Humans were once thought to have evolved from Neanderthals, but the evidence is pretty clear today that Neanderthal, while related as a member of the group *homo,* was of a different lineage. Neanderthal vanished about 30,000 years ago along with *Homo erectus.* Modern humans—like us—have been alone on the planet for only a short period of our 200,000-year or so history. Remember that classic drawing with the silhouette of an ape at one end and a human at the other? It had Neanderthal as an evolutionary step behind us. A more accurate representation should have Neanderthal, *Homo erectus* and *Homo sapiens* walking side by side.

Ian Tattersall, curator of anthropology at the American Museum of Natural History in New York, made a sojourn around the world a

---

few years ago to examine personally every hominid fossil that has been found. Rick Potts, head of paleontology at the Smithsonian's National Museum of Natural History, recalls bumping into Tattersall outside a small museum in east Africa. Tattersall was sitting alone on a bench, head in hands, in apparent distress.

"He said, 'Rick, we've got it all wrong,'" Potts says.

How so? Tattersall had arrived at the conclusion, based on more careful observation of their structures, that many of the fossils presumed to be directly related to each other were, in fact, from different groups. "And there [are] a lot more species out there than we have had the courage to recognize," Tattersall says.

Tattersall discusses the latest theories about human origins in his latest book, *The Monkey in the Mirror: Essays on the Science of Human Evolution,* and makes the case that the family tree is a bushy one indeed.

He and many other leading paleontologists believe the world once was populated by many different creatures, neither ape nor quite yet human, that were living at the same time and competing for food and resources.

"There are lots of different ways to be a hominid, and ours is only one of the them," Tattersall says. "The new skull will have to be added to the hominid tree, but there is no way you can shoehorn this discovery into any scenario that exists today."

The newly discovered skull is dated at between 6 million and 7 million years old, based on estimates of the age of surrounding fossilized fauna. Most experts have accepted the date as solid.

From behind, it looks like a chimpanzee, but its face is flat, more like human ancestors that lived about 1.5 million years ago. Its teeth are small like a chimpanzee's, but the enamel is thicker like that of hominids. Its nose also is like those of later hominids, and the spot where the spinal cord would have been is moved forward, similar to hominids known to walk upright. Also of note is a pronounced brow ridge found only on hominids. Paleontologist Bernard Wood, who viewed the new skull, known as Toumai, says it illustrates the conundrum facing scientists: The skull is the oldest ever found, but it has features of a modern face not seen again on fossils until about 1.5 million years ago. If it is a direct human ancestor, then everything else in between must be regarded as mere sideshows in the drama of hominid and human evolution. "That's a lot of babies to throw out with a lot of bath water," he says.

More likely, Wood says, nature was experimenting with many different designs for the hominids, which had recently diverged from an ancestor they shared with chimpanzees. Most experts agree the split occurred sometime between 6 million and 8 million years ago, so Toumai is no doubt one of our earliest ancestors. Wood says Toumai could have had a modern face and still become extinct. In nature, sometimes similar features evolve in different species independently. This is called convergent evolution. *Paranthropus,* another group of ancestors that went extinct, also shared some humanlike features.

Wood says one important conclusion that may arise from the new discovery is that human evolution is no different from that observed in other animals, such as birds and cats: Nature allows many different designs of the same basic model to develop. This appears to have been the case with hominids. Now, as the last remaining hominids, perhaps we should be declared an endangered species.

Questions

1. Why and how did the discovery of the Toumai skull "shake [the] human family tree"?

2. Locate the following on Tattersall's tree: *Sahelanthropus tchadensis, Ardipithecus ramidus (Ardi), Australopithecus afarensis* (Lucy), *Paranthropus boisei* (Dear Boy), *Australopithecus africanus* (Taung child), and *Homo sapiens* (modern humans). How, if at all, are these "human ancestors" related to one another? Across how many years? What does this tree, together with White's *USA Today* article, suggest about the modern picture of human evolution?

3. What does coverage of new paleoanthropological finds like the Toumai skull in the *New York Times, USA Today,* and other reporting venues suggest about our fascination with, and the newsworthiness of, the ever-changing story of human evolution?

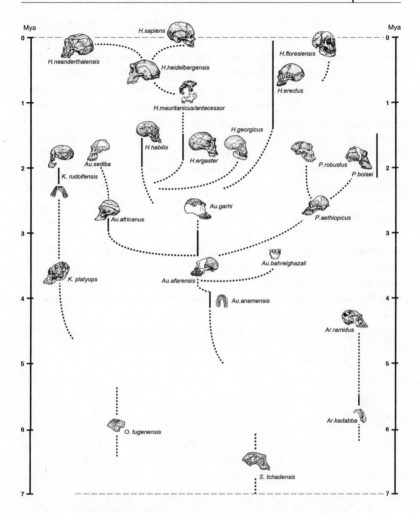

What Foraging Hadza Grandmothers Suggest about *Homo erectus* Lifestyle (1.8 million years ago and 1999)

Ethnography is the careful study of a particular group of people, including their customs, their beliefs, their social organization, and their ways of interacting with their environment. Scholars can hypothesize ethnographic parallels between their observations of modern groups they study firsthand and similar groups that lived long in the past. Modern hunter-gatherer communities, like the Hadza, offer useful parallels for making sense of the community structures of long-ago hunter-gatherers, including not only *Homo sapiens* from our inception until the changes that came with the agricultural revolution (from c. 200,000 to 12,000 years before the present), but also other hominid species, like *Homo erectus* (as long as 1.8 million years ago). The Hadza of east Africa are some of the world's last surviving hunter-gatherers. The one thousand remaining Hadza live in bands of twenty to thirty people and forage in several areas in modern Tanzania. Individual Hadza own very little—perhaps a bow and arrows, a knife, a smoking pipe, a cooking pot—and share almost everything, from food to shelter to child-care responsibilities. As hard as their life may seem to Westerners, theirs is often described as the ultimate life of leisure, given that they spend on average only four to six hours a day at work, gathering food. Compare that to the 40+-hour workweek, plus commute, of most Americans. In the following passage, anthropologists attempt to apply the "grandmother hypothesis," using parallels with modern Hadza women, to understand how adjustments in women's foraging brought about by climate change had a significant impact on *Homo erectus*'s evolutionary success.

Our model is grounded on the results of fieldwork with the Hadza, a small population of traditional foragers living in the arid savanna woodlands of the Eastern Rift, northern Tanzania.

Apart from the very old and very young, Hadza of all ages are active, productive foragers. Time allocation and foraging returns are particularly striking for senior females and younger children. Women in their 60s and early 70s work long hours in all seasons, often with return rates equal to (sometimes greater than) those of their reproductive-age female kin. Hadza children are involved in the food quest virtually from the time they can walk, and by the age of

SOURCE: J. F. O'Connell, K. Hawkes, and N. G. Blurton Jones, "Grandmothering and the Evolution of *Homo erectus*," *Journal of Human Evolution* 36 (1999), pp. 465–66, 475.

five can and do supply, in some seasons, up to 50% of their daily nutritional requirements by their own efforts.

Hadza mothers and grandmothers routinely capitalize on children's foraging capabilities by targeting resources that youngsters can take at high rates, notably fruit. Sometimes this involves bypassing items from which women earn better returns, but that children cannot handle. These choices mark an effort to maximize "team" returns, those earned by women and children together. In the wet season, when fruit is widely available, children's foraging opportunities largely determine adult female foraging strategies.

When resources easily taken by children are unavailable (especially in the dry season), Hadza women provision their off-spring with foods they can procure reliably and efficiently. A good example is the woody rootstock, *Vigna frutescens* (Hadza: *Ilekwa*), which favors deep stony soils and requires both substantial upper body strength and endurance to collect and the ability to make and control fire to process. Adult women, including seniors, take it often in all seasons, routinely earning up to 2000 kcal/h as a result. Preadolescents seldom pursue it, and rarely gain more than about 200 kcal/h when they do. Youngsters under 8 years old ignore it entirely.

This provisioning has an important ecological implication: it allows the Hadza to operate in habitats from which they would otherwise be excluded if, as among other primates, weanlings were responsible for their own subsistence.

It also creates the opportunity for another adult to influence a mother's birth-spacing: if someone else supplies food for her weaned but still dependent child, she can have the next baby sooner. Under these circumstances, grandmother, whose fertility has declined, can have a large impact on her own fitness by feeding the weaned children of her younger kin. Analyses of time allocation, foraging returns, and children's nutritional status (measured by seasonal changes in weight) provide a compelling measure of her effect. In families where mother is *not* nursing, children's nutritional status varies in accordance with mother's own foraging effort. At the arrival of a newborn, however, mother's foraging time drops and the correlation between her foraging effort and her weaned children's weight changes disappears. Instead, those weight changes vary closely with the effort of a related senior female, usually grandmother.

This suggests an hypothesis to account for the differences in average adult lifespans among the hominoids. Child-bearing careers in humans and apes are similar in length, but humans survive far longer after menopause. The dependence of weaned children on food from adults would have allowed ancestral human grandmothers to affect their fitness in ways that other apes could not, increasing the strength of selection against senescence, lowering adult mortality rates, and so lengthening average adult lifespans.

* * *

AN EVOLUTIONARY SCENARIO GROUNDED IN THE PLIO-PLEISTOCENE

Data on *H. erectus* life history, climate, and resource use developed and integrated so far can be summarized along the following lines. By ca. 1–8 Ma, a long-term trend toward cooler, drier climate led to sharp reductions, at least seasonally, in the availability of plant foods previously exploited by hominids, especially juveniles. In some populations, adults and older juveniles increased a previously infrequent practice of using resources that younger children could not acquire on their own, with mothers and older siblings providing shares to the younger ones. Without weanlings of their own, aging females were able to feed their daughter's youngsters. Those more vigorous could support a weanling fully, allowing their daughters to wean early and begin their next pregnancies sooner, with less impact on their weanlings' welfare. This increased selection against senescence, thereby lowering adult mortality rates and in turn favoring later maturity. Extended lifespans did not favor delaying menopause since females who continued to have babies of their own were unable to enhance their daughters' fertility. Lineages with higher fertility rates were those with post-menopausal helpers. Relaxation of the limits previously imposed on adult foraging by children's resource handling capabilities opened a broader range of habitats to exploitation. Longer-lived, and so later-maturing, larger-bodied, bigger-brained hominids, identified as *H. erectus*, quickly spread throughout the Old World tropics and into temperate latitudes.

Questions

1. What does this passage reveal about the Hadza, a modern hunter-gatherer community? In particular, what is the relationship between children, childbearing women, and post-menopausal women, especially with regard to foraging for food?

2. How does a Hadza, and by parallel a *Homo erectus*, grandmother extend her own life span and improve the chances of her own genetic line—her daughter and her daughter's children—surviving?

3. How do the authors apply the ethnography of the Hadza to an understanding of *Homo erectus* communities? What does an ethnographic approach add to an understanding of our human ancestors that cannot be gleaned from the sources/methods in "Rachael Moeller Gorman," Cooking Up Bigger Brains, and "What Happened to the Neanderthals?" (both in this chapter)

Rachael Moeller Gorman, Cooking Up Bigger Brains (1.8 million years ago and 2008)

Reconstructing human evolution is very difficult. For one thing, because only a tiny percentage of people become fossils that we later find, dating the first appearance of any change is always provisional; statistical analysis of genetic divergence can sometimes yield more precise dates, but only sometimes. And without an established chronology, explaining change becomes very difficult.

We know that humans' powerful brains—though obviously a huge evolutionary advantage—also posed problems that required additional evolutionary adaptations in order to make bigger brains sustainable. For instance, female anatomy had to change so that such large-headed creatures could be born safely; an organ easily damaged by overheating required a better cooling system (which is why humans have lots of skin not covered by hair and unusually efficient sweat glands); and an organ requiring lots of calories necessitated more efficient gathering and digesting of food. In each case, the relationships among changes are hard to pinpoint. Did A come first and make B possible? Did B come first, and then create a problem solved by A, allowing B to be selected for more strongly than when it first appeared? Did the two somehow emerge together?

In the case of the brain-nutrition link, another complication appears: the adjustment to increased nutritional demands may well have been learning new behavior, rather than a change encoded in our genes. In her January 2008 article in *Scientific American*, Rachael Moeller Gorman introduces us to Richard Wrangham's suggestion that learning to cook, presumably made possible by a more powerful brain, may have been the key to further increases in brain power.

Richard Wrangham has tasted chimp food, and he doesn't like it. "The typical fruit is very unpleasant," the Harvard University biological anthropologist says of the hard, strangely shaped fruits endemic to the chimp diet, some of which look like cherries, others like cocktail sausages. "Fibrous, quite bitter. Not a tremendous amount of sugar. Some make your stomach heave." After a few tastings in western Uganda, where he works part of the year on his 20-year-old project studying wild chimpanzees, Wrangham came to the conclusion that no human could survive long on such a diet. Besides the unpalatable taste, our weak jaws, tiny teeth and small guts would never be able to chomp and process enough calories from the fruits to support our large bodies.

Then, one cool fall evening in 1997, while gazing into his fireplace in Cambridge, Mass., and contemplating a completely different question—"What stimulated human evolution?"—he remembered the chimp food. "I realized what a ridiculously large difference cooking would make," Wrangham says. Cooking could have made the fibrous fruits, along with the tubers and tough, raw meat that chimps also eat, much more easily digestible, he thought—they could be consumed quickly and digested with less energy. This innovation could

---

SOURCE: Rachael Moeller Gorman, "Cooking Up Bigger Brains," *Scientific American*, January 2008, pp. 102–105.

have enabled our chimp-like ancestors' gut size to shrink over evolutionary time; the energy that would have gone to support a larger gut might have instead sparked the evolution of our bigger-brained, larger-bodied, humanlike forebears.

In the 10 years since coming on his theory, Wrangham has stacked up considerable evidence to support it, yet many archaeologists, paleontologists and anthropologists argue that he is just plain wrong. Wrangham is a chimp researcher, the skeptics point out, not a specialist in human evolution. He is out of his league. Furthermore, archaeological data does not support the use of controlled fire during the period Wrangham's theory requires it to.

Wrangham, who first encountered chimps as a student of Jane Goodall's in 1970, began his career looking at the way ecological pressures, especially food distribution, affect chimp society. He famously conducted research into chimp violence, leading to his 1996 book *Demonic Males*. But ever since staring into that fire 10 years ago, he has been plagued with thoughts of how humans evolved. "I tend to think about human evolution through the lens of chimps," he remarks. "What would it take to convert a chimpanzee-like ancestor into a human?" Fire to cook food, he reasoned, which led to bigger bodies and brains.

And that is exactly what he found in *Homo erectus*, our ancestor that first appeared 1.6 million to 1.9 million years ago. *H. erectus*'s brain was 50 percent larger than that of its predecessor, *H. habilis*, and it experienced the biggest drop in tooth size in human evolution. "There's no other time that satisfies expectations that we would have for changes in the body that would be accompanied by cooking," Wrangham says.

The problem with his idea: proof is slim that any human could control fire that far back. Other researchers believe cooking did not occur until perhaps only 500,000 years ago. Consistent signs of cooking came even later, when Neanderthals were coping with an ice age. "They developed earth oven cookery," says C. Loring Brace, an anthropologist at the University of Michigan at Ann Arbor. "And that only goes back a couple hundred thousand years." He and others postulate that the introduction of energy-rich, softer animal products, not cooking, was what led to *H. erectus*'s bigger brain and smaller teeth.

So Wrangham did more research. He examined groups of modern hunter-gatherers all over the world and found that no human group currently eats all their food raw. Humans seem to be well adapted to eating cooked food: modern humans need a lot of high-quality calories (brain tissue requires 22 times the energy of skeletal muscle); tough, fibrous fruits and tubers cannot provide enough. Wrangham and his colleagues calculated that *H. erectus* (which was in *H. sapiens*'s size range) would have to eat roughly 12 pounds of raw plant food a day, or six pounds of raw plants plus raw meat, to get enough calories to survive. Studies on modern women show that those on a raw vegetarian diet often miss their menstrual periods because of lack of energy. Adding high-energy raw meat does not help much, either—Wrangham found data showing that even at chimps' chewing rate, which can deliver them 400 food calories per hour, *H. erectus* would have needed to chew raw meat for 5.7 to 6.2 hours a day to fulfill its daily energy needs. When it was not gathering food, it would literally be chewing that food for the rest of the day.

To prove that cooking actually does save energy, Wrangham partnered with Stephen Secor, a University of Alabama biologist who studies the evolutionary design of the digestive system. They found that the python—an animal model with easily studied gut responses—expends less effort breaking down cooked food than raw. Heat alters the physical structure of proteins and starches, thereby making enzymatic breakdown easier.

Wrangham's theory would fit together nicely if not for that pesky problem of controlled fire. Wrangham points to some data of early fires that may indicate that *H. erectus* did indeed tame fire. At Koobi Fora in Kenya, anthropologist Ralph Rowlett of the University of Missouri–Columbia has found evidence of scorched earth from 1.6 million years ago that contains a mixture of burned wood types, indicating purposely made fire and no signs of roots having burned underground (a tree struck by lightning would show only one wood type and burned roots). The discoveries are consistent with human-controlled fire. Rowlett plans next to study the starch granules found in the area to see if food could have been cooked there.

Still, most researchers state that unless evidence of controlled fire can be regularly confirmed at most *H. erectus* sites, they will remain skeptical of Wrangham's theory. Moreover, other food-based theories can explain the body and brain expansion without flames. One is the expensive tissue hypothesis, proposed in 1995 by Leslie C. Aiello, professor emeritus of biological anthropology at University College London, and physiologist Peter Wheeler of Liverpool John Moores University in England. The main idea of the hypothesis—that smaller guts correlate with bigger brains in primates—fits with Wrangham's theory, but Aiello and Wheeler think that energy-dense animal-derived foods, such as soft bone marrow and brain matter, were the reason humans developed these characteristics, not cooking.

Lacking the proof for widespread fire use by *H. erectus*, Wrangham hopes that DNA data may one day help his cause. "It would be very interesting to compare the human and *Homo erectus* genetics data to see when certain characteristics arose, such as, When did humans evolve improved defenses against Maillard reaction products?" he says, referring to the chemical products of cooking certain foods that can lead to carcinogens.

Even without such evidence yet, some think Wrangham's theory is just the thing to shake up the field of human evolution. "It doesn't matter who develops these ideas," says Aiello, who is also president of the Wenner-Gren Foundation, which supports anthropological research. "You have to listen to what Richard is saying because he has some very interesting, original data. Sometimes the most creative ideas come from unexpected places." She points to Goodall, who surprised the world by proving that humans were not the only toolmakers. "It's one of the best illustrations I know of the value of primate research informing our knowledge of human evolution and adaptation," Aiello says.

If Wrangham's strange ideas turn out to be true, we can thank an early hominid Emeril Lagasse who picked a charred tuber out of a campfire and swallowed it. Without that person, we might never have been able to examine our origins—or enjoy a good grilled steak—in the first place.

Questions

1. How does Wrangham use evidence gathered from contemporary humans and chimpanzees to support his hypothesis?

2. Why is the roughly simultaneous increase in brain size and decline in tooth size of *Homo erectus* significant for this hypothesis?

3. What are the objections raised against Wrangham's hypothesis? Who do you find most convincing, and why?

What Happened to the Neanderthals? (45,000–30,000 years ago and 2008)

Homo neanderthalis, named for the German valley in which the first remains of the species were found, lived from around 200,000 to 30,000 years ago. As the closest species to our own *Homo sapiens* and one that was a contemporary with our own until relatively recently in the long span of human evolution, questions about them abound: Did *Homo sapiens* and *Homo neanderthalis* interact with one another? If so, what was the nature of their communication with one another? Did they interbreed? What, if any, division of labor marked women's from men's labor? Neanderthals' stocky bodies and even their facial bone structure seem to have been particularly well adapted to the colder climate of northern Europe. Their brains were bigger, their eyesight was likely better than ours, and even their ears had a different internal bone structure that may indicate they heard the world in different ways. These clothes-wearing, tool-using, fire-controlling, shelter-living Neanderthals are the only human ancestors who appear to have practiced symbolic behavior, like intentional burying of their dead accompanied with grave goods. Notched eagle talons, which were found in a Neanderthal-occupied cave in Croatia from around 130,000 years ago, may well have been crafted into necklaces or bracelets adorning Neanderthal bodies.

Perhaps the most enduring question about Neanderthals, however, is what happened to them as a species. Arguments to explain their demise have ranged from their inability to adapt to changes in climate, to a massive volcanic eruption around 40,000 years ago precipitating their decline, to *Homo sapiens'* use of a barely domesticated wolf-dog for hunting advantage (see Temple Grandin, Dogs Make Us Human, in this chapter). The following excerpt from an article in *National Geographic* reviews the evidence, from El Sidrón in northern Spain, for understanding Neanderthals' life patterns and fate, as well as a startling reason that the evidence may have survived so well.

On a damp, fog-shrouded morning in September 2007, I stood before the entrance to El Sidrón [a cave network in Northern Spain] with Antonio Rosas of the National Museum of Natural Sciences in Madrid, who heads the paleoanthropological investigation [of the El Sidrón cave system, discovered by Spelunkers in 1994]. One of his colleagues handed me a flashlight, and I gingerly lowered myself into the black hole. As my eyes adjusted to the interior, I began to make out the fantastic contours of a karstic cave. An underground river had hollowed out a deep vein of sandstone, leaving behind a limestone cavern extending hundreds of yards, with side galleries spidering out to at least 12 entrances. Ten minutes into the cave, I arrived at the Galería del Osario—the "tunnel of bones." Since 2000, some 1,500 bone fragments have been unearthed from this side gallery, representing the remains of at least nine Neanderthals—five young adults, two adolescents, a child of about eight, and a three-year-old toddler. All showed signs of nutritional stress in their teeth—not unusual in young Neanderthals late in their time on Earth. But a deeper desperation is etched in their bones. Rosas picked up a recently unearthed fragment of a skull and another of a long bone of an arm, both with jagged edges.

"These fractures were—*clop*—made by humans," Rosas said, imitating the blow of a stone tool. "It means these fellows went after the brains and into long bones for the marrow." In addition to the fractures, cut marks left on the bones by stone tools clearly indicate that the individuals were cannibalized. Whoever ate their flesh, and for whatever reason—starvation? ritual?—the subsequent fate of their remains bestowed upon them a distinct and marvelous kind of immortality.

SOURCE: Stephen S. Hall, *National Geographic* 214.4 (October 2008), pp. 34, 36, 38–47, 49–55, 57–59. [Editorial insertions appear in square brackets—*Ed.*]

* * *

Prehistoric cannibalism has been very good for modern-day molecular biology. Scraping flesh from a bone also removes the DNA of microorganisms that might otherwise contaminate the sample. The bones of El Sidrón have not yielded the most DNA of any Neanderthal fossil—that honor belongs to a specimen from Croatia, also cannibalized—but so far they have revealed the most compelling insights into Neanderthal appearance and behavior. In October 2007 Lalueza-Fox, Holger Römpler of the University of Leipzig, and their colleagues announced that they had isolated a pigmentation gene from the DNA of an individual at El Sidrón (as well as another Neanderthal fossil from Italy). The particular form of the gene, called MClR, indicated that at least some Neanderthals would have had red hair, pale skin, and, possibly, freckles. The gene is unlike that of redhaired people today, however— suggesting that Neanderthals and modern humans developed the trait independently, perhaps under similar pressures in northern latitudes to evolve fair skin to let in more sunlight for the manufacture of vitamin D. Just a few weeks earlier, Svante Pääbo, who now heads the genetics laboratory at the Max Planck Institute in Leipzig, Lalueza-Fox, and their colleagues had announced an even more astonishing find: Two El Sidrón individuals appeared to share, with modern humans, a version of a gene called FOXP2 that contributes to speech and language ability, acting not only in the brain but also on the nerves that control facial muscles. Whether Neanderthals were capable of sophisticated language abilities or a more primitive form of vocal communication (singing, for example) still remains unclear, but the new genetic findings suggest they possessed some of the same vocalizing hardware as modern humans . . .

* * *

To coax a Neanderthal fossil to reveal its secrets, you can measure it with calipers, probe it with a CT scan, or try to capture the ghost of its genetic code. Or if you happen to have at your disposal a type of particle accelerator called a synchrotron, you can put it in a lead-lined room and blast it with a 50,000-volt x-ray beam, without disturbing so much as a single molecule.

Over a sleep-deprived week in October 2007, a team of scientists gathered at the European Synchrotron Radiation Facility (ESRF) in Grenoble, France, for an unprecedented "convention of jawbones." The goal was to explore a crucial question in the life history of the Neanderthals: Did they reach maturity at an earlier age than their modern human counterparts? If so, it might have implications for their brain development, which in turn might help explain why they disappeared. The place to look for answers was deep inside the structure of Neanderthal teeth . . .

When teeth are imaged at high resolution, they reveal a complex, three-dimensional hatch of daily and longer periodic growth lines, like tree rings, along with stress lines that encode key moments in an individual's life history. The trauma of birth etches a sharp neonatal stress line on the enamel; the time of weaning and episodes of nutritional deprivation or other environmental stresses similarly leave distinct marks on developing teeth. "Teeth preserve a continuous, permanent record of growth, from before birth until they finish growing at the end of adolescence," Smith explained . . .

To address this question, Smith, Tafforeau, and colleagues had previously used the synchrotron to demonstrate that an early modern human child from a site called Jebel Irhoud in Morocco (dated to around 160,000 years ago) showed the modern human life history pattern [of later puberty]. In contrast, the "growth rings" in the 100,000-year-old tooth of a young Neanderthal discovered in the Scladina cave in Belgium indicated that the child was eight years old when it died and appeared to be on track to reach puberty several years sooner than the average for modern humans. Another research team, using a single Neanderthal tooth, had found no such difference between its growth pattern and that of living humans. But while a full analysis from the "jawbone convention" would take time, preliminary results, Smith said, were "consistent with what we see in Scladina."

"This would certainly affect Neanderthal social organization, mating strategy, and parenting behavior," says Hublin. "Imagine a society where individuals start to reproduce four years earlier than in modern humans. It's a very different society. It could also mean the Neanderthals' cognitive abilities may have been different from modern humans" . . .

When the coldest fingers of the Ice Age finally reached southern Iberia in a series of abrupt fluctuations between 30,000 and 23,000 years ago, the landscape was transformed into a semi-arid steppe. On this more open playing field, perhaps the tall, gracile modern humans moving into the region with projectile spears gained the advantage over the stumpy, muscle-bound Neanderthals. But [the Gibraltar Museum's evolutionary biologist, Clive] Finlayson argues that it was not so much the arrival of modern humans as the dramatic shifts in climate that pushed the Iberian Neanderthals to the brink. "A three-year period of intense cold, or a landslide, when you're down to ten people, could be enough," he said. "Once you reach a certain level, you're the living dead."

The larger point may be that the demise of the Neanderthals is not a sprawling yet coherent paleoanthropological novel; rather, it is a collection of related, but unique, short stories of extinction. "Why did the Neanderthals disappear in Mongolia?" Stringer asked. "Why did they disappear in Israel? Why did they disappear in Italy, in Gibraltar, in Britain? Well, the answer could be different in different places, because it probably happened at different times. So we're talking about a large range, and a disappearance and retreat at different times, with pockets of Neanderthals no doubt surviving in different places at different times. Gibraltar is certainly one of their last outposts. It could be the last, but we don't know for sure."

Questions

1. What techniques do scientists employ for analyzing Neanderthal remains? From your reading of Johanson's description in Finding Lucy (in this chapter) and the study of the Toumai skull (New Skulls and a "Bushy" Human Family Tree, in this chapter), how is the analysis of Neanderthal remains similar? How is it different?

2. What does the evidence suggest about Neanderthals' physical features and ways of life?

3. How and why does this article suggest Neanderthals became extinct? Why should we *Homo sapiens* care?

Temple Grandin, Dogs Make Us Human (2005)

Like "Cooking Up Bigger Brains," this document summarizes a controversial argument about how culturally learned behaviors may have given humans important advantages that also shaped subsequent biological evolution. In this case, however, the hypothesis involves more than one species. It claims that when humans domesticated wolves, creating dogs, both species were able to specialize, and to stop wasting precious resources on tasks that the other species could help with. At the same time, it suggests that when humans changed their environment by bringing in wolves/dogs, they positioned themselves to observe and then learn a series of very advantageous behaviors for which they (like other primates) were not hard-wired.

The thesis is controversial for many reasons. Among others, the dates at which dogs began diverging from wolves as estimated by DNA differ dramatically from the earliest dates at which we find unambiguous evidence of domestication by humans; and while this might simply reflect gaps in the fossil record, there are also some technical reasons to worry about the dating of DNA divergence in this case.

The summary of the research here comes from Temple Grandin, an expert on animal behavior (especially cattle) who was diagnosed in early childhood with autism, and has argued that mental differences reflected in that diagnosis actually make it easier for her than for most humans to understand the way many animals think.

[A] study by Robert K. Wayne and his colleagues at UCLA of DNA variability in dogs found that dogs had to have diverged from wolves as a separate population 135,000 years ago. The reason the fossil record doesn't show any dogs with humans before 14,000 years ago is probably that before then people were partnered with wolves, or with wolves that were evolving into dogs. Sure enough, fossil records do show lots of wolf bones close to human bones before 100,000 years ago.

SOURCE: Temple Grandin and Catherine Johnson, *Animals in Translation* (New York: Scribner, 2005), pp. 304–306.

If Dr. Wayne is right, wolves and people were together at the point when *homo sapiens* had just barely evolved from *homo erectus*. When wolves and humans first joined together people only had a few rough tools to their name, and they lived in very small nomadic bands that probably weren't any more socially complicated than a band of chimpanzees. Some researchers think these early humans may not even have had language.

This means that when wolves and people first started keeping company they were on a lot more equal footing than dogs and people are today. Basically, two different species with complementary skills teamed up together, something that had never happened before and has really never happened since.

Going over all the evidence, a group of Australian anthropologists believes that during all those years when early humans were associating with wolves *they learned to act and think like wolves.* Wolves hunted in groups; humans didn't. Wolves had complex social structures; humans didn't. Wolves had loyal same-sex and nonkin friendships; humans probably didn't, judging by the lack of same-sex and nonkin friendships in every other primate species today. (The main relationship for chimpanzees is parent-child.) Wolves were highly territorial; humans probably weren't—again, judging by how nonterritorial all other primates are today.

By the time these early people became truly modern, they had learned to do all these wolfie things. When you think about how different we are from other primates, you see how doglike we are. A lot of the things we do that the other primates don't are dog things. The Australian group thinks it was the dogs who showed us how.

They take their line of reasoning even further. Wolves, and then dogs, gave early humans a huge survival advantage, they say, by serving as lookouts and guards, and by making it possible for humans to hunt big game in groups instead of hunting small prey as individuals. Given everything wolves did for early man, dogs were probably a big reason why early man survived and Neanderthals didn't. Neanderthals didn't have dogs.

But dogs didn't just help people stay alive long enough to reproduce. Dogs probably also made it possible for humans to pull ahead of all their primate cousins. Paul Tacon, principal research scientist at the Australian Museum, says that the development of human friendship "was a tremendous survival advantage because that speeds up the exchange of ideas between groups of people." All cultural evolution is based on cooperation, and humans learned from dogs how to cooperate with people they aren't related to.

Maybe the most amazing new finding is that wolves didn't just teach us a lot of useful new behaviors. Wolves probably also changed the structure of our brains. Fossil records show that whenever a species becomes domesticated its brain gets smaller. The horse's brain shrank by 16 percent; the pig's brain shrank as much as 34 percent; and the dog's brain shrank 10 to 30 percent. This probably happened because once humans started to take care of these animals, they no longer needed various brain functions in order to survive. I don't know what functions they lost, but I do know all domestic animals have reduced fear and anxiety compared to wild animals.

Now archaeologists have discovered that 10,000 years ago, just at the point when humans began to give their dogs formal burials, the human brain began to shrink, too. It shrank by 10 percent, just like the dog's brain. And what's interesting is what *part* of the human brain shrank. In all of the domestic animals the *forebrain*, which holds the frontal lobes, and the *corpus callosum*, which is the connecting tissue between the two sides of the brain, shrank. But in humans it was the *midbrain*, which handles emotions and sensory data, and the *olfactory bulbs*, which handle smell, that got smaller while the corpus callosum and the forebrain stayed pretty much the same. Dog brains and human brains specialized: humans took over the planning and organizing tasks, and dogs took over the sensory tasks. Dogs and people coevolved and became even better partners, allies, and friends.

Questions

1. What are the changes in human behavior that some scholars think might have come about as a result of the domestication of wolves/dogs? What are the changes in human and animal physiology?

2. What evidence is presented for those changes?

3. If true, what implications would this have for our understanding of human evolution? What if we don't have enough evidence to either accept or reject these hypotheses for certain?

Clive Gamble, Human Tool Use and the "Pioneer Phase" of Technological and Behavioral Development (1993)

What sets humans apart from other primates: brain size, complex language, bipedalism, domestication of dogs, or the sophistication of our tools? From these basic characteristics, other markers of human society followed: permanent hearths, burial sites, body ornaments, long-distance trade, and settlement in a broad range of ecosystems, including mountains, deserts, and rainforests.

Many of the elements associated with distinctively human behavior have left reliable archaeological traces only in the last 40,000 years—

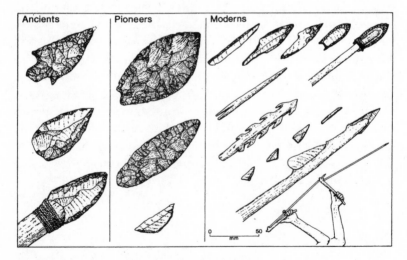

Technological changes in hunting weapons

SOURCE: Redrawn from Clive Gamble, *Timewalkers: The Prehistory of Global Colonization* (New York: Penguin Books, 1994).

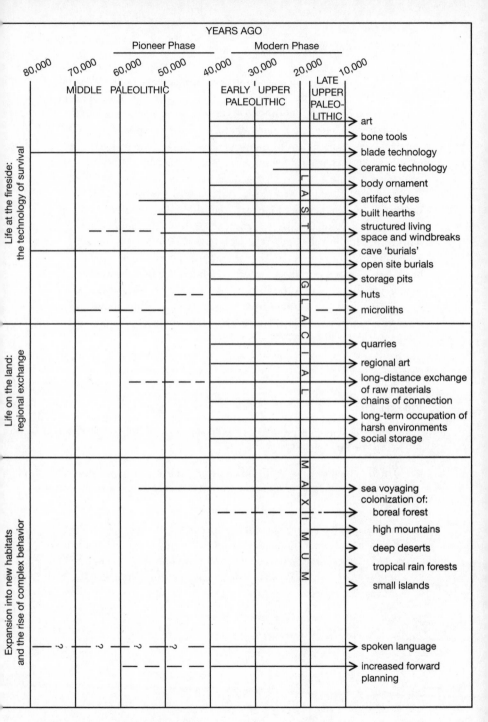

The change in behavior between the Ancients and Moderns, as captured in the archaeological record

though there were significant precursors. Archaeologist Clive Gamble describes a "Pioneer phase" of human behavioral change that happened in the period between 60,000 and 40,000 years ago. He designed the chart presented here to compare when people began to demonstrate "modern" practices. Dates for many of these achievements have been established even earlier; ongoing research will no doubt provide continued revisions.

Gamble further supports this periodization by grouping tools representative of Ancients, Pioneers, and Moderns. The oldest tools show the simplest design. The three spearheads in the right-hand box are flint tools from Middle Paleolithic; the style goes back at least as far as 300,000 BCE. The second group includes bifacial (two-sided) points found across much of Europe as well as a microlith from southern Africa, which shows that the Pioneer phase had wide geographic distribution. The third group, from the Upper Paleolithic, shows even more changes in size, shape, and materials, including bone and antler.

Questions

1. Which behaviors have the oldest archaeological record? Which emerge in the "Pioneer phase"?

2. Which behaviors appear in the Upper Paleolithic (after 40,000 BCE)? Do you see a relationship between tools and behavior in this period? Why?

3. Note that behaviors important for "life at the fireside" generally tend to have older archaeological traces, while many of the behaviors associated with expanding into new habitats are relatively recent—the last 10,000 years. Which behaviors do not fit into this generalization? Can you suggest any reasons why?

Chapter 2

RIVERS, CITIES, AND FIRST STATES, 3500–2000 BCE

Royal Standard of Ur (c. 2600–2400 BCE)

A wooden box 8½ inches high and 19½ inches long, decorated with shell, red limestone, and lapis lazuli, and dating from c. 2600–2400 BCE, was found in the 1920s in the section of the city of Ur known as the Royal Graves. Its function is unknown. Sir Leonard Woolley, who discovered it, thought it was carried on a pole as a standard. It has also been hypothesized to be the sound box of a musical instrument. One of the two main panels, known as "War" shows war chariots, infantry, enemy soldiers being trampled underneath the chariots and killed with axes, and naked prisoners being presented to the king. The other main panel, known as "Peace" (illustrated here), shows a banquet and various animals and other goods being brought to it.

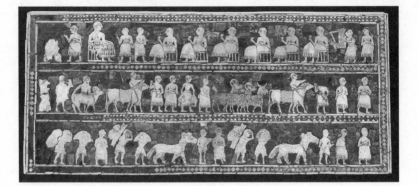

Questions

1. What range of occupations does the "Peace" panel show, both explicitly in the scenes it depicts on each of the three registers and implicitly in the efforts that went into its creation?

2. What ways of life are depicted on each register? What might they suggest about urban versus rural communities, as well as the relationships between settled peoples and pastoralists in the mid-third millennium?

3. If the object was a standard, paraded about on a pole, or if it was the sound box of a musical instrument, how would its use impact the way we read its imagery? Why does an object's use matter for modern scholars' interpretation of its meaning?

Mencius, On the Legendary Sage Kings
(c. 2400–2200 BCE)

Mencius (c. 371–289 BCE), eventually recognized as the most important follower of Confucius, spent much of his life lecturing various rulers of Chinese states, trying to persuade them that following a Confucian philosophy would benefit both their subjects and themselves. Here he describes the labors of Yao, Shun, and Yü, legendary civilizers who paved the way for China's first dynasty, the Xia—though they chose their successors based on merit, not heredity. (Very little about the Xia is verifiable, but its founding is commonly dated between 2200 and 2000 BCE.) Note the connections made between agriculture, land and water management, and human struggles to "rise above" nature. Mencius also hoped that the contemporary rulers would take these men as their role models. (For an example of Mencius trying to improve rulers' behavior, see Mencius, *"Humane Government,"* in Chapter 5.)

In the time of Yao, the Empire was not yet settled. The Flood still raged unchecked, inundating the Empire; plants grew thickly; birds and beasts multiplied; the five grains did not ripen; birds and beasts encroached upon men, and their trail criss-crossed even the Central Kingdoms. The lot fell on Yao to worry about this situation. He raised Shun to a position of authority to deal with it. Shun put Yi in charge of fire. Yi set the mountains and valleys alight and burnt them, and the birds and beasts went into hiding. Yü dredged the Nine Rivers, cleared the courses of the [Ji] and the [Ta] to channel the water into the Sea, deepened the beds of the Ju and the Han, and raised the dykes of the Huai and the [Si] to empty them into the River. Only then were the people of the Central Kingdoms able to find food for themselves. During this time Yü spent eight years abroad and passed the door of his own house three times without entering. Even if he had wished to plough the fields, could he have done it?

Hou [Ji] taught the people how to cultivate land and the five kinds of grain. When these ripened, the people multiplied. This is the way of the common people: once they have a full belly and warm clothes on their back they degenerate to the level of animals if they are allowed to lead idle lives, without education and discipline. This gave the sage King further cause for concern, and so he appointed [Xie] as the Minister of Education whose duty was to teach the

---

SOURCE: *Mencius*, translated by D. C. Lau (Harmondsworth: Penguin Books, 1970), pp. 102–3.

people human relationships: love between father and son, duty between ruler and subject, distinction between husband and wife, precedence of the old over the young, and faith between friends. Fang [Xun] said,

Encourage them in their toil,
Put them on the right path,
Aid them and help them,
Make them happy in their station,
And by bountiful acts further relieve them of hardship.

The Sage worried to this extent about the affairs of the people. How could he have leisure to plough the fields? Yao's only worry was that he should fail to find someone like Shun, and Shun's only worry was that he should fail to find someone like Yü and [Gao] Yao. He who worries about his plot of a hundred *mu* not being well cultivated is a mere farmer.

* * *

Confucius said, "Great indeed was Yao as a ruler! Heaven alone is great, and it was Yao who modelled himself on Heaven. So great was he that the people could not find a name for him. What a ruler Shun was! He was so lofty that while in possession of the Empire he held aloof from it."

It is not true that Yao and Shun did not have to use their minds to rule the Empire. Only they did not use their minds to plough the fields.

Questions

1. How do the great rulers benefit the people? What marks them as not only capable, but virtuous?

2. How are agriculture, state interests, and popular interests connected in this document?

3. What constitutes civilization in Mencius' view? How is this account of its origins similar to and different from others you have encountered in this text?

The Curse of Agade (c. 2150–2000 BCE)

This epic describes events in the reign of Naram Sin (c. 2190–2154 BCE), grandson of Sargon I, during a period when the Akkadian empire built by Sargon encountered numerous setbacks, including a catastrophic drought (since confirmed by analysis of wind-blown sand deposited as sediment in the Persian Gulf) and an invasion by Gutians from the Zagros Mountains. In the epic's account (written sometime between 2150 and 2000 BCE), the problems begin when Naram Sin conquers Nippur and plunders its temple to the god Enlil. Enlil wants to destroy all of Mesopotamia in revenge; other gods intervene to limit the devastation to Agade (Akkad).

It sunk low as the foundation of the land,
He set axes against its branches, and
The temple, like a dead soldier, fell prostrate—
All the foreign lands fell prostrate—
He ripped out its drain pipes, and
The heavens' rains came down into it,
He removed its door frames, and the land's vigor was subverted.
At its "Gate from Which Grain Is Never Diverted," he diverted
    grain(-offerings), and
Grain was thereby diverted from the "hand" of the (home)land,
At its "Gate of Well-Being," the pickax struck, and
Well-being was subverted in all the foreign lands,

               *   *   *

The people saw the bedchamber, its room which knows no
    daylight,
Akkad saw the holy vessels of the gods,
Naramsin cast down into the fire
Its *lahama*-figures, standing in the great gateway at the temple,
Though they had committed no sacrilege.

SOURCE: Jerrold S. Cooper, *The Curse of Agade* (Baltimore: The Johns Hopkins University Press, 1983), pp. 57, 59, 61, 63.

* * *

He put its gold in containers,
He put its silver in leather bags,
He filled the docks with its copper, as if he were delivering huge
    ears of grain.
Metalsmiths were to work its precious metals,
Lapidaries were to work its precious stones,
Smiths were to beat its copper.
Though they were not the goods of a plundered city . . .

* * *

Large ships were docked at Enlil's temple, and
The goods were removed from the city.
As the goods were removed from the city,
So was the good sense of Agade removed . . .

* * *

IV. *Enlil and Gutium*

* * *

Enlil, because his beloved Ekur was destroyed, what should he
    destroy (in revenge) for it?
He looked toward the Gubin mountains,
He *scoured* all of the broad mountain ranges—
Not classed among people, not reckoned as part of the land,
Gutium, a people who know no inhibitions,
With human instincts, but canine intelligence, and monkeys'
    features—
Enlil brought them out of the mountains.
Like hordes of locusts they lie over the land,
Their arms are stretched over the plain for him (Enlil) like a snare
    for animals,
Nothing leaves their arms,
No one escapes their arms.
Messengers no longer travel the highways,

The courier's boat no longer takes to the rivers.
They (the Guti) drive the trusty goats of Enlil from the fold, and
    make their herdsmen follow,
They drive the cows from the pens, and make their cowherds follow.
The *criminal* manned the watch,
The brigand occupied the highways,
The doors of all the city-gates of the land lay dislodged in the dirt,
    and
All the foreign lands uttered bitter cries from the walls of their cities.
In the cities' midst, though not the widespread exterior plains,
    they planted gardens,
(For the first time) since cities were built and founded,
The great agricultural tracts produced no grain,
The inundated tracts produced no fish,
The irrigated orchards produced neither syrup nor wine,
The gathered clouds did not rain, the *mašgurum* did not grow.
At that time, one shekel's worth of oil was only one-half quart,
One shekel's worth of grain was only one-half quart,
One shekel's worth of wool was only one-half mina,
One shekel's worth of fish filled only one *ban*-measure—
These sold at such (prices) in the markets of all the cities!
He who slept on the roof, died on the roof,
He who slept in the house, had no burial,
People were flailing at themselves from hunger.
In the *ki'ur*, Enlil's great place,
Dogs were gathered together in the silent streets,

*   *   *

Three men would come, and be eaten together,

*   *   *

Honest people were confounded with liars,
Young men lay upon young men,
The blood of liars ran upon the blood of honest men.
At that time, Enlil remodeled
His great sanctuaries into tiny reed sanctuaries, and
From east to west he reduced their stores.

* * *

V. *The Gods Curse Agade*

At that time, Sin, Enki, Inanna, Ninurta, Iškur, Utu, Nusku, and
　　Nisaba, the great gods,
Cooled Enlil's (angry) heart with cool water, and prayed to him:
"Enlil, may the city that destroyed your city, be done to as your city,
"That defiled your *giguna*, be done to as Nippur!
"(Because of) your city, may heads fill its wells!
"May no one find his acquaintance there,
"May brother not recognize brother!
"May its young woman be cruelly killed in her woman's domain,
"May its old man cry bitterly for his slain wife!
"May its pigeons moan in their holes,
"May its birds be smitten in their nooks,
"May they, like frightened pigeons, become immobilized!"
Once again, Sin, Enki, Inanna, Ninurta, Iškur, Utu, Nusku, and
　　Nisaba—all the gods whosoever—
Turned their attention to the city, and
Cursed Agade severely:
"City that attacked Ekur—it was Enlil!
"Agade that attacked Ekur—it was Enlil!
"May your holy walls, to their highest point, resound with mourning!

.　　　　　* * *

"May your grain be returned to its furrow,
"May it be grain cursed by Ezinu!
"May your timber be returned to its forest,
"May it be timber cursed by Ninildum!
"May the cattle slaughterer slaughter his wife,
"May your sheep butcher butcher his child,
"May your pauper drown the child who seeks money for him!
"May your prostitute hang herself at the entrance to her brothel,
"May your cult prostitutes and hierodules, who are mothers, kill
　　their children!

"May your gold be bought for the price of silver,
"May your silver be bought for the price of *pyrite*,
"May your copper be bought for the price of lead!
"Agade, may your athlete be deprived of his strength,
"May he be unable to lift his gear bag *onto its stand*!
"May your *niskum*-ass not enjoy its strength, but lie about all day,
"May that city thereby die of hunger!
"May your aristocrats, who eat fine food, lie (hungry) in the grass,
"May your upstanding nobleman
"Eat the *thatching* on his roof,
"The leather hinges on the main door of his father's house—
"May he *gnaw* at those hinges!
"May depression descend upon your palace, constructed in joy!
"May the 'evil one' of the silent plains scream out!
"In your fattening pens, established for purification ceremonies,
"May foxes that frequent ruined mounds sweep with their tails!
"In your city-gate, established for the land,
"May the 'sleep bird,' the bird of depression, establish its nest!
"In your city that couldn't sleep because of the *tigi*-drum music,
"That couldn't rest because of its rejoicing,
"The cattle of Nanna, that fill the pens—
"May they shriek like the 'wandering one' of the silent plains!
"May long grass grow on your canal bank tow-paths,
"May 'mourning grass' grow on your highways laid for coaches!
"Moreover, on your tow-paths, places (built up) with canal
    sediment,
"May *recurved* mountain sheep and mountain *ul*-snakes allow no
    one to pass!
"On your plains, where fine grass grows, may 'lamentation reeds'
    grow!
"Agade, may your flowing sweet water flow as brackish water!

*   *   *

And with the *rising* of the sun, so it was!

*   *   *

Agade is destroyed—hail Inanna!

Questions

1. What can you tell about the economy and society of Agade from the account of its devastation?

2. Why are the Gutians chosen as the instrument of Enlil's wrath?

3. What kinds of relationships seem to exist between gods and human affairs? (Note: Though it is not mentioned here, Naram Sin, unlike his predecessors, claimed to be a divinity himself.)

Ptah-Hotep, Precepts (2300 BCE)

Ptah-hotep was an Egyptian official of the Fifth Dynasty who served as a first minister to Pharaoh Djedkare Isesi. He compiled a set of maxims as advice for young people. Although the document reads as counsel from a father to his son, this format is most likely a rhetorical strategy rather than a specific letter of instruction. The genre—rules for behavior appropriate to social position and gender—is widespread. This text repeatedly emphasizes the importance of learning, humility, and stratified social relationships, exhorting readers to defer to superiors, extend kindness to dependents, and observe proper relationships between husbands and wives. Papyrus copies of Ptah-hotep's instructions exist today in the French Bibliothèque Nationale and the British Museum. The most notable is the Prisse Papyrus from the Twelfth Dynasty, at least five centuries after Ptah-hotep's life, so this idealized representation of good behavior must have remained relevant.

Precepts of the prefect the feudal lord Ptah-hotep, under the Majesty of the King of the South and North, Assa, living eternally forever.

* * *

SOURCE: Charles F. Horne, ed., *The Sacred Books and Early Literature of the East* (New York: Parke, Austin, and Lipscomb, Inc., 1917), pp. 62–66, 68–71, 74–76.

The prefect, the feudal lord Ptah-hotep, says: * * * Who will cause me to have authority to speak, that I may declare to him the words of those who have heard the counsels of former days? And the counsels heard of the gods, who will give me authority to declare them? Cause that it be so and that evil be removed from those that are enlightened.

*　*　*

Be not arrogant because of that which thou knowest; deal with the ignorant as with the learned; for the barriers of art are not closed. * * * But good words are more difficult to find than the emerald, for it is by slaves that that is discovered among the rocks of pegmatite.

*　*　*

Let no one inspire men with fear; this is the will of [Ptah]. Let one provide sustenance for them in the lap of peace; it will then be that they will freely give what has been torn from them by terror.

*　*　*

If thou art an agriculturist, gather the crops in the field which the great [Ptah] has given thee, fill not thy mouth in the house of thy neighbors; it is better to make oneself dreaded by the possessor. As for him who, master of his own way of acting, being all-powerful, seizes the goods of others like a crocodile in the midst even of watchmen, his children are an object of malediction, of scorn, and of hatred on account of it, while his father is grievously distressed, and as for the mother who has borne him, happy is another rather than herself. But a man becomes a god when he is chief of a tribe which has confidence in following him.

*　*　*

Be active during the time of thy existence, doing more than is commanded. Do not spoil the time of thy activity; he is a blameworthy person who makes a bad use of his moments. Do not lose the daily opportunity of increasing that which thy house possesses.

Activity produces riches, and riches do not endure when it slackens.

* * *

If thou desirest to excite respect within the house thou enterest, for example the house of a superior, a friend, or any person of consideration, in short everywhere where thou enterest, keep thyself from making advances to a woman, for there is nothing good in so doing. There is no prudence in taking part in it, and thousands of men destroy themselves in order to enjoy a moment, brief as a dream, while they gain death, so as to know it. It is a villainous intention, that of a man who thus excites himself; if he goes on to carry it out, his mind abandons him. For as for him who is without repugnance for such an act, there is no good sense at all in him.

If thou desirest that thy conduct should be good and preserved from all evil, keep thyself from every attack of bad humor. It is a fatal malady which leads to discord, and there is no longer any existence for him who gives way to it. For it introduces discord between fathers and mothers, as well as between brothers and sisters; it causes the wife and the husband to hate each other; it contains all kinds of wickedness, it embodies all kinds of wrong. When a man has established his just equilibrium and walks in this path, there where he makes his dwelling, there is no room for bad humor.

* * *

If thou art wise, look after thy house; love thy wife without alloy. Fill her stomach, clothe her back; these are the cares to be bestowed on her person. Caress her, fulfil her desires during the time of her existence; it is a kindness which does honor to its possessor. Be not brutal; tact will influence her better than violence; * * *

Treat thy dependents well, in so far as it belongs to thee to do so; and it belongs to those whom [Ptah] has favored. When there comes the necessity of showing zeal, it will then be the dependents themselves who say: "Come on, come on," if good treatment has not quitted the place; if it has quitted it, the dependents are defaulters.

* * *

If thou art a son of the guardians deputed to watch over the public tranquillity, execute thy commission without knowing its meaning, and speak with firmness. Substitute not for that which the instructor has said what thou believest to be his intention; the great use words as it suits them. Thy part is to transmit rather than to comment upon.

* * *

If thou takest a wife, * * * Let her be more contented than any of her fellow-citizens. She will be attached to thee doubly, if her chain is pleasant. Do not repel her; grant that which pleases her; it is to her contentment that she appreciates thy direction.

If thou hearest those things which I have said to thee, thy wisdom will be fully advanced.

In attending to instruction, a man loves what he attends to, and to do that which is prescribed is pleasant. When a son attends to his father, it is a twofold joy for both; when wise things are prescribed to him, the son is gentle toward his master. Attending to him who has attended when such things have been prescribed to him, he engraves upon his heart that which is approved by his father; and the recollection of it is preserved in the month of the living who exist upon this earth.

When a son receives the instruction of his father there is no error in all his plans. Train thy son to be a teachable man whose wisdom is agreeable to the great. Let him direct his mouth according to that which has been said to him; in the docility of a son is discovered his wisdom. His conduct is perfect, while error carries away the unteachable. To-morrow knowledge will support him, while the ignorant will be destroyed.

As for the man without experience who listens not, he effects nothing whatsoever. He sees knowledge in ignorance, profit in loss; he commits all kinds of error, always accordingly choosing the contrary of what is praiseworthy.

Questions

1. Why is it important for Ptah-hotep to instruct readers to be kind and fair to their dependents? What can you infer from his instructions for husbands?

2. Consider the instructions for farmers, just a small segment of the text. What are a farmer's duties? How would you characterize Ptah-hotep's attitude toward agricultural resources?

3. Given the intended audience of this document, do you think the tidy division of class and gender roles accurately depicts ancient Egyptian life?

Domesticated Animals (c. 2000 BCE) and Egyptian Labor (2125–1795 BCE)

The wooden models shown here date to a time of transition between the late Old Kingdom (2686–2181 BCE) and early Middle Kingdom Egypt (2055–1650 BCE). The industry they depict represents the culmination of the dramatic changes that the agricultural revolution brought to the fertile lands along the Nile in the third millennium BCE. The tomb of the local governor Djehutynakht and his wife, who lived around 2000 BCE, was found in Deir el-Bersha on the Nile in Middle Egypt. It contained nearly 100 wooden models, each of which was meant to provide a service for the afterlife of the tomb's occupants. The Djehutynakhts' wooden models enacted a wide range of industry, including farming, tending to cattle, fishing and transport of goods by boat, processing grain, baking, brick-making, loom-weaving, and carpentry, to name a few. The first group of models shown here (each one about 12×3.5 inches), depicts cattle being force-fed by hand. The second model (just over 21 inches in length), also from the Djehutynakhts' tomb, portrays cattle straining forward to pull a plow guided by a field worker. Another tomb in Middle Egypt, that of a governor's servant named Sebekhetepi buried in Beni Hasan during the early Middle Kingdom, also contains impressive wooden models, though nowhere near as many as the Djehutynakhts' tomb. The c. 20×10-inch model shown here depicts (from left to right) bread-making and beer-brewing—the two main products of wheat grown along the Nile—as well as the butchering of an ox. While cattle were more likely to be used for plowing fields, cattle were also slaughtered

SOURCE: *Model of a man feeding an ox.* Egyptian, Middle Kingdom, late Dynasty 11–early Dynasty, 2010–1961 BCE. Findspot: Egypt, Deir el-Bersha, Tomb 10, shaft A (Djehutynakht), Wood, plaster, length x width: 30 x 9 cm (11 13/16 x 9/16 in.). Museum of Fine Arts, Boston. Harvard University–Boston Museum of Fine Arts Expedition, 21.16702. Photograph © Museum of Fine Arts, Boston

Model scene of workers ploughing a field. Egyptian, Middle Kingdom, late Dynasty 11–early Dynasty, 2010–1961 BCE. Findspot: Egypt, Deir el-Bersha, Tomb 10, shaft A (Djehutynakht), wood, length x width: 54 cm (21 1/4 in.). Museum of Fine Arts, Boston.Harvard University–Boston Museum of Fine Arts Expedition, 21.408. Photograph © Museum of Fine Arts, Boston

as a grave offering for the wealthy. For instance, the painted tomb-chapel of Nebamun, an official who lived around 1350 BCE, includes a scene of funerary offerings: an ox's head, rear leg, and its heart piled in the midst of bread, plucked birds, and fruits (see Nebamun Inspecting Flocks and Herds, in Chapter 3, for more information on Nebamun).

Questions

1. Examine the detail on each of the force-fed cattle and compare the force-fed cattle with those pulling a plow. Given the depiction of ox parts in the later funerary offering scene of Nebamun (described above), why do you think these cattle, which were so important for farming, would be force-fed?

2. What do you make of the care with which each scene of industry is shown, as well as the details of each worker? Note that the baker and brewer, both of whom work indoors, have lighter skin; but the water carrier and butcher (as well as those working with the cattle in the other models) have darker skin. What might account for the differ-

ences in skin color? Why do you think the artisans who crafted these models took such care with detail?

3. What does the range of industry depicted in these models reveal about the economy of early Middle Kingdom Egypt and perhaps, by extension, earlier Old Kingdom Egypt? Consider also the craftsmanship necessary to produce these models and the wealth of the individuals with whom they were interred. What does that suggest about the nature of Egyptian society at the end of the third millennium?

Domesticated Corn (c. 4000 BCE)

Today, corn is one of the world's biggest crops; but its domestication was later (probably beginning over 6,000 years ago in what is now Mexico, versus 10,000 years ago for some Eurasian crops) and slower than those of major Afro-Eurasian cereals: wheat, rice, barley, and sorghum. It also resembles its wild ancestor, teosinte, much less than those crops resemble theirs. Teosinte had a number of features that made it less immediately useful to people than wild wheat or barley; those features changed gradually during this slow domestication. In fact, had barley or wheat been available in the Americas, one wonders whether teosinte would have seemed worth bothering with. One major change—larger cobs and seeds—is obvious here. Some very early cultivated cobs reached one-half inch; around 1500 BCE, some were six inches; today some are eighteen inches. These changes have made corn more useful to humans—and more dependent on us.

Evolution of corn. Domesticated corn gradually
increased in size.

SOURCE: Photo courtesy of John Doebley; www.plosbiology.org/article
/info:doi/10.1371/journal/pbio.0000008.

Questions

1. How might domestication and changes in corn cob size be related?

2. Teosinte ears would fall to the ground and scatter their seeds (covered by a tough skin) as soon as they ripened. How might this have suited a wild plant, but not a domesticated one?

3. Corn was probably pre-Columbian America's most important crop. How might its particular characteristics matter?

Casebook

HUMANS AND THE ENVIRONMENT IN THE SECOND MILLENNIUM BCE

Climate change and other environmental events have influenced life on earth for millions of years. Many have heard of the comet/meteor impact that wiped out 75 percent of life on earth, including nearly all dinosaurs, around 65 million years ago. Perhaps less well known is the release of large amounts of carbon into the atmosphere that caused significant changes in the earth's environment—including higher global temperatures ($>5°$ C) and elevated sea levels—around 56 million years ago, during a 150,000-year-long period called the Paleocene-Eocene Maximum Thermal. These dramatic events occurred long before Lucy wandered the earth 3.2 million years ago (see Finding Lucy in Chapter 1) or even the time when the owner of the Toumai skull lived, 7 million years ago (see New Skulls and a "Bushy" Human Family Tree in Chapter 1).

The intimate relationship of humans with our global environment extends to our beginnings as a species more than 250,000 years ago. The ability of *Homo sapiens* to manipulate fire and fashion warm clothing and useful tools enabled our migrations across the planet, living in sustainable hunter-gatherer communities for the vast majority of our existence as a species (see What Foraging Hadza Grandmothers Suggest about *Homo erectus* Lifestyle in Chapter 1). Shortly after another global warming phase around 12,000 years ago, ushering in the beginning of what scientists refer to as the Holocene period, humans began to exploit easily domesticated plants and animals. Thus began a period known as the agricultural revolution. Within several thousand years (by around 3000 BCE), humans were learning to take advantage of the annual flooding of major river systems to produce agricultural surplus to support complex urban societies (see Chapter 2).

Global cooling and warming patterns have shaped human developments (like the river basin societies), while human settlements—through such activities as deforestation to build urban areas and the industry of bronze working and later iron smelting—have had adverse impacts on their environment whose consequences were realized over thousands of years. By 2000 BCE, in part because of such environmental challenges, Old Kingdom Egypt had fallen, the Kingdom of Akkad in Mesopotamia was faltering, and Harappan civilization in the Indus Valley was in decline. Natural disasters, on the other hand, could deal a more abrupt, tremendous, and decisive blow. The dramatic eruption of a volcano on the Mediterranean island of Thera, modern-day Santorini, is one such example. C14-dating of an olive branch from Thera places the eruption of that volcano around 1600 BCE. This volcanic island's eruption was so massive that it caused tsunamis in the Mediterranean and shot debris into the atmosphere that likely influenced climate, and hence human settlements, across the globe, and especially in the immediate Mediterranean region (Egypt and Southwest Asia included). Whether due to long-term developments such as deforestation or abrupt events such as volcanic eruption, human struggles with the environment were a striking feature of the second millennium.

Details about the environment and its impact on human communities abound in sources for the second millennium BCE, including laments and other religious texts, historical annals, personal letters, and archaeological evidence for—and even satellite imagery of—long dried-up river channels. As you read and analyze the sources in this casebook, watch for details about ecological crises, both natural and possibly human-caused. Note the ways that people in different regions, from Egypt to Mesopotamia to the Indus Valley to East Asia—and even different communities within the same region—remembered and adapted to the environmental changes that were taking place in the second millennium BCE.

Lament for Ur (c. 2000 BCE)

This excerpt, from an approximately 500-line Sumerian lament, is difficult to date, but it is suggestive of calamity in the city of Ur (Urim). Ur was a Sumerian city-state that flourished during the third millennium in ancient Mesopotamia near the mouth of the Euphrates (in modern-day Iraq). Among the world's first cities, Ur was an economic and spiritual center. Not only was Ur home to the impressive ziggurat honoring the moon god Nanna, but it also was the site of the rich royal tombs in which objects such as the "Royal Standard" (see Royal Standard of Ur in Chapter 2) and the famous "Queen's Lyre" were found. The lament excerpted here mentions various gods: Enlil, the god of earth, wind, and air, whose chief city was Nippur (Nibru) up the Euphrates from Ur; Nanna, the moon god also called Suen; Ningal, the goddess of reeds and consort of Nanna; and An/Anu, chief god of the heavens. Interpretations of similar, shorter laments have described them as liturgies, or religious rituals, performed as a sort of spring cleaning in a temple after the winter storms. This longer text, however, may point to a time, around 2000 BCE, when Ur was suffering from various environmental crises and violent nomadic incursions.

292–302. Enlil threw open the door of the grand gate to the wind. In Urim no one went to fetch food, no one went to fetch water. Its people rushed around like water being poured from a well. Their strength ebbed away, they could not even go on their way. Enlil afflicted the city with an evil famine. He afflicted the city with that which destroys cities, that which destroys houses. He afflicted the city with that which cannot be withstood with weapons. He afflicted the city with dissatisfaction and treachery. In Urim, which was like a solitary reed, there was not even fear. Its people, like fish being grabbed in a pond, sought to escape. Its young and old lay spread about, no one could rise.

303–317. At the royal station there was no food on top of the platform. The king who used to eat marvellous food grabbed at a mere ration. As the day grew dark, the eye of the sun was eclipsing, the people experienced hunger. There was no beer in the beer-hall,

---

SOURCE: Electronic Text Corpus of Sumerian Literature, at http://etcsl .orinst.ox.ac.uk/cgi-bin/etcsl.cgi?text=t.2.2.3#. © Copyright 2003, 2004, 2005, 2006. The ETCSL project, Faculty of Oriental Studies, University of Oxford.

there was no more malt for it. There was no food for him in his palace, it was unsuitable to live in. Grain did not fill his lofty store-house, he could not save his life. The grain-piles and granaries of Nanna held no grain. The evening meal in the great dining hall of the gods was defiled. Wine and syrup ceased to flow in the great dining hall. The butcher's knife that used to slay oxen and sheep lay hungry. Its mighty oven no longer cooked oxen and sheep, it no longer emitted the aroma of roasting meat . . . The mortar, pestle and grinding stone lay idle; no one bent down over them.

318–327. The Shining Quay of Nanna was silted up. The sound of water against the boat's prow ceased, there was no rejoicing . . . Boats and barges ceased docking at the Shining Quay. Nothing moved on your watercourse which was fit for barges. The plans of the festivals at the place of the divine rituals were altered. The boat with first-fruit offerings of the father who begot Nanna no longer brought first-fruit offerings. Its food offerings could not be taken to Enlil in Nibru. Its watercourse was empty, barges could not travel.

328–339. There were no paths on either of its banks, long grass grew there. The reed fence of the well-stocked cattle-pen of Nanna was split open. The garden's fence was violated and breached. The cows and their young were captured and carried off to enemy terri-tory. The munzer-fed cows took an unfamiliar path in an open coun-try that they did not know. Gayau, who loves cows, dropped his weapon in the dung. Šuni-dug, who stores butter and cheese, did not store butter and cheese. Those who are unfamiliar with butter were churning the butter. Those who are unfamiliar with milk were curdling (?) the milk. The sound of the churning vat did not resound in the cattle-pen. Like mighty coals that once burnt, its smoke is extinguished.

340–349. Suen wept to his father Enlil: "O father who begot me, why have you turned away from my city which was built (?) for you? O Enlil, why have you turned away from my Urim which was built (?) for you? The boat with first-fruit offerings no longer brings first-fruit offerings to the father who begot him. Your food offer-ings can no longer be brought to Enlil in Nibru. The priests of the countryside and city have been carried off by phantoms. Urim, like a city raked by a hoe, is to be counted as a ruin-mound. The Du-ur,

Enlil's resting-place, has become a haunted shrine. O Enlil, gaze upon your city, an empty wasteland. Gaze upon your city Nibru, an empty wasteland."

". . . May you restore the divine powers of Sumer that have been forgotten."

* * *

360–370. Enlil then answered his son Suen: "There is lamentation in the haunted city, reeds of mourning grow there . . . Oh Nanna, the noble son . . . why do you concern yourself with crying? The judgment uttered by the assembly cannot be reversed. The word of An and Enlil knows no overturning. Urim was indeed given kingship but it was not given an eternal reign. From time immemorial, since the Land was founded, until people multiplied, who has ever seen a reign of kingship that would take precedence forever? The reign of its kingship had been long indeed but had to exhaust itself. O my Nanna, do not exert yourself in vain, abandon your city."

371–377. Then my king, the noble son, became distraught. . . . Nanna who loves his city left his city. Suen took an unfamiliar path away from his beloved Urim. In order to go as an exile from her city to foreign territory, Ningal quickly clothed herself and left the city . . . The trees of Urim were sick, its reeds were sick. Laments sounded all along its city wall. Daily there was slaughter before it. Large axes were sharpened in front of Urim. The spears, the arms of battle, were prepared. The large bows, throw-sticks and shields gathered together to strike. The barbed arrows covered its outer side like a raining cloud. Large stones fell together with great thuds. . . . Urim, confident in its own strength, stood ready for the murderers. Its people, oppressed by the enemy, could not withstand their weapons.

* * *

389–402. In the city, those who had not been felled by weapons succumbed to hunger. Hunger filled the city like water, it would not cease. This hunger contorted people's faces, twisted their muscles. Its people were as if drowning in a pond, they gasped for breath. Its king breathed heavily in his own palace. Its people dropped their weapons, their weapons hit the ground. They struck their necks with their hands and cried. They sought counsel with each other, they searched for clarification: "Alas, what can we say about it? What more can we add to it? How long until we are finished off by this catastrophe? Inside Urim there is death, outside it there is death. Inside it we are to be finished off by famine. Outside it we are to be finished off by Elamite weapons. In Urim the enemy oppresses us, oh, we are finished." . . .

* * *

435–448 . . . There was no eloquence in the Dubla-maḫ, the place where oaths used to be taken. The throne was not set up at its place of judgment, justice was not administered. Alamuš threw down his sceptre, his hands trembling. In the sacred bedchamber of Nanna musicians no longer played the balaĝ drum. The sacred box that no one had set eyes upon was seen by the enemy. The divine bed was not set up, it was not spread with clean hay. The statues that were in the shrine were cut down. The cook, the dream interpreter, and the seal keeper did not perform the ceremonies properly. They stood by submissively and were carried off by the foreigners. The priests of the holy uzga shrine and the sacred lustrations, the linen-clad priests, forsook the divine plans and sacred divine powers, they went off to a foreign city.

Questions

1. What specific crises is Ur (Urim) facing?

2. To what causes does the lament attribute the crises?

3. What does the imagery evoked in this lament suggest about the community? What in the lament suggests an urban context? An agricultural context?

Ḥeḳanakhte's Household (2002/1 BCE)

The Ḥeḳanakhte archive includes eight documents that illustrate the household economy of an Egyptian landholder around the year 2000 BCE. In his letters and accounts, Ḥeḳanakhte refers to himself as a *ka*-servant, which means that he was responsible for the various rituals that should take place in a tomb to honor and nourish the *ka* (spirit) of the deceased. Given that Ḥeḳanakhte's letters were ultimately excavated from the tomb of a dependent of the vizier Ip and that Ḥeḳanakhte invokes Ip in this letter, he may have been *ka*-servant to this vizier. The letters of the Ḥeḳanakhte archive are written in hieratic, which is a cursive form of hieroglyphs, in vertical columns from right to left, on sheets of papyrus. Each sheet was then folded several times before being delivered from Ḥeḳanakhte, who had traveled to the South, to the recipients he left behind to manage his home estate at Nebesēyet. The letter here appears to be written at a time of famine, and makes reference to "the inundation," by which Ḥeḳanakhte means the level of Nile flooding. This letter followed within months of another letter Ḥeḳanakhte had written to Merisu (perhaps the eldest son of Ḥeḳanakhte), who is addressed in the second part of the letter here. In that first letter, Ḥeḳanakhte had exhorted Merisu several times to "take great care!" and that "this is not the year for a man to be last in respect of his master, his father, or his brother."

---

(1) A son speaks to his mother: the *ka*-servant Ḥeḳanakhte to his mother Ipi, and to Ḥetepet: How are you? Are you alive, prosperous and healthy? In the favour of Monthu, Lord of Uaset! (2)—and to the whole household: How are you? How are you? Are you alive, prosperous and healthy? Do not worry about me. See! I am healthy and alive. (3) See! you are that one who ate until he was satisfied and hungered until his eyes sunk (into his head) (?). See! the whole land is perished while [you] are not hungry. [See!] (4) when I came hither southwards I had fixed your rations properly. [Now] is the inundation

---

SOURCE: T. G. H. James, *The Ḥeḳanakhte Papers* (New York: Publications of the Metropolitan Museum of Art, 1962), pp. 32–33.

[very great (?)] See! [our] rations are fixed for us (5) according to the state of the inundation. Be patient, like names. See! I have reached today among you, nourishing you.

—Rations should be measured for Sinebnut (6) from his barley which he had on his threshing-floor (?), until he leaves Perha'a—

(7) Account of the rations of the household:

(8) Ipi	8 ḥeḳat (?)
(9) Her maidservant	
(10) Ḥetepet	
(11) Her maidservant	8 ḥeḳat (?)
(12) Ḥeti's son Nakhte	8 ḥeḳat (?)
(13) Together with his family	
(14) Merisu <and> his family	8 ḥeḳat (?)
(15) Siḥathor	8 ḥeḳat (?)
(16) Sinebnut	7 ḥeḳat (?)
(17) Anupu	4 ḥeḳat (?)
(18) Snofru	4 ḥeḳat (?)
(19) Si-inut (?)	4 ḥeḳat (?)
(20) Mcay's daughter Ḥetepet	5 ḥeḳat (?)
(21) Nofret	3½ ḥeḳat (?)
(22) Situret	2 ḥeḳat (?)
(23) Total	7 khar 9½ ḥeḳat (?)

(24) If you avoid being angry about this, (25) See! the whole household are like my children, (26) everything is mine—(for it is said) that half-life is better than death outright. (27) See! one says 'hunger' about hunger. See! they are beginning (28) to eat men here. See! there are no people to whom those rations are given anywhere. You shall conduct yourselves with stout hearts until I have reached (29) you. See! I shall spend the *shõmu* here.

Communication by the *ka*-servant Ḥeḳanakhte to Merisu and to Ḥeti's son Nakhte subordinately. You are to give those (30) rations to my people while they are doing work. Take great care; hoe all my land; sieve with the sieve; hack with your noses (31) in the work. See! if they are diligent god will be praised for you and I shall not have to make things unpleasant for you. Now one should begin by giving the

(32) rations about which I have written to you, on the first day of Khentkhetiperty, for a new first day. Do not be neglectful then (33) about the 10 *arouras* of land which are in the neighbourhood and which were given to Ip the Younger's son Khentykhe—about hoeing it. Be very diligent. See! you are eating my rations.

(34) Now, any possession of Anupu's which you have, give it (back) to him; whatever is lost, make it up to him. Don't make me write to you about it another (35) time. See! I have written to you twice about it. Now if Snofru does want to be in charge of those bulls, you should put him (36) in charge of them. Now he did not want to be with you cultivating, going up and down; nor did he want to come hither with me. Whatever else he wants (37) you should let him enjoy what he wants. Now anyone who will reject those rations out of the women and men, (38) he should come to me here (to be) with me and live as I live. Now there is no one who has come here to me.

I said to you: "Do not keep away (39) a companion of Ḥetepet's from her, whether her hair-dresser or her domestic servant (?)." Take great care of her. May you prosper (40) in all things thus. Now (if) you do not want her, then you should send Iutenḥeb to me. As this man lives for me—I speak of (41) Ip—he who shall commit any act upon the person (?) of (my) concubine, he is against me and I am against him. See! this is my concubine (42) and it is known what should be done for a man's concubine. See! whoever will do for her the like of what I have done—Indeed, would anyone of you (43) be patient if his wife had been denounced to him? Then shall I be patient! How can I be with you in the same establishment? (44) No! You will not respect (my) concubine for my sake.

(*vs.* I) Now see! I have sent you by Siḥatḥor 24 copper *debens* for the renting of land. Now let (*vs.* 2) 5(?) *arouras* of land be cultivated for us on rent in Perha'a beside Hau the Younger('s land), with copper or with clothes or with barley (*vs.* 3) [or with anything (else)], but only when you have collected the value [there(?)] of oil or of anything (else). Take great care; be very diligent; be watchful. (*vs.* 4) Now [see!] you are on good unworked (?) land of Khepeshēyet.

(*vs.* 5) What the *ka*-servant Ḥeḳanakhte gives (*vs.* 6) to his household of Nebesēyet.

Questions

1. What people are mentioned in this letter and what do they suggest about domestic relationships on a small estate in Egypt, c. 2000 BCE?

2. What are the issues that Ḥeḳanakhte is attempting to resolve in this letter?

3. What comments in the letter might suggest that Ḥeḳanakhte is writing in a time of famine?

Natural Disasters and the End of the Xia Dynasty (c. 1550 BCE)

While the Shang dynasty of the second millennium BCE is considered China's first "historic" dynasty, the legendary Xia dynasty holds an important place in Chinese memory. The Xia dynasty ended when its emperor Gui (Jie) was overthrown and banished by Cheng Tang, the first leader of the Shang dynasty in 1556 BCE. The *Bamboo Annals,* a hotly contested text, contain one description of this transition of power. According to tradition, the *Bamboo Annals* were allegedly buried with King Xiang of Wei around 300 BCE and were found again in 280 CE. These texts, heavily reconstructed in both ancient and modern times, offer a host of philological and historiographical challenges to scholars of earliest Chinese history. David Nivison, from whose reconstruction of the *Bamboo Annals* this excerpt is drawn, has argued that even though the text may have gone through many editorial stages prior to its burial with King Xiang, it represents a fairly accurate annalistic narrative. In reading Nivison's reconstruction of the account of the transition from the Xia to the Shang dynasty, we should recognize that these texts may be at best a 300 BCE version of events that transpired more than a millennium before.

SOURCE: *The Riddle of the Bamboo Annals,* translated by David S. Nivison (Taipei: Airiti Press, 2009), pp. 140, 142.

* * *

110 [The emperor] died. Tai Shan suffered an [earth] quake. *The Emperor Gui [i.e., Jie].*

111 First year: The emperor took his position as ruler. He dwelt in Zhenxun. 3rd year: He built the Qing Palace. He tore down the Rong Tower: The Quan Yi entered the Qi [area] in rebellion. 6th year: The [chiefs of the] Qizhong *rong* came as guests [in submission]. 10th year: The five planets moved in succession: at night

112 stars fell like rain. There was an earthquake. The Yi and Luo (Rivers] ran dry. 11th year: He assembled the regional lords in Reng. [The lord of] You Min fled back home. Following that, [the emperor] destroyed You Min. 13th year: He moved to south of the Yellow River. He began the use of an imperial chariot drawn by human beings

113 [14th year: Bian led an army attacking Min Shan. 15th year: Lü, *hou* of Shang, moved to Bo . . .

* * *

115 . . . 17th year: Shang sent Yi Yin to the [Xia] court. 20th year: Yi Yin went back to Shang, and met with Ru

116 Jiu and Ru Fang at the North Gate. 21st year: The Shang army made a punitive expedition against You Luo, and conquered it. After that, [Shang] made a punitive expedition against Jing; Jing fell. 22nd year: Lü, *hou* of Shang, came to court; he was ordered to be imprisoned in the Tower of Xia.

117 23rd year: Lü, *hou* of Shang, was released. After that, the regional lords came as guests to Shang, [acknowledging submission]. 26th year: Shang destroyed Wen. 28th year: Kunwu attacked Shang. Shang assembled the regional lords in Jing Bo.

118 After that [Shang] made a punitive expedition against Wei. The Shang army took Wei. Then they made an expedition against Gu. Zhonggu, the [Xia] chief grand recorder, left [Xia] and fled to Shang. 29th year: The Shang army took Gu. Three suns rose at the same time. Chang, *bo* of Fei, left [Xia] and fled to Shang. In winter. 10th month,

119 they bored through mountains and tunneled through hills, to [let water flow] through to the Yellow River. 30th year: There was a landslide on Mount Qu. [Di Gui] killed his great officer Guan Longfeng. The Shang army made a punitive attack on Kunwu. In the winter, there was a fire in Lingsui. 31st year: From Er, Shang made a punitive attack

120 on the City of Xia, and defeated Kunwu. In a great thunder storm, a battle was fought at Mingtiao, where the Xia army was routed. Jie escaped and fled to Sanzong. The Shang army made a punitive attack on Sanzong, doing battle at Zheng. Jie was captured in Jiaomen, and was banished to Nanchao.

* * *

122 Yin-Shang: Cheng Tang, personal name Lü. Tang had seven names and made nine punitive military campaigns. When he had banished Jie to Nanchao and had returned, there were

123 1800 regional lords who came to his court, some being [from so far away that] eight translations [were needed to communicate with them]. [Even the chief off the Qigong ("wonderful arms") people came in his chariot. All alike extolled "Tiun Yi Lü" as Son of Heaven. Three times he declined, but then he did take the position of Son of Heaven. Earlier, in the times of Gao Xin (i.e., the emperor Ku).

124 [the emperor] had a wife named Jiandi. At the time of the spring equinox, in the days when the dark birds arrive, she went with the emperor to sacrifice outside the city to pray for a son. She was bathing together with her sister in a stream by the Dark Hill, when a dark bird came holding an egg in its mouth

125 and then dropping it. It was of five colors and very beautiful. The two ladies each tried to be the first to get it and cover it with a gem basket. Jiandi got there first and swallowed it. She then became pregnant. [When her time came] her breast split open and she gave birth to Xie. When he grew to manhood he became Yao's minister of instruction.

126 and was successful in serving the people, so that he was given the fief of Shang. Thirteen generations later Zhu Gui was born. Zhu Gui had a wife named Fudu, who saw a white vapor vapor

penetrating the moon and then felt herself pregnant. [In due time], on an yl day, she bore Tang.

127 who was called Tian Yi ("Heaven's Yi"). [His face] was broad below and tapered above, white and bearded. He had a crooked body and a loud voice. He grew to be nine feet tall. His arms had four joints. This was Cheng Tang. When Tang was in Bo he was able to cultivate his virtue.

128 When Yi Zhi was about to respond to Tang's summons, he dreamed that he was riding in a boat passing by the sun and moon. Tang then went east as far as Luo, and seeing the altar of the emperor Yao he dropped a jade disc into the water and stood back. Yellow fish leaped up in pairs, and a black

129 bird followed him, stopping at the altar, where it turned into a piece of black jade. There was also a black turtle, with red marks forming characters, which said that Jie of Xia lacked moral principles, and that Cheng Tang ought later to attack him. The spirit Taowu

130 was seen on Mount Pei. There was a spirit pulling a white wolf with a hook in its mouth into the Shang court. The Power of Metal was about to flourish. Silver flowed out of the mountains. When Tang was about to do Heaven's bidding and banish Jie, he dreamed that he reached the sky and

131 licked it. Subsequently he possessed the empire. The men of Shang after that changed the name of the empire to Yin. 18th year: The king took his position as ruler. He lived in Bo. He for the first time built a building over the Xia alter to the soil. 19th year: There was a great drought. The Di and the Qiang

132 came as guests [in submission]. 20th year: There was a great drought. Jie of Xia died in Ting Shan. The playing of stringed instruments, the singing of songs, and performing of dances were forbidden. 21st year: There was a great drought. Metal money was coined. 22nd year:

133 There was a great drought. 23rd year: There was a great drought. 24th year: There was a great drought. The king prayed in the Mulberry Grove, and it rained. 25th year: He made the "Da Huo" ("Downpour") music. He made his first tour of inspection. He set

the rules for offerings [to the court]. 27th year: He moved the Nine Cauldrons to the city of Shang.

134 29th year: He died . . .

Questions

1. What types of events—human, natural, and even supernatural—does the text describe?

2. To what extent do natural phenomena and political events appear to be intertwined?

3. If this text is not an accurate account as Nivison suggests but rather the result of post–Song dynasty (960–1279 CE) reconstruction, what might later reconstructors of the *Annals* be attempting to suggest about the relationship between natural and human events?

Competing Flood Narratives in the Second Millennium BCE

The *Epic of Gilgamesh,* a collection of Sumerian poems, recounts the story of Gilgamesh's search for immortality in the midst of his grief over the death of his friend Enkidu. On his search, Gilgamesh learns of a man named Utnapishtim who has gained eternal life. Gilgamesh searches for Utnapishtim to hear the story of how he achieved this feat. Genesis preserves the story of the relationship between the Hebrew God and God's people, from Adam and Eve through Abraham and Sarah and their descendants. A pivotal moment in that narrative occurs when God finds fault with humanity and sends a flood, from which only a righteous man, Noah, and his family are spared.

Each of these flood narratives that circulated in the second millennium BCE experienced a long oral history, evident when one considers that Gilgamesh was a legendary king of Uruk in the mid-third millennium and that Genesis places Noah ten long generations (each many hundreds of years in length) after creation. And both texts have a complicated textual tradition. For example, the flood portion of the *Epic of Gilgamesh* owes a debt to another ancient Mesopotamian epic called the *Atrahasis,* while proponents of the biblical documentary hypothesis point to two textual traditions, the Jahwist and Priestly accounts, that can be traced in the Genesis account of Noah's flood. Nonetheless, both the *Epic of Gilgamesh* and Genesis reached their final form by 400 BCE: Gilgamesh's story during the court of Ashurbanipal in late seventh-century BCE Nineveh and the Hebrew Bible begin to come together during, and in the century after, the Babylonian captivity of the sixth century BCE.

Given the Mesopotamian connections of early Judaism (Genesis 11:27–31 places Abraham in Ur of the Chaldeans), it is reasonable to expect some overlap between the texts. The goal in presenting them together here is not to suggest one text borrowed from the other or to "prove" that a flood happened at some point in the Levantine distant past, but rather to examine how two very different but interacting population groups in the second millennium—the urbanites of Mesopotamia and the more pastoral nomadic Jewish peoples—preserved a remembrance of their experience of environmental calamity.

THE STORY OF THE FLOOD

'You know the city Shurrupak, it stands on the banks of Euphrates? That city grew old and the gods that were in it were old. There was Attu, lord of the firmament, their father, and warrior Enlil their counselor, Ninurta the helper, and Ennugi watcher over canals; and with them also was Ea. In those days the world teemed, the people multiplied, the world bellowed like a wild bull, and the great god was aroused by the clamour. Enlil heard the clamour and he said to the gods in council, "The uproar of mankind is intolerable and sleep is no longer possible by reason of the babel." So the gods agreed to exterminate mankind. Enlil did this, but Ea because of his oath warned me in a dream. He whispered their words to my house of reeds, "Reed-house, reed-house! Wall, O wall, hearken

---

SOURCE: *The Epic of Gilgamesh,* translated by N. K. Sandars (New York: Penguin, 1972), pp. 108–13, and Genesis 6:9–8:22, Revised Standard Version Bible, National Council of the Churches of Christ, 1952.

reed-house, wall reflect; O man of Shurrupak, son of Ubara-Tutu;
tear down your house and build a boat, abandon possessions and
look for life, despise worldly goods and save your soul alive. Tear
down your house, I say, and build a boat. These are the measure-
ments of the barque as you shall build her: let her beam equal her
length, let her deck be roofed like the vault that covers the abyss;
then take up into the boat the seed of all living creatures."

'When I had understood I said to my lord, "Behold, what you
have commanded I will honour and perform, but how shall I answer
the people, the city, the elders?" Then Ea opened his mouth and said
to me, his servant, "Tell them this: I have learnt that Enlil is wrath-
ful against me, I dare no longer walk in his land nor live in his city; I
will go down to the Gulf to dwell with Ea my lord. But on you he will
rain down abundance, rare fish and shy wild-fowl, a rich harvest-
tide. In the evening the rider of the storm will bring you wheat in
torrents."

'In the first light of dawn all my household gathered round me,
the children brought pitch and the men whatever was necessary.
On the fifth day I laid the keel and the ribs, then I made fast the
planking. The ground-space was one acre, each side of the deck
measured one hundred and twenty cubits, making a square. I built
six decks below, seven in all, I divided them into nine sections with
bulkheads between. I drove in wedges where needed, I saw to the
punt-poles, and laid in supplies. The carriers brought oil in baskets,
I poured pitch into the furnace and asphalt and oil; more oil was
consumed in caulking, and more again the master of the boat took
into his stores. I slaughtered bullocks for the people and every day
I killed sheep. I gave the shipwrights wine to drink as though it
were river water, raw wine and red wine and oil and white wine.
There was feasting then as there is at the time of the New Year's
festival; I myself anointed my head. On the seventh day the boat
was complete.

'Then was the launching full of difficulty; there was shifting of
ballast above and below till two thirds was submerged. I loaded
into her all that I had of gold and of living things, my family, my
kin, the beast of the field both wild and tame, and all the crafts-
men. I sent them on board, for the time that Shamash had ordained

was already fulfilled when he said, "In the evening, when the rider of the storm sends down the destroying rain, enter the boat and batten her down." The time was fulfilled, the evening came, the rider of the storm sent down the rain. I looked out at the weather and it was terrible, so I too boarded the boat and battened her down. All was now complete, the battening and the caulking; so I handed the tiller to Puzur-Amurri the steersman, with the navigation and the care of the whole boat.

'With the first light of dawn a black cloud came from the horizon; it thundered within where Adad, lord of the storm was riding. In front over hill and plain Shullat and Hanish, heralds of the storm, led on. Then the gods of the abyss rose up; Nergal pulled out the dams of the nether waters, Ninurta the war-lord threw down the dykes, and the seven judges of hell, the Annunaki, raised their torches, lighting the land with their livid flame. A stupor of despair went up to heaven when the god of the storm turned daylight to darkness, when he smashed the land like a cup. One whole day the tempest raged, gathering fury as it went, it poured over the people like the tides of battle; a man could not see his brother nor the people be seen from heaven. Even the gods were terrified at the flood, they fled to the highest heaven, the firmament of Anu; they crouched against the walls, cowering like curs. Then Ishtar the sweet-voiced Queen of Heaven cried out like a woman in travail: "Alas the days of old are turned to dust because I commanded evil; why did I command this evil in the council of all the gods? I commanded wars to destroy the people, but are they not my people, for I brought them forth? Now like the spawn of fish they float in the ocean." The great gods of heaven and of hell wept, they covered their mouths.

'For six days and six nights the winds blew, torrent and tempest and flood overwhelmed the world, tempest and flood raged together like warring hosts. When the seventh day dawned the storm from the south subsided, the sea grew calm, the flood was stilled; I looked at the face of the world and there was silence, all mankind was turned to clay. The surface of the sea stretched as flat as a roof-top; I opened a hatch and the light fell on my face. Then I bowed low, I sat down and I wept, the tears streamed down my face, for on every side was the waste of water. I looked for land in vain, but fourteen leagues distant there appeared a mountain, and there the boat grounded; on the mountain of Nisir the boat held fast, she held fast and did not budge. One day she held, and a second day on the mountain of Nisir she held fast and did not budge. A third day, and a fourth day she held fast on the mountain and did not budge; a fifth day and a sixth day she held fast on the mountain. When the seventh day dawned I loosed a dove and let her go. She flew away, but finding no resting-place she returned. Then I loosed a swallow, and she flew away but finding no resting-place she returned. I loosed a raven, she saw that the waters had retreated, she ate, she flew around, she cawed, and she did not come back. Then I threw everything open to the four winds, I made a sacrifice and poured out a libation on the mountain top. Seven and again seven cauldrons I set up on their stands, I heaped up wood and cane and cedar and myrtle. When the gods smelled the sweet savour, they gathered like flies over the sacrifice. Then, at last, Ishtar also came, she lifted her necklace with the jewels of heaven that once Anu had made to please her. "O you gods here present, by the lapis lazuli round my neck I shall remember these days as I remember the jewels of my throat; these last days I shall not forget. Let all the gods gather round the sacrifice, except Enlil. He shall not approach this offering, for without reflection he brought the flood; he consigned my people to destruction."

'When Enlil had come, when he saw the boat, he was wrath and swelled with anger at the gods, the host of heaven, "Has any of these mortals escaped? Not one was to have survived the destruction." Then the god of the wells and canals Ninurta opened his mouth and said to the warrior Enlil, "Who is there of the gods that can devise without Ea? It is Ea alone who knows all things." Then Ea opened his mouth and spoke to warrior Enlil, "Wisest of gods, hero Enlil, how could you so senselessly bring down the flood?

> *Lay upon the sinner his sin,*
> *Lay upon the transgressor his transgression,*
> *Punish him a little when he breaks loose,*
> *Do not drive him too hard or he perishes;*
> *Would that a lion had ravaged mankind*

Rather than the flood,
Would that a wolf had ravaged mankind
Rather than the flood,
Would that famine had wasted the world
Rather than the flood,
Would that pestilence had wasted mankind
Rather than the flood.

It was not I that revealed the secret of the gods; the wise man learned it in a dream. Now take your counsel what shall be done with him."

'Then Enlil went up into the boat, he took me by the hand and my wife and made us enter the boat and kneel down on either side, he standing between us. He touched our foreheads to bless us saying, "In time past Utnapishtim was a mortal man; henceforth he and his wife shall live in the distance at the mouth of the rivers." Thus it was that the gods took me and placed me here to live in the distance, at the mouth of the rivers.'

GENESIS 6:9–8:23

. . . Noah was a righteous man, blameless in his generation; Noah walked with God. [10] And Noah had three sons, Shem, Ham, and Japheth.

[11] Now the earth was corrupt in God's sight, and the earth was filled with violence. [12] And God saw the earth, and behold, it was corrupt; for all flesh had corrupted their way upon the earth. [13] And God said to Noah, "I have determined to make an end of all flesh; for the earth is filled with violence through them; behold, I will destroy them with the earth. [14] Make yourself an ark of gopher wood; make rooms in the ark, and cover it inside and out with pitch. [15] This is how you are to make it: the length of the ark three hundred cubits, its breadth fifty cubits, and its height thirty cubits. [16] Make a roof[k] for the ark, and finish it to a cubit above; and set the door of

[k] Or *window*

the ark in its side; make it with lower, second, and third decks. ¹⁷ For behold, I will bring a flood of waters upon the earth, to destroy all flesh in which is the breath of life from under heaven; everything that is on the earth shall die. ¹⁸ But I will establish my covenant with you; and you shall come into the ark, you, your sons, your wife, and your sons' wives with you. ¹⁹ And of every living thing of all flesh, you shall bring two of every sort into the ark, to keep them alive with you; they shall be male and female. ²⁰ Of the birds according to their kinds, and of the animals according to their kinds, of every creeping thing of the ground according to its kind, two of every sort shall come in to you, to keep them alive. ²¹ Also take with you every sort of food that is eaten, and store it up; and it shall serve as food for you and for them." ²² Noah did this; he did all that God commanded him.

7 Then the LORD said to Noah, "Go into the ark, you and all your household, for I have seen that you are righteous before me in this generation. ² Take with you seven pairs of all clean animals, the male and his mate; and a pair of the animals that are not clean, the male and his mate; ³ and seven pairs of the birds of the air also, male and female, to keep their kind alive upon the face of all the earth. ⁴ For in seven days I will send rain upon the earth forty days and forty nights; and every living thing that I have made I will blot out from the face of the ground." ⁵ And Noah did all that the LORD had commanded him.

⁶ Noah was six hundred years old when the flood of waters came upon the earth. ⁷ And Noah and his sons and his wife and his sons' wives with him went into the ark, to escape the waters of the flood. ⁸ Of clean animals, and of animals that are not clean, and of birds, and of everything that creeps on the ground, ⁹ two and two, male and female, went into the ark with Noah, as God had commanded Noah. ¹⁰ And after seven days the waters of the flood came upon the earth.

¹¹ In the six hundredth year of Noah's life, in the second month, on the seventeenth day of the month, on that day all the fountains of the great deep burst forth, and the windows of the heavens were opened. ¹² And rain fell upon the earth forty days and

forty nights. [13] On the very same day Noah and his sons, Shem and Ham and Japheth, and Noah's wife and the three wives of his sons with them entered the ark, [14] they and every beast according to its kind, and all the cattle according to their kinds, and every creeping thing that creeps on the earth according to its kind, and every bird according to its kind, and every bird according to its kind, every bird of every sort. [15] They went into the ark with Noah, two and two of all flesh in which there was the breath of life. [16] And they that entered, male and female of all flesh, went in as God had commanded him; and the LORD shut him in.

[17] The flood continued forty days upon the earth; and the waters increased, and bore up the ark, and it rose high above the earth. [18] The waters prevailed and increased greatly upon the earth; and the ark floated on the face of the waters. [19] And the waters prevailed so mightily upon the earth that all the high mountains under the whole heaven were covered; [20] the waters prevailed above the mountains, covering them fifteen cubits deep. [21] And all flesh died that moved upon the earth, birds, cattle, beasts, all swarming creatures that swarm upon the earth, and every man; [22] everything on the dry land in whose nostrils was the breath of life died. [23] He blotted out every living thing that was upon the face of the ground, man and animals and creeping things and birds of the air; they were blotted out from the earth. Only Noah was left, and those that were with him in the ark. [24] And the waters prevailed upon the earth a hundred and fifty days.

8 But God remembered Noah and all the beasts and all the cattle that were with him in the ark. And God made a wind blow over the earth, and the waters subsided; [2] the fountains of the deep and the windows of the heavens were closed, the rain from the heavens was restrained, [3] and the waters receded from the earth continually. At the end of a hundred and fifty days the waters had abated; [4] and in the seventh month, on the seventeenth day of the month, the ark came to test upon the mountains of Ar'arat. [5] And the waters continued to abate until the tenth month; in the tenth month, on the first day of the month, the tops of the mountains were seen.

⁶ At the end of forty days Noah opened the window of the ark which he had made, ⁷ and sent forth a raven; and it went to and fro until the waters were dried up from the earth. ⁸ Then he sent forth a dove from him, to see if the waters had subsided from the face of the ground; ⁹ but the dove found no place to set her foot, and she returned to him to the ark, for the waters were still on the face of the whole earth. So he put forth his hand and took her and brought her into the ark with him. ¹⁰ He waited another seven days, and again he sent forth the dove out of the ark; ¹¹ and the dove came back to him in the evening, and lo, in her mouth a freshly plucked olive leaf; so Noah knew that the waters had subsided from the earth. ¹² Then he waited another seven days, and sent forth the dove; and she did not return to him any more.

¹³ In the six hundred and first year, in the first month, the first day of the month, the waters were dried from off the earth; and Noah removed the covering of the ark, and looked, and behold, the face of the ground was dry. ¹⁴ In the second month, on the twenty-seventh day of the month, the earth was dry. ¹⁵ Then God said to Noah, ¹⁶ "Go forth from the ark, you and your wife, and your sons and your sons' wives with you. ¹⁷ Bring forth with you every living thing that is with you of all flesh—birds and animals and every creeping thing that creeps on the earth—that they may breed abundantly on the earth, and be fruitful and multiply upon the earth." ¹⁸ So Noah went forth, and his sons and his wife and his sons' wives with him. ¹⁹ And every beast, every creeping thing, and every bird, everything that moves upon the earth, went forth by families out of the ark.

²⁰ Then Noah built an altar to the LORD, and took of every clean animal and of every clean bird, and offered burnt offerings on the altar. ²¹ And when the LORD smelled the pleasing odor, the LORD said in his heart, "I will never again curse the ground because of man, for the imagination of man's heart is evil from his youth; neither will I ever again destroy every living creature as I have done. ²³ While the earth remains, seedtime and harvest, cold and heat, summer and winter, day and night, shall not cease."

Questions

1. Describe the flood in each story. Why does it happen? How long does it last? What destruction does it cause?

2. Who is the protagonist of each flood story and what reasons does the text give for why he is saved from the flood? Whom does each protagonist save from the flood and how? What are some of the details of the ship each protagonist builds, and what goes on the ship?

3. What hints in the Utnapishtim flood story in the *Epic of Gilgamesh* point to an urban context? What hints in the Noah flood story in Genesis point to a more pastoral nomadic context? How might you account for these different contextual clues?

Environmental Changes Influence Harappan Civilization (1700–1500 BCE)

Harappan civilization was the first urban culture of the Indus Valley. It was populated with city centers such as Harappa (the first excavated by modern archaeologists and hence after which the civilization is named), Mohenjo Daro, Dholavira, and Lothal. Complex city plans, which included large structures that scholars have interpreted as administrative buildings (perhaps even granaries), suggest a degree of central organization. Semiprecious stones such as carnelian, which is native to the region, are found in Egyptian and Mesopotamian grave goods. Such finds demonstrate that long-distance trade connected these regions. The urban and connected Harappan culture is also referred to as Indus Valley Civilization, for the river along which many of its settlements were established. However, like Mesopotamia, watered by its two rivers the Tigris and Euphrates, Harappan civilization was also settled along two rivers, the Indus and the Sarasvati (modern Ghaggar-Hakra River).

While there were earlier settlements in the region, Harappan civilization began to thrive around 2500 BCE, reached its height around 2000 BCE, and then declined by 1500 BCE. Scholars have long debated why, and the extent to which, Harappan civilization faded. Possible reasons used as an explanation for Harappan decline have included population movements, changes in transregional trade and agricultural patterns, deforestation, tectonic shifts, and climate change (in particular, shifts in the monsoons that fed its mighty rivers). Contemporary Egyptian and Mesopotamian writings offer scholars a wealth of source material for their respective civilizations; but the writing of Harappan peoples, namely the Indus Valley script as preserved on seal stones and the Dholavira gate inscription, is yet to be deciphered. Consequently, scholars must rely on a different range of evidence in their attempt to understand this civilization. The passage included here is excerpted from a recent article published in a modern scientific journal. The article describes Indian scientists' use of satellite data to trace the course of the now dried-up Sarasvati River and its relationship with Harappan-period settlements that have been identified through archaeological survey.

The region of northwestern India (covering the states of Punjab, Haryana, Gujarat and Rajasthan) and flood plains of [the] river Indus and its tributaries in Pakistan is geographically diverse, geologically active and rich in archaeological sites of the Harappan civilization (2500 BC–1500 BC). In the past few decades a large amount of work has been carried out to map palaeochannels in this region using multi-sensor satellite data and to understand their migration and evolution. These studies have shown evidence of a prominent river system, which has become buried under the sand cover of [the] Thar Desert sometime during [the] late Holocene. This major river has been identified as Sarasvati, a legendary river mentioned in ancient Indian texts including the Rigveda. The Sarasvati river is inferred to flow from [the] Himalayas to [the] Arabian Sea through [the] present states of Punjab, Haryana, Rajasthan, and, in Pakistan, Bahawalpur and Sind.

An IRS-1C WiFS [Indian Space Research Satellite 1C, Wide Field Sensor] mosaic provid[es] a synoptic view of the study area covering [the] Indus basin and the Thar desert. [A] large portion of the study area appears as [a] light bluish to white tone due to the presence of aeolian [wind-blown] sand. However, the synoptic

SOURCE: M. B. Rajani and A. S. Rajawat, *Journal of Archaeological Science* 38:9 (September 2011), pp. 2010–16.

cover in this data distinctly shows the pattern of palaeochannels in north-western India and adjoining parts of Pakistan. Present day dried Ghaggar bed is identified as [the] palaeochannel of the river Sarasvati.

The present study aimed to analyse multisensor satellite data using digital interpretation techniques in conjunction with [a] Geographical Information System (GIS) to reconfirm as well as identify hitherto unknown palaeochannels in the Indus basin [,] in particular [the] Thar desert [,] and [to] correlate with spatial distribution of Harappan settlements. The study also aimed to utilize [a] 3D view of the terrain using SRTM DEM [Shuttle Research Topography Mission—Digital Elevation Map] in conjunction with enhanced satellite data to identify geomorphological guides for archaeological exploration.

* * *

Extensive archaeological survey and exploration between 1954 and 1975 have identified around seven hundred sites belonging to different phases of Indus civilization within the political boundaries of India, and about two hundred and fifty sites in Pakistan. The geographical extent of this culture spreads over 1.5 million sq km extending beyond the confines of the Indus Valley [,] therefore archaeologists have redesignated it as Harappan Culture, named after the first discovered site, Harappa. Considering the area of its spread and span of time [,] there has been a remarkable uniformity and standardization in weights, measures, ceramics, construction, town planning, arts and crafts which binds them as one culture. The outer limits of Harappan culture include Surkagendor (Makran) in the west, Alamgirpur (UP, India) in the east, Rupar in the north and Bhagatrav in south Gujarat, India. The total period has also been divided into three: the early Harappan (2500–2200 BC), the mature Harappan (2200–1700 BC) and the later Harappan (1700–around 1500 BC).

The Harappans were great city planners. They based their city streets on a grid system and [the city] was surrounded by massive walls and gateways. The walls were built to control trade and also to stop the city from being flooded. Each part of the city was made up of walled sections. Streets were oriented east to west. Each street had a well-organized drain system. If the drains were not cleaned, the water ran into the houses and silt built up. Then the Harappans would build another story on top of it. This raised the level of the city over the years, and today archaeologists call these high structures "mounds."

Joshi and Bisht (1994) have compiled the data on Harappan sites in India. Mughal (1982) has mapped 414 sites in a 16–24 km wide strip along the Hakra bed in Cholistan desert (Bahawalpur, Pakistan) extending over a distance of 480 km starting from Fort Abbas on [the] Indo-Pakistan border to Rahim Yar Khan, Pakistan. Sahai (1999) has attempted to superimpose [the] location of Harappan sites on the palaeochannels as deciphered by Pal et al. (1980) using [a] GIS environment. In the present study we have superimposed mature and late Harappan sites on Resourcesat-1 AWiFS data covering the entire basin of the ancient river system in the north-western Indian subcontinent. The observations show that there is fairly good distribution of Mature Harappan sites along the palaeochannels of [the] ancient river system in northern Rajasthan and [the] Bahawalpur region of Pakistan.

The distribution of Late Harappan sites is mainly along the Bahawalpur region in Pakistan. Late Harappan sites are not observed along the palaeochannel upstream on the India side and parts of the upper Indo-Gangetic plain [,] indicating that by this time the bed identified as Sarasvati must have dried. A large number of Mature Harappan sites are observed in the Kachchh and Saurashtra peninsula in Gujarat state.

A 3D view of the palaeochannel of the Sarasvati (Ghagga region) seen on IRS 1D LISS-III [Linear Imaging Self-Scanning Sensor] along with Mature Harappan sites plotted as black dots [shows that] these sites occupy the adjoining relict natural levees seen as raised mounds. It suggests that other relict natural levees or raised mounds adjoining the identified palaeochannel courses may be taken up for further archaeological exploration. Most of the sites are located at the fringe of the Thar Desert (western boundary) with the Indo-Gangetic plain. It is observed that only five or six mature Harappan sites are located within the aeolian cover of [the]

Thar Desert seen as [a] bluish-white tone of AWiFS FCC [Advanced Wide Field Sensor False Colour Composites] mosaic. Five of these sites coincide with courses of the river Sarasvati identified in the present study. Further exploration along the identified courses of this river system may yield fruitful results in terms of finding new sites. The reduction in the number of sites between the Mature and Late period and also the shrinkage in the geographical area covered by Late Harappan sites as compared with the Mature Harappan ones is very significant. A large number of sites of the Mature period must have ceased to exist, perhaps due to the channels' drying up and not having sufficient water supply for sustenance of the settlements. The inhabitants of these sites might have abandoned them and migrated elsewhere. The cluster of sites in the region further west might have lasted into [a] later period because of [a] continued supply of water although from a different course. The area in Pakistan where there is a cluster of later sites has a cluster of Mature period sites too. It could be due to the water supply to this area continuing for longer. Presence of [a] large spread of Mature Harappan (2200–1700 BC) sites along the palaeochannel of the Sarasvati and its tributaries in north-west India and occurrence of Late Harappan sites limited to further west in adjoining regions of Pakistan suggests that the shift of cluster of settlements have followed the pattern of river migration towards [the] west. These are questions for further investigation. One would raise also the possibility of palaeoclimatic changes and related studies for detailed investigation.

Questions

1. What does the excerpt argue happened to the Sarasvati River?

2. What evidence does the excerpt use to make this argument? What other evidence do you wish you had for considering this issue?

3. According to the excerpt, how did changes in the course of the Sarasvati River have an impact on later Harappan settlement patterns?

Chapter **3**

Nomads, Territorial States, and Microsocieties, 2000–1200 BCE

The Code of Hammurapi (c. 1792 BCE)

Hammurapi (also spelled Hammurabi) became king of the Mesopotamian city-state of Babylon in 1792 BCE. His career as a conqueror began when the Elamite state, which controlled the trade routes through the Zagros mountains, tried to expand its influence into the Mesopotamian plain. Allying with other Mesopotamian rulers, Hammurapi defeated the Elamites. He then turned on his former allies and conquered the lands to his south and, later, those to his north. The empire he ruled over contained virtually all of Mesopotamia. To facilitate the rule of such a large state, Hammurapi issued one of the earliest known codes of law. Carved on a stone stele, it was displayed in a public place. In the twelfth century BCE it was acquired as war booty by the Elamites, who took it to Susa, their capital, which is located in modern Iran. French archaeologists discovered it in 1901. Spelling has been updated in the following excerpt to reflect modern orthography.

When the lofty Anu, King of the Anunnaki, and Ellil, lord of heaven and earth, he who determines the destiny of the land, committed the rule of all mankind to Marduk, the chief son of Ea; when they made him great among the Igigi; when they pronounced the lofty name of Babylon; when they made it famous among the quarters of the world and in its midst established an everlasting kingdom whose foundations were firm as heaven and earth—at that time, Anu and Enlil called me, Hammurapi the exalted prince, the worshipper of the gods, to cause justice to prevail in the land, to destroy the wicked and the evil, to prevent the strong from oppressing the weak, to go forth like the Sun over the Black Head Race, to enlighten the land, and to further the welfare of the people.

* * *

15. If a man aid a male or female slave of the palace, or a male or female slave of a freeman [former slave], to escape from the city gate, he shall be put to death.

16. If a man harbour in his house a male or female slave who has fled from the palace or from a freeman, and do not bring him (the slave) forth at the call of the commandant, the owner of that house shall be put to death.

17. If a man seize a male or female slave, a fugitive, in the field, and bring that (slave) back to his owner, the owner of the slave shall pay him two shekels of silver.

* * *

128. If a man take a wife and do not arrange with her the (proper) contracts, that woman is not a (legal) wife.

129. If the wife of a man be taken in lying with another man, they shall bind them and throw them into the water. If the husband of the woman would save his wife, or if the king would save his male servant (he may).

SOURCE: Percy Handcock, *The Code of Hammurabi* (New York: Macmillan, 1920), pp. 6, 11, 22–24, 27, 33–34.

130. If a man force the (betrothed) wife of another who has not known a male and is living in her father's house, and he lie in her bosom and they take him, that man shall be put to death and that woman shall go free.

131. If a man accuse his wife and she has not been taken in lying with another man, she shall take an oath in the name of the god and she shall return to her house.

132. If the finger have been pointed at the wife of a man because of another man, and she have not been taken in lying with another man, for her husband's sake she shall throw herself into the river.

* * *

137. If a man set his face to put away a concubine who has borne him children, or a wife who has presented him with children, he shall return to that woman her dowry and shall give to her the income of field, garden, and goods, and she shall bring up her children; from the time that her children are grown up, from whatever is given to her children, they shall give to her a portion corresponding to that of a son, and the man of her choice may marry her.

138. If a man would put away his wife who has not borne him children, he shall give her money to the amount of her marriage settlement, and he shall make good to her the dowry which she brought from her father's house and then he may put her away.

* * *

141. If the wife of a man who is living in his house set her face to go out and play the part of a fool, neglect her house, belittle her husband, they shall call her to account; if her husband say: "I have put her away," he shall let her go. On her departure nothing shall be given to her for her divorce. If her husband say: "I have not put her away," her husband may take another woman. The first woman shall dwell in the house of her husband as a maid-servant.

142. If a woman hate her husband, and say: "Thou shalt not have me," they shall inquire into her antecedents for her defects, and if she have been a careful mistress and be without reproach,

and her husband have been going about and greatly belittling her, that woman has no blame. She shall receive her dowry and shall go to her father's house.

* * *

167. If a man take a wife and she bear him children, and that woman die, and after her (death) he take another wife and she bear him children, and later the father die, the children of the mothers shall not divide (the estate). They shall receive the dowries of their respective mothers and they shall divide equally the goods of the house of the father.

* * *

195. If a son strike his father, they shall cut off his fingers.
196. If a man destroy the eye of a man (gentleman), they shall destroy his eye.
198. If one destroy the eye of a freeman or break the bone of a freeman, he shall pay 1 mana of silver.
199. If one destroy the eye of a man's slave, or break a bone of a man's slave, he shall pay one-half his price.

* * *

209. If a man strike a man's daughter and bring about a miscarriage, he shall pay 10 shekels of silver for her miscarriage.

Questions

1. Hammurapi's code contains several decrees concerning slaves. What seems to be the importance of slavery in Babylonia? Are offenses involving slaves punished more severely than other types of offenses?

2. What can we deduce from the code about the nature of the Babylonian family?

3. Why would Hammurapi put his laws on public display at a time when almost everyone was illiterate?

Nebamun Inspecting Flocks and Herds (1350 BCE)

Right around the time that Jean-François Champollion cracked Egyptian hieroglyphs using the trilingual Rosetta Stone, documents written by British diplomats and travelers mention the appearance of Nebamun's paintings on the antiquities scene of Egypt. The paintings of the tomb-chapel of Nebamun were acquired by the British Museum in the early nineteenth century, when Europeans' fascination with all things Egypt was surging. The exact find-spot of Nebamun's tomb was not clear, but later scholars have dated it to around 1350 BCE in the necropolis of Thebes along the Nile River. As might be expected in a tomb, the paintings show offerings made at Nebamun's death and a funerary banquet attended by friends and family, living and dead, as well as dancers, musicians, and other servants. Presented here, however, are two scenes that depict Nebamun's life and work as "Scribe and Grain Accountant of the Granary of the Divine Offerings of Amun." In the first scene, on the top level, you can just make out the lower body of the scribes sitting cross-legged as they take notes about the flock before them. On the lower level of the scene, from left to right, there is a table piled high with offerings, a scribe reading an account surrounded

by the tools of his trade (writing kit in front, scroll chests behind), geese offered in baskets, and a flock of geese being driven forward by the gooseherders. In the second scene, an elderly man stands in his wheat field next to a boundary stone as two chariot drivers await the return of the surveyors.

Questions

1. Examine the pictures for details in the way the artist(s) drew the various individuals: the scribe, the gooseherders, the farmer, and the chariot drivers. Note also the detail in the representation of the geese and the horses. Why do you think the artists took such care with the details—of clothes, posture, movement, etc.—of their animal and human subjects (especially the scribe)?

2. What do these images suggest about the economy and social context of New Kingdom Egypt?

3. Why do you think the British Museum would have acquired these paintings in the early nineteenth century, even without clear records on where they had come from?

SOURCE: HIP/Art Resource, NY.

Amarna Letters (c. 1340–1320 BCE)

The Amarna correspondence is a cache of nearly 350 letters written in cuneiform script, primarily in Akkadian, with a few in other languages including Assyrian, Hittite, and Hurrian. The collection of letters demonstrates the complex nexus of diplomatic relations between Egyptian pharaohs and Babylonian and Hittite leaders in the late fourteenth century BCE. The letters make reference to alliances between leaders as "brotherhoods" and close friendships. Topics include marriage alliances and gift exchange, and the obligations that come with both. The first letter included here (EA 10 = BM 29786) was sent by Burra-Buriyaš, a king of Babylon, to Naphurareya, thought by modern scholars to be Akhenaten (reigned c. 1351–1334 BCE). Akhenaten, also known as Amenhotep IV, was the father of Tutankhamun (the King Tut made famous by his tomb) and husband of Nefertiti (famed for her regal beauty). Yet Akhenaten is most significant in Egyptian history for his adoption of a short-lived form of monotheism that focused on the worship of Aten, a sun deity, and his founding of a city dedicated to Aten. That city was Akhetaten, modern el-Amarna, where these letters were found. The second letter included here (EA 41) was sent by the Hittite king Šuppiluliumaš (reigned c. 1344–1322 BCE) to an Egyptian pharaoh, possibly Tutankhamun.

Letter EA 10: Burra-Buriyaš, King of Babylon, to Naphurareya/Akhenaten (?) of Egypt

[Say t]o [Naphu]rar[ey]a, the king of [Egypt: T]hus Burra-Buriyaš, the king of Karad[uniyaš]. For me all goes wel[l]. For you, for your household, for your wives, fo[r your sons], for your magnates, for your troops, for your chariots, for your horses, and for your country, may all go very well.

8–24 From the time of Karaindaš, since the messengers of your ancestors came regularly to my ancestors, up to the present, they

Source: *The Amarna Letters*, edited and translated by William L. Moran (Baltimore: Johns Hopkins University Press, 1992), pp. 19–20, 114.

(the ancestors) have been friends. Now, though you and I are friends, 3 times have your messengers come to me and you have not sent me a single beautiful greeting-gift: nor have I for my part sent you a beautiful greeting-gift. (I am one for whom nothing is scarce, and you are one for whom nothing is scarce.) As for your messenger whom you sent to me, the 20 minas of gold that were brought here were not all there. When they put it into the kiln, not 5 minas of gold appeared. [The . . . th]at did appear, on cooling off looked like ashes. Was [the gold ev]er . . . identifi[ed] (as gold)? [. . .] friends with e[ach other] [. . .] . . . 25–28 [. . .] 29–42 [. . .] of a wild ox for . . . [. . .] when your messenger . . . [. . .] let him bring to me. There are skilled carpenters where you are. Let them represent a wild animal, land or aquatic, lifelike, so that the hide is exactly like that of a live animal. Let your messenger bring it to me. But if there are some old ones already on hand, then as soon as Šindišugab, my messenger, reaches you, let him immediately, posthaste, borrow chariot[s] and get here. Let them make some n[e]w ones for future delivery, and then when my messenger comes here with your messenger, let them bring (them) here together. 43–49 I send as your greeting-gift 2 minas of lapis lazuli, and concerning your daughter Mayati, having heard (about her), I send to her as her greeting-gift a necklace of cricket-(shaped) gems, of lapis lazuli, 1048 their number. And when the messenger [comes] along with Šindišugab, I will make [. . .] and have (it) brough[t to h]er . . .

LETTER EA 41: HITTITE KING ŠUPPILULIUMAŠ TO EGYPTIAN PHARAOH (POSSIBLY TUTANKHAMUN)

[Thus the Sun], Šuppiluliumaš, G[reat] King, [king of Har]ti. Say to Huriy[a, the king of Eg]ypt, my brother:

* * *

4–6 [For me all goes w]ell. For you may all go wel[l. For yo]ur [wives], your sons, your household, your troops, your chariot[ts, and i]n your country, may all go very well.

7–13 Neither my messengers, whom I sent to your father, nor the request that your father made, saying, "Let us establish only the most friendly relations between us," did I indeed re[fus]e. What-soever your father said to me, I indeed did absolutely eve[ry]thing. And my own request, indeed, that I made to your father, he never refused; he gave me absolutely everything.

14–15 Why, my brother, have you held back the presents that your father made to me when he was al[iv]e?

16–22 Now, my brother, [yo]u have ascended the throne of your father, and just as your father and I were desirous of peace between us, so now too should you and I be friendly with one another. The request (that) I expressed to your father [I shall express] to my brother, too. Let us be helpful to each other.

23–28 My brother, do not hold back anything that [I asked] of your father. [As to the 2 st]atues of gold, one [should be standing], one should be seated. And, my brother, [send me] the 2 [silve]r statues of women, and a large piece of lapis lazuli, and a large stand for [. . .].

29–38 [. . .] . . . If my brother [wants to give them], let my [broth]er give the[m. But i]f my brother does not want to give them, when my chariots hav[e been r]eadied for . . . *linenhuzzi*, I will return them to my brother. Whatever you want, my brother, write to me so I can send it to you.

39–43 I herewith send you as your-greeting-gift: 1 silver rhyton, a stag, 5 minas its weight; 1 silver rhyton, a young ram, 3 minas its weight; 2 silver disks, 10 minas their weight, as 2 large nikiptu-trees.

Questions

1. What is the occasion for each letter? How does each letter's sender justify the request in the letter?

2. How does the sender of each letter greet the recipient? What does the set of relationships implied in the greetings and throughout the text of each letter suggest about the interactions among the "community of major powers" in the eastern Mediterranean in the late fourteenth century BCE?

3. What commodities are listed in each letter? What does this suggest about the economy and trade networks of the "community of major powers" among the territorial states of Egypt and Southwest Asia Minor?

Egyptian Account of the Battle of Qadesh (c. 1274 BCE)

The battle of Qadesh, fought c. 1274 BCE, was possibly the largest chariot battle in history. The Egyptians had been expanding their power into Canaan and Syria, gaining control of Qadesh in what is now Syria under the reign of the Pharaoh Seti I. However, the Hittite kingdom, based in what is now Turkey, was expanding its influence southward into Syria. Seti I handed Qadesh over to the Hittite ruler, Muwatalli I. Seti's successor, Ramses II, attempted to recover control of the city, which led to the battle. Egyptian records, excerpted below, indicate that the Egyptians won. Hittite sources, however, suggest that the Hittites won. In any case, Ramses had to abandon Qadesh. Spelling has been updated in the following excerpt to reflect modern orthography.

307. Behold, his majesty prepared his infantry and his chari-otry, the Sherden of the captivity of his majesty from the victories of his sword * * * they gave the plan of battle. His majesty proceeded northward, his infantry and his chariotry being with him. * * * Every country trembled before him, [fear] was in their hearts; all the rebels came bowing down for fear of the fame of his majesty, when his [army] came upon the narrow road, being like one who is upon the highway. * * *

308. * * * His majesty proceeded northward, and he then arrived at the high-land of Qadesh. Then his majesty * * * marched before, like his father, Montu lord of Thebes, and crossed over the channel of the Orontes there being with him the first division of Amon (named): "Victory-of-King-Usermare-Setepnere. * * *"

309. When his majesty * * * reached the city, behold, the wretched, vanquished chief of Kheta had come, having gathered together all countries from the ends of the sea to the land of Kheta,

SOURCE: James Henry Breasted, ed. and trans., *Ancient Records of Egypt: Historical Documents from the Earliest Times to the Persian Conquest* (Chicago: University of Chicago Press, 1906), Vol. 3, pp. 136–41, 143–47.

which came entire: the Naharin likewise, and Arvad, Mesa, Kesh-kesh, Kelekesh, Luka, Kezweden, Carchemish, Ekereth, Kode, the entire land of Nuges, Mesheneth, and Qadesh. He left not a country which was not brought, to[gether with] their chiefs who were with him, every man bringing his chariotry, an exceeding great multi-tude, without its like. They covered the mountains and the valleys; they were like grasshoppers with their multitudes. He left not silver nor gold in his land (but) he plundered it of all its possessions and gave to every country, in order to bring them with him to battle.

310. Behold, the wretched, vanquished chief of Kheta, together with the numerous allied countries, were stationed in battle array, concealed on the northwest of the city of Qadesh, while his maj-esty was alone by himself, [with] his bodyguard, and the division of Amon was marching behind him. The division of Re crossed over the river-bed on the south side of the town of Shabtuna, at the dis-tance of an iter from the [division of Amon]; the division of Ptah was on the south of the city of Aranami; and the division of Sutekh was marching upon the road. His majesty had formed the first rank of all the leaders of his army, while they were on the shore in the land of the Amor. Behold, the wretched vanquished chief of Kheta was stationed in the midst of the infantry which was with him, and he came not out to fight, for fear of his majesty. Then he made to go the people of the chariotry, an exceedingly numerous multitude like the sand, being three people to each span. Now, they had made their combinations (thus): among every three youths was one man of the vanquished of Kheta, equipped with all the weapons of battle. Lo, they had stationed them in battle array, concealed on the north-west the city of Qadesh.

311. They came forth from the southern side of Qadesh, and they cut through the division of Re in its middle, while they were march-ing without knowing and without being drawn up for battle. The infantry and chariotry of his majesty retreated before them. Now, his majesty had halted on the north of the city of Qadesh, on the western side of the Orontes. Then came one to tell it to his majesty. * * *

312. His majesty * * * shone like his father Montu, when he took the adornments of war; as he seized his coat of mail, he was like Baal in his hour. The great span which bore his majesty * * * called:

"Victory-in-Thebes," from the great stables of Ramses (II), was in the midst of the leaders. His majesty halted in the rout; then he charged into the foe, the vanquished of Kheta, being alone by himself and none other with him. When his majesty went to look behind him, he found 2,500 chariotry surrounding him, in his way out, being all the youth of the wretched Kheta, together with its numerous allied countries: from Arvad, from Mesa, from Pedes, from Keshkesh, from Erwenet, from Kezweden, from Aleppo, Eketeri, Qadesh, and Luka, being three men to a span, acting in unison.

*   *   *

319. When his majesty appeared like the rising of Re, he assumed the adornments of his father, Montu. When the king proceeded northward, and his majesty had arrived at the locality south of the town of Shabtuna, there came two Shasu, to speak to his majesty as follows: "Our brethren, who belong to the greatest of the families with the vanquished chief of Kheta, have made us come to his majesty, to say: 'We will be subjects of Pharaoh * * * and we will flee from the vanquished chief of Kheta; for the vanquished chief of Kheta sits in the land of Aleppo, on the north of Tunip. He fears because of Pharaoh * * * to come southward.'" Now, these Shasu spake these words, which they spake to his majesty, falsely, (for) the vanquished chief of Kheta made them come to spy where his majesty was, in order to cause the army of his majesty not to draw up for fighting him, to battle with the vanquished chief of Kheta.

320. Lo, the vanquished chief of Kheta came with every chief of every country, their infantry and their chariotry, which he had brought with him by force, and stood, equipped, drawn up in line of battle behind Qadesh the Deceitful, while his majesty knew it not. Then his majesty proceeded northward and arrived on the northwest of Qadesh; and the army of his majesty [made camp] there.

321. Then, as his majesty sat upon a throne of gold, there arrived a scout who was in the following of his majesty, and he brought two scouts of the vanquished chief of Kheta. They were conducted into the presence, and his majesty said to them: "What are ye?" They said: "As for us, the vanquished chief of the Kheta has caused that we should come to spy out where his majesty is." Said his majesty to

them: "He! Where is he, the vanquished chief of Kheta? Behold, I have heard, saying: 'He is in the land of Aleppo.'" Said they: "See, the vanquished chief of Kheta is stationed, together with many countries, which he has brought with him by force, being every country which is in the districts of the land of Kheta, the land of Naharin, and all Kode. They are equipped with infantry and chariotry, bearing their weapons; more numerous are they than the sand of the shore. See, they are standing, drawn up for battle, behind Qadesh the Deceitful."

322. Then his majesty had the princes called into the presence, and had them hear every word which the two scouts of the vanquished chief of Kheta, who were in the presence, had spoken. Said his majesty to them: "See ye the manner wherewith the chiefs of the peasantry and the officials under whom is the land of Pharaoh * * * have stood, daily, saying to the Pharaoh: 'The vanquished chief of Kheta is in the land of Aleppo, he has fled before his majesty, since hearing that, behold, he came.' So spake they to his majesty daily. But see, I have held a hearing in this very hour, with the two scouts of the vanquished chief of Kheta, to the effect that the vanquished chief of Kheta is coming, together with the numerous countries [that are with] him, being people and horses, like the multitudes of the sand. They are stationed behind Qadesh the Deceitful. But the governors of the countries and the officials under whose authority is the land of Pharaoh * * * were not able to tell it to us."

* * *

324. Then the vizier was ordered to hasten the army of his majesty, while they were marching on the south of Shabtuna, in order to bring them to the place where his majesty was.

325. Lo, while his majesty sat talking with the princes, the vanquished chief of Kheta came, and the numerous countries, which were with him. They crossed over the channel on the south of Qadesh, and charged into the army of his majesty while they were marching, and not expecting it. Then the infantry and chariotry of his majesty retreated before them, northward to the place where his majesty was. Lo, the foes of the vanquished chief of Kheta surrounded the bodyguard of his majesty, who were by his side.

326. When his majesty saw them, he was enraged against them, like his father, Montu, lord of Thebes. He seized the adornments of battle, and arrayed himself in his coat of mail. He was like Baal in his hour. Then he betook himself to his horses, and led quickly on, being alone by himself. He charged into the foes of the vanquished chief of Kheta, and the numerous countries which were with him. His majesty was like Sutekh, the great in strength, smiting and slaying among them; his majesty hurled them headlong, one upon another into the water of the Orontes.

Questions

1. How does Ramses II represent his role in the battle?

2. What does this document tell us about the "community of major powers" that was taking shape in the Near East?

3. What military tactics were employed during the battle?

Shang Dynasty Oracle Bones (c. 1200 BCE)

Oracle bones offer the earliest written documents for Chinese history. Using oracle bones, diviners would ask the ancestors about a range of topics, including weather, crops, military undertakings, health issues, and childbirth. In 1899, a large cache of these documents was found near the Shang dynasty capital at Anyang. Given the thousands of Chinese characters and their change over time, a great deal of interpretation is necessary for the translation of the bones. David N. Keightley, one of the world's leading experts on Shang dynasty oracle bones, has drawn attention to the rituals and labor hours that would have gone into the production of a series of oracle bones: the preparation of the turtle shell or ox scapula, the dramatic firing of the bone as the diviner called out the charge or question, watching and listening for cracks, the inscribing by a specialized engraver of the charges on the bone (although some have argued the inscribing came before the firing), and then the interpretation of the cracks that formed. A complete divination series—often on multiple shells or bones—would include the name of the diviner, the date of the questioning, a charge or topic (or a group of charges) often asked in multiple ways, and then sometimes other notations inscribed after the cracking, such as an interpretation by the diviner and even the outcome of the issues about which the diviner was questioning the ancestors. The oracle bone series provided here appears on a series of plastrons (the flat underbelly portion of a turtle shell). It dates to the reign of the Shang king Wu Ding (c. 1200 BCE) and mentions several ancestors (Fu Chia, Fu Keng, Fu Hsin, and Fu Yi).

PAIRS OF COMPLEMENTARY CHARGES	
Negative charge (left side)	Positive charge (right side)
(Preface:) (2) Crack-making on hsin-yu (day 58), Ch'üeh divined:	(1) Crack-making on hsin-yu (day 58), Ch'üeh divined:
(Charge:) "This season, the king should not follow Wang Ch'eng to attack the Hsia Wei, (for if he does, we) will not perhaps receive assistance in this case."	"This season, the king should follow Wang Ch'eng to attack the Hsia Wei, (for if he does, we) will receive assistance in this case."
(Preface:) (4) Crack-making on hsin-yu (day 58), Ch'üeh divined:	(3) Crack-making on hsin-yu (day 58), Ch'üeh divined:
(Charge:) "(This season) the king should not follow Chih Kuo (to attack the Pafang, for if he does, we will not perhaps receive assistance in this case)."	"(This season) the king should follow Chih Kuo (to attack the Pa-fang, for if he does, we will receive assistance in this case)."
(Preface:) (6) Crack-making on hsin-yu (day 58), Ch'üeh divined:	(5) Crack-making on hsin-yu (day 58), Ch'üeh divined:

SOURCE: David N. Keightley, *Sources of Shang History: The Oracle-Bone Inscriptions of Bronze Age China* (Berkeley: University of California Press, 1978), pp. 78–80.

(Charge:)	"(This season) it should not be Chih Kuo that the king follows (to attack the Pa-fang, for if he does we will not perhaps receive assistance in this case)."	"(This season) it should be Chih Kuo that the king follows (to attack the Pa-fang, for if he does we will receive assistance in this case)."
(Preface:)		(7) Divined:
(Charge:)	(8) "Praying to lead away this sick tooth (?), the *ting* sacrifice will be favorable."	"*Yu* sacrifice a dog to Fu Keng (and) *mao* sacrifice a sheep."
(Charge:)	(10) "(Sick tooth) will perhaps not be favorable."	(9) "Sick tooth will be favorable."

	Negative charge (left side)	Positive charge (right side)
(Subcharge:) (1)	It is because of Fu Chia.	(2) It is not because of Fu Chia.
(Subcharge:) (3)	It is because of Fu Keng.	(4) It is not because of Fu Keng.
(Subcharge:) (5)	It is because of Fu Hsin.	(6) It is not because of Fu Hsin.
(Subcharge:) (7)	It is because of Fu Yi.	(8) It is not because of Fu Yi.

NONCOMPLEMENTARY RECORDS

(First prognostication, 17:9:)	The king [reading the cracks] said: "There will perhaps be a natural phenomenon. If it be a wu day when there is a natural phenomenon, it will be inauspicious."
(Second prognostication, 19.9:)	The king, reading the cracks, said: "On ting-ch'ou (day 14), there will perhaps be a natural phenomenon; it will be inauspicious. If it be a chia day when there is a natural phenomenon, it will be auspicious. If it be a hsin day when there is a natural phenomenon, it will also be inauspicious.

Questions

1. Concerning what issues is this series of oracle bones seeking guidance? Based on the headnote to this selection and the information in the excerpt, how do you imagine the scene of this divination series as it took place?

2. What are the limits of oracle bones as documents for Shang dynasty history?

3. How does this earliest Shang writing—its purpose, its topics, its medium—compare with the contemporary and earlier written sources from other river basin civilizations (such as Mesopotamian, Egyptian, and Harappan) as seen in this chapter, in Chapter 2, and in the casebook "Humans and the Environment in the Second Millennium BCE"?

Catalog of the Greek Ships that Sailed to Troy (c. 1200 BCE)

The Mycenaean Greeks, with their dispersed island communities, walled fortresses, and chariot warfare, were a fierce Mediterranean microsociety, especially when united with a singular purpose. The legendary Trojan War was fought c. 1200 BCE, when a great host of Greek forces assaulted the citadel of Troy in northwest Asia Minor. The *Iliad*, Homer's account of the ninth year of that war, was composed more than 400 years later. Homer's *Iliad* likely compiled oral histories of the war that had been preserved across centuries by wandering bards. Scholars debate which elements of the socio-historic context evident in Homer's epics date from the time of the war (the twelfth century) as opposed to Homer's own times (the eighth century). And even after Homer wove these many stories into a unified poetic narrative, the story was edited further. The sixth-century Athenian tyrant Peisistratos, for instance, is credited with commissioning the first official version of Homer's epics, which perhaps accounts for Athens's suspicious prominence in the catalog of Greek ships sent to fight the Trojan War even though Athens was a backwater in the twelfth century. Despite the *Iliad*'s complicated transmission, set pieces like the "Catalog of Ships" (*Iliad* 2.494–759), included here, are thought to be among the oldest in the epic and can be mined for what they suggest about Mycenaean Greece or at least archaic Greek memory of the Trojan War.

SOURCE: *The Iliad of Homer*, translated by Richmond Lattimore (Chicago: University of Chicago Press, 1951), pp. 89–95.

Tell me now, you Muses who have your homes on
    Olympos.
485   For you, who are goddesses, are there, and you know all things,
    and we have heard only the rumour of it and know nothing.
    Who then of those were the chief men and the lords of the
        Danaans?
    I could not tell over the multitude of them nor name them,
    not if I had ten tongues and ten mouths, not if I had
490   a voice never to be broken and a heart of bronze within me,
    not unless the Muses of Olympia, daughters
    of Zeus of the aegis, remembered all those who came beneath
        Ilion.
    I will tell the lords of the ships, and the ships numbers.
      Leïtos and Peneleos were leaders of the Boiotians,
495   with Arkesilaos and Prothoenor and Klonios;
    they who lived in Hyria and in rocky Aulis,
    in the hill-bends of Eteonos, and Schoinos, and Skolos,
    Thespeia and Graia, and in spacious Mykalessos;
    they who dwelt about Harma and Eilesion and Erythrai,
500   they who held Eleon and Hyle and Peteon,
    with Okalea and Medeon, the strong-founded citadel,
    Kopai, and Eutresis, and Thisbe of the dove-cotes;
    they who held Koroneia, and the meadows of Haliartos,
    they who held Plataia, and they who dwelt about Glisa,
505   they who held the lower Thebes, the strong-founded citadel,
    and Onchestos the sacred, the shining grove of Poseidon;
    they who held Arne of the great vineyards, and Mideia,
    with Nisa the sacrosanct and uttermost Anthedon.
    Of these there were fifty ships in all, and on board
510   each of these a hundred and twenty sons of the Boiotians.
      But they who lived in Aspledon and Orchomenos of the
        Minyai,
    Askalaphos led these, and Ialmenos, children of Ares,
    whom Astyoche bore to him in the house of Aktor
    Azeus' son, a modest maiden; she went into the chamber
515   with strong Ares, who was laid in bed with her secretly.
    With these two there were marshaled thirty hollow vessels.

* * *

Swift Aias son of Oïleus led the men of Lokris,
the lesser Aias, not great in size like the son of Telamon,
but far slighter. He was a small man armoured in linen,
yet with the throwing spear surpassed all Achaians and
    Hellenes.   530
These were the dwellers in Kynos and Opoeis and Kalliaros,
and in Bessa, and Skarphe, and lovely Augeiai,
in Thronion and Tarphe and beside the waters of Boagrios.
Following along with him were forty black ships
of the Lokrians, who dwell across from sacred Euboia.   535
    They who held Euboia, the Abantes, whose wind was fury,
Chalkis, and Eretria, the great vineyards of Histiaia,
and seaborne Kerinthos and the steep stronghold of Dion,
they who held Karystos and they who dwelt about Styra,
of these the leader was Elephenor, scion of Ares,   540
son of Chalkodon and lord of the great-hearted Abantes.
And the running Abantes followed with him, their hair grown
long at the back, spearmen furious with the out-reached ash
    spear
to rip the corselets girt about the chests of their enemies.
Following along with him were forty black ships.   545
    But the men who held Athens, the strong-founded citadel,
the deme of great-hearted Erechtheus, whom once Athene
Zeus' daughter tended after the grain-giving fields had born
    him,
and established him to be in Athens in her own rich temple;
there as the circling years go by the sons of the Athenians   550
make propitiation with rams and bulls sacrificed;
of these men the leader was Peteos' son Menestheus.
Never on earth before had there been a man born like him
for the arrangement in order of horses and shielded fighters.
Nestor alone could challenge him, since he was far older.   555
Following along with him were fifty black ships.
    Out of Salamis Aias brought twelve ships and placed them
next to where the Athenian battalions were drawn up.

    They who held Argos and Tiryns of the huge walls,
560 Hermione and Asine lying down the deep gulf,
    Troizen and Eïonai, and Epidauros of the vineyards,
    they who held Aigina and Mases, sons of the Achaians,
    of these the leader was Diomedes of the great war cry
    with Sthenelos, own son to the high-renowned Kapaneus,
565 and with them as a third went Euryalos, a man godlike,
    son of Mekisteus the king, and scion of Talaos;
    but the leader of all was Diomedes of the great war cry.
    Following along with these were eighty black ships.
    But the men who held Mykenai, the strong-founded citadel,
570 Korinth the luxurious, and strong-founded Kleonai;
    they who dwelt in Orneai and lovely Araithyrea,
    and Sikyon, where of old Adrestos had held the kingship;
    they who held Hyperesia and steep Gonoëssa,
    they who held Pellene and they who dwelt about Aigion,
575 all about the sea-shore and about the wide headland of Helike,
    of their hundred ships the leader was powerful Agamemnon,
    Atreus' son, with whom followed far the best and bravest
    people; and among them he himself stood armoured in
      shining
    bronze, glorying, conspicuous among the great fighters,
580 since he was greatest among them all, and led the most people.
    They who held the swarming hollow of Lakedaimon,
    Pharis, and Sparta, and Messe of the dove-cotes,
    they who dwelt in Bryseiai and lovely Augeiai,
    they who held Amyklai and the seaward city of Helos,
585 they who held Laas, and they who dwelt about Oitylos,
    of these his brother Menelaos of the great war cry
    was leader, with sixty ships marshaled apart from the others.
    He himself went among them in the confidence of his valour,
    driving them battleward, since above all his heart was eager
590 to avenge Helen's longing to escape and her lamentations.
    They who dwelt about Pylos and lovely Arene,
    and Thryon, the Alpheios crossing, and strong-built Aipy;
    they who lived in Kyparisseeis and Amphigeneia,
    Pteleos and Helos and Dorion, where the Muses

encountering Thamyris the Thracian stopped him from singing   595
as he came from Oichalia and Oichalian Eurytos;
for he boasted that he would surpass, if the very Muses,
daughters of Zeus who holds the aegis, were singing against
    him,
and these in their anger struck him maimed, and the voice of
    wonder
they took away, and made him a singer without memory;   600
of these the leader was the Gerenian horseman, Nestor,
in whose command were marshaled ninety hollow vessels.
    They who held Arkadia under the sheer peak, Kyllene,
beside the tomb of Aipytos, where men fight at close
    quarters,
they who dwelt in Orchomenos of the flocks, and Pheneos,   605
about Rhipe and Stratia and windy Enispe;
they who held Tegea and Mantineia the lovely,
they who held Stymphalos, and dwelt about Parrhasia,
their leader was Angkaios' son, powerful Agapenor.
Sixty was the number of their ships, and in each ship   610
went many men of Arkadia, well skilled in battle.
Agamemnon the lord of men himself had given
these for the crossing of the wine-blue sea their strong-
    benched vessels,
Atreus' son, since the work of the sea was nothing to these
    men.

                    *   *   *

    They who came from Doulichion and the sacred Echinai,   625
islands, where men live across the water from Elis,
Meges was the leader of these, a man like Ares,
Phyleus' son, whom the rider dear to Zeus had begotten,
Phyleus, who angered with his father had settled
    Doulichion.
Following along with him were forty black ships.   630
    But Odysseus led the high-hearted men of Kephallenia,
those who held Ithaka and leaf-trembling Neriton,
those who dwelt about Krokyleia and rigged Aigilips,

those who held Zakynthos and those who dwelt about Samos,
those who held the mainland and the places next to the
635   crossing.
All these men were led by Odysseus, like Zeus in counsel.
Following with him were twelve ships with bows red painted

*   *   *

645   Idomeneus the spear-famed was leader of the Kretans,
those who held Knosos and Gortyna of the great walls,
Lyktos and Miletos and silver-shining Lykastos,
and Phaistos and Rhytion, all towns well established,
and others who dwelt beside them in Krete of the hundred
    cities.
650 Of all these Idomeneus the spear-famed was leader,
with Meriones, a match for the murderous Lord of Battles.
Following along with these were eighty black ships.
    Herakles' son Tlepolemos the huge and mighty
led from Rhodes nine ships with the proud men of Rhodes
    aboard them,
those who dwelt about Rhodes and were ordered in triple
655   division,
Ialysos and Lindos and silver-shining Kameiros.
Of all these Tlepolemos the spear-famed was leader,
he whom Astyocheia bore to the strength of Herakles.
Herakles brought her from Ephyra and the river Selleëis
660 after he sacked many cities of strong, god-supported fighters.
Now when Tlepolemos was grown in the strong-built mansion,
he struck to death his own father's beloved uncle,
Likymnios, scion of Ares, a man already ageing.
At once he put ships together and assembled a host of
    people
665 and went fugitive over the sea, since the others threatened,
the rest of the sons and the grandsons of the strength of
    Herakles.
And he came to Rhodes a wanderer, a man of misfortune,
and they settled there in triple division by tribes, beloved
of Zeus himself, who is lord over all gods and all men,

Kronos' son, who showered the wonder of wealth upon them.   670
  Nireus from Syme led three balanced vessels,
Nireus son of Aglaia and the king Charopos,
Nireus, the most beautiful man who came beneath Ilion
beyond the rest of the Danaans next after perfect Achilleus.
But he was a man of poor strength and few people with him.   675
  They who held Nisyros and Krapathos and Kasos,
and Kos, Eurypylos' city, and the islands called Kalydnai,
of these again Pheidippos and Antiphos were the leaders,
sons both of Thessalos who was born to the lord Herakles.
In their command were marshalled thirty hollow vessels.   680
  Now all those who dwelt about Pelasgian Argos,
those who lived by Alos and Alope and at Trachis,
those who held Phthia and Hellas the land of fair women,
who were called Myrmidons and Hellenes and Achaians,
of all these and their fifty ships the lord was Achilleus.   685
But these took no thought now for the grim clamour of
      battle
since there was no one who could guide them into close order,
since he, swift-footed brilliant Achilleus, lay where the ships
      were,
angered over the girl of the lovely hair, Briseis,
whom after much hard work he had taken away from Lyrnessos   690
after he had sacked Lyrnessos and the walls of Thebe
and struck down Epistrophos and Mynes the furious
      spearmen,
children of Euenos, king, and son of Selepios.
For her sake he lay grieving now, but was soon to rise up.
  They who held Phylake and Pyrasos of the flowers,   695
the precinct of Demeter, and Iton, mother of sheepflocks,
Antron by the sea-shore, and Pteleos deep in the meadows,
of these in turn fighting Protesilaos was leader
while he lived; but now the black earth had closed him under,
whose wife, cheeks torn for grief, was left behind in Phylake   700
and a marriage half completed; a Dardanian man had killed
      him
as he leapt from his ship, far the first of all the Achaians.

Yet these, longing as they did for their leader, did not go
  leaderless,
but Podarkes, scion of Ares, set them in order,
705 child of Iphikles, who in turn was son to Phylakos
rich in flocks, full brother of high-hearted Protesilaos,
younger born; but the elder man was braver also,
Protesilaos, a man of battle; yet still the people
lacked not a leader, though they longed for him and his valour.
710   Following along with Podarkes were forty black ships.

Questions

1. How does the "Catalog of Ships" itemize and describe the contingent
    supplied by each people? Map the places from which these ships and
    fighters come. What does this "catalog," with its list of city-states,
    leaders, and forces, suggest about the nature of Mycenaean political
    organization?

2. With what qualities are men described? When mentioned, how are
    women—like Astyoche, Helen, Astyocheia, Briseis, and Protesilaus's
    otherwise unnamed wife—described? What might these contrast-
    ing descriptions suggest about differing gender roles in Mycenaean
    Greece?

3. What role do gods and goddesses play in this passage? Why do you
    think the archaic Greeks included divine figures as historical agents?
    Why would later Greeks perpetuate in their retelling of the epic sto-
    ries that involvement of the divine in human affairs?

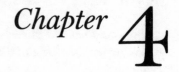

Chapter 4

First Empires and Common Cultures in Afro-Eurasia, 1250–325 bce

Rig-Veda (c. 1700–1100 bce)

The Rig-Veda is a collection of sacred hymns; it is among the oldest examples of Sanskrit literature and of Hindu religious texts. The name comes from the Sanskrit words *rg* (praise) and *veda* (knowledge). The Rig-Veda is one of four canonical Hindu texts, each of which has a specific religious and social function. Sections of these Vedas are still recited as prayers, an indication of long cultural continuities that survived processes of political change. The text originated between 1700 and 1100 bce in the ancient kingdoms of northwestern India—and so coincides with the period of Vedic migrations.

For at least a millennium, the Vedas survived only orally, with specific formulas, performance, and mnemonic markers serving to maintain remarkable continuity. The Rig-Veda is organized into 10 *mandalas* (books) of varying lengths and purposes: religious ritual, prayers, hymns, sacrifices, and commentary on everyday life. The following selection, from Hymn 90 in Book 10, tells a story of creation through sacrifice.

———————

Thousand-headed Purusha, thousand-eyed, thousand-footed—
he, having pervaded the earth on all sides, still extends ten fingers
beyond it.

Purusha alone is all this—whatever has been and whatever is
going to be. Further, he is the lord of immortality and also of what
grows on account of food.

Such is his greatness; greater, indeed, than this is Purusha. All
creatures constitute but one-quarter of him, his three-quarters are
the immortal in the heaven.

With his three-quarters did Purusha rise up; one-quarter of
him again remains here. With it did he variously spread out on all
sides over what eats and what eats not.

From him was Virāj born, from Virāj the evolved Purusha. He,
being born, projected himself behind the earth as also before it.

When the gods performed the sacrifice with Purusha as the
oblation, then the spring was its clarified butter, the summer the
sacrificial fuel, and the autumn the oblation.

The sacrificial victim, namely, Purusha, born at the very beginning, they sprinkled with sacred water upon the sacrificial grass.
With him as oblation, the gods performed the sacrifice, and also
the Sādhyas [a class of semidivine beings] and the rishis [ancient
seers].

From that wholly offered sacrificial oblation were born the
verses [ṛc] and the sacred chants; from it were born the meters
[chandas]; the sacrificial formula was born from it.

From it horses were born and also those animals who have double rows [i.e., upper and lower] of teeth; cows were born from it,
from it were born goats and sheep.

When they divided Purusha, in how many different portions
did they arrange him? What became of his mouth, what of his two
arms? What were his two thighs and his two feet called?

His mouth became the brāhman; his two arms were made into
the rājanya; his two thighs the vaishyas; from his two feet the
shūdra was born.

SOURCE: *Sources of Indian Tradition*, edited by Ainslie T. Embree (New
York: Columbia University Press, 1988), vol. 1, pp. 18–19.

The moon was born from the mind, from the eye the sun was born; from the mouth Indra and Agni, from the breath [*prāṇa*] the wind [vāyu] was born.

From the navel was the atmosphere created, from the head the heaven issued forth; from the two feet was born the earth and the quarters (the cardinal directions) from the ear. Thus did they fashion the worlds.

Seven were the enclosing sticks in this sacrifice, thrice seven were the fire-sticks made when the gods, performing the sacrifice, bound down Purusha, the sacrificial victim.

With this sacrificial oblation did the gods offer the sacrifice. These were the first norms [*dharma*] of sacrifice. These greatnesses reached to the sky wherein live the ancient Sādhyas and gods.

Questions

1. Paragraph 11 is an explicit discussion of varna (later called castes, after the Portuguese term). How does this hymn describe or justify the hierarchical relationships among Brahmin (priests and nobles), Rājanya (warriors and administrators), Vaiśya (merchants, cattle herders, artisans), and Śūdra (servants and unfree peasants)?

2. How does this hymn characterize the relationships between humans and the natural world?

3. On one level, this hymn is a creation story—the birth of the cosmos, people, and animals from various parts of Puruṣa. How is sacrifice related to creation here? Why might such a tale be appealing in a society with strong memories of recent conflict?

Upanishads (first millennium BCE)

The *Upanishads*, a collection of Indian sacred texts, have grown over centuries; some have even been added in modern times. The earliest ones, however, date to the middle of the first millennium BCE, and include many of the fundamental principles of Hinduism. They also influenced the development of Buddhism and other faiths. The excerpt here lays out some of the basic ideas of *karma* and reincarnation, linking people's conduct and desires in their current life to the fate of their soul in the future.

According as one acts, according as one conducts himself, so does he become. The doer of good becomes good. The doer of evil becomes evil. One becomes virtuous by virtuous action, bad by bad action.

But people say: "A person is made [not of acts, but] of desires only." [In reply to this I say:] As is his desire, such is his resolve; as is his resolve, such the action he performs; what action (*karma*) he performs, that he procures for himself.

On this point there is this verse:—

Where one's mind is attached—the inner self
Goes thereto with action, being attached to it alone.

> Obtaining the end of his action,
> Whatever he does in this world,
> He comes again from that world
> To this world of action.

—So the man who desires.

* * *

Now the man who does not desire.—He who is without desire, who is freed from desire, whose desire is satisfied, whose desire is the Soul—his breaths do not depart. Being very Brahma, he goes to Brahma.

* * *

Accordingly, those who are of pleasant conduct here—the prospect is, indeed, that they will enter a pleasant womb, either the womb of a Brahman, or the womb of a Kshatriya, or the womb of a Vaiśya. But those who are of stinking conduct here—the prospect is, indeed, that they will enter a stinking womb, either the womb of a dog, or the womb of a swine, or the womb of an outcast (*caṇḍāla*).

SOURCE: Robert Ernst Hume, *The Thirteen Principal Upanishads* (Oxford: Oxford University Press, 1931), pp. 140–41, 233.

Questions

1. What happens to the person who is free of earthly desires?

2. For those who are reborn in this world, what determines what kind of body they are reborn in?

3. What are the possible outcomes for those who have not behaved well in their current life? What does this suggest about social hierarchy in this world?

When Sennacherib's Forces Met Hezekiah
(c. 700 BCE)

As recorded on many reliefs in imperial palaces—most notably Sennacherib's reliefs of the siege of Lachish displayed at Nineveh and Tiglath Pileser III's earlier reliefs at Nimrud—one way the Neo-Assyrians maintained tight control over their centralized empire was through brutal conquest and deportation of any who would resist the "yoke of Ashur." One such resistance against Neo-Assyrian rule took place in Judah, the southern kingdom of Israel, led at the time by King Hezekiah. Records survive that offer both the Neo-Assyrian and the Jewish perspective on this particular moment around the year 700 BCE. From the Neo-Assyrian perspective, the so-called Taylor prism records on its six sides, in 500 lines of cuneiform script in Akkadian, the first eight campaigns of Sennacherib. Sennacherib (r. 705–681 BCE) ruled the Neo-Assyrian Empire at its height. His third campaign described on the prism includes the fight against Judah, among other opponents such as Hittite, Amorite, and Egyptian contingents. From the Jewish perspective, the biblical text 2 Kings 18–19 records the exchanges between Sennacherib's envoys and the people of Judah, Hezekiah's anxiety over his resistance to Sennacherib, and his consultation with the prophet Isaiah about what to do in the face of Neo-Assyrian might. 2 Kings, from which this passage comes, was part of a series of historical texts preserved in the Hebrew Bible and was likely composed in the sixth century BCE. The chronicle of Sennacherib's campaigns on the Taylor prism and 2 Kings together offer a valuable opportunity to compare completely separate reports, in different genres, from diametrically opposed sides, reflecting

on the exact same moment in time, and offering an evocative challenge
to the truism often attributed to Winston Churchill that "history is
written by the victors."

TAYLOR PRISM OF SENNACHERIB

Sennacherib, the great king, the mighty king, king of the world,
king of Assyria, king of the four quarters, the wise shepherd, favor-
ite of the great gods, guardian of right, lover of justice, who lends
support, who comes to the aid of the destitute, who performs pious
acts, perfect hero, mighty man, first among all princes, the powerful one who consumes the insubmissive, who strikes the wicked
with the thunderbolt; the god Assur, the great mountain, an unri-
valed kinship has entrusted to me, and above all those who dwell in
palaces, has made powerful my weapons; from the upper sea of the
setting sun to the lower sea of the rising sun, he has brought the
black-headed people in submission at my feet; and mighty kings
feared my warfare, leaving their homes and flying alone, like the
sidinnu, the bird of the cave, to some inaccessible place . . .

* * *

In my third campaign, I went against the Hittite-land. Lulê, king of
Sidon, the terrifying splendor of my sovereignty overcame him, and
far off into the midst of the sea he fled. There he died. Great Sidon,
Little Sidon, Bît-Zitti, Zaribtu, Mahalliba, Ushu, Akzib, Akko, his
strong, walled cities, where there were fodder and drink, for his
garrisons, the terrors of the weapon of Assur, my lord, overpowered
them and they bowed in submission at my feet. I seated Tuba'lu on
the royal throne over them, and tribute, gifts for my majesty, I
imposed upon him for all time, without ceasing. From Menachem,

SOURCE: Daniel David Luckenbill, ed., *Ancient Records of Assyria and
Babylonia* (New York: Greenwood Publishers, 1968 [1927]), pp. 115–16,
118–21, and 2 Kings 18–19, Revised Standard Version Bible, National
Council of the Churches of Christ, 1952.

the Shamsimurunite, Tuba'lu the Sidonite, Abdi-liti the Arvadite, Uru-milki the Gublite, Mitinti the Ashdodite Budu-ilu the Beth Ammonite, Kammusu-nadbi the Moabite, Malik-rammu the Edomite, kings of Amurru, all of them, numerous presents as their heavy tribute, they brought before me for the fourth time, and kissed my feet. But Sidka, the king of Ashkelon, who had not submitted to my yoke, the gods of his father's house, himself, his wife, his sons, his daughters, his brothers, the seed of his paternal house, I tore away and brought to Assyria. Sharru-lu-dari, son of Rukibti, their former king, I set over the people of Ashkelon, and I imposed upon him the payment of tribute: presents to my majesty. He accepted my yoke. In the course of my campaign, Beth-Dagon, Joppa, Banaibarka, Asuru, cities of Sidka, who had not speedily bowed in submission at my feet, I besieged, I conquered, I carried off their spoil. The officials, nobles, and people of Ekron, who had thrown Padi their king; bound by oath and curse of Assyria; into fetters of iron and had given him over to Hezekiah, the Judahite; he kept him in confinement like an enemy; their heart became afraid, and they called upon the Egyptian kings, the bowmen, chariots and horses of the king of Meluhha [Ethiopia], a countless host, and these came to their aid. In the neighborhood of Eltekeh, their ranks being drawn up before me, they offered battle. With the aid of Assur, my lord, I fought with them and brought about their defeat. The Egyptian charioteers and princes, together with the Ethiopian king's chari-oteers, my hands captured alive in the midst of the battle. Eltekeh and Timnah I besieged, I captured, and I took away their spoil. I approached Ekron and slew the governors and nobles who had rebelled, and hung their bodies on stakes around the city. The inhabitants who rebelled and treated (Assyria) lightly I counted as spoil. The rest of them, who were not guilty of rebellion and con-tempt, for whom there was no punishment, I declared their pardon. Padi, their king, I brought out to Jerusalem, set him on the royal throne over them, and imposed upon him my royal tribute.

As for Hezekiah the Judahite, who did not submit to my yoke: forty-six of his strong, walled cities, as well as the small towns in their area, which were without number, by levelling with battering-rams and by bringing up seige-engines, and by attacking and storming on foot, by mines, tunnels, and breeches, I besieged and took them. 200,150 people, great and small, male and female, horses, mules, asses, camels, cattle and sheep without number, I brought away from them and counted as spoil. (Hezekiah) himself, like a caged bird I shut up in Jerusalem, his royal city. I threw up earthworks against him; the one coming out of the city-gate, I turned back to his misery. His cities, which I had despoiled, I cut off from his land, and to Mitinti, king of Ashdod, Padi, king of Ekron, and Silli-bêl, king of Gaza, I gave (them). And thus I diminished his land. I added to the former tribute, and I laid upon him the surrender of their land and imposts; gifts for my majesty. As for Hezekiah, the terrifying splendor of my majesty overcame him, and the Arabs and his mercenary troops which he had brought in to strengthen Jerusalem, his royal city, deserted him. In addition to the thirty talents of gold and eight hundred talents of silver, gems, antimony, jewels, large carnelians, ivory-inlaid couches, ivory-inlaid chairs, elephant hides, elephant tusks, ebony, boxwood, all kinds of valu-able treasures, as well as his daughters, his harem, his male and female musicians, which he had brought after me to Nineveh, my royal city. To pay tribute and to accept servitude, he dispatched his messengers.

EXCERPT FROM 2 KINGS 18–19

Chapter 18 . . . Hezeki'ah the son of Ahaz, king of Judah, began to reign. 2 He was twenty-five years old when he began to reign, and he reigned twenty-nine years in Jerusalem . . . 3 And he did what was right in the eyes of the LORD, according to all that David his father had done. 4 He removed the high places, and broke the pil-lars, and cut down the Ashe'rah. And he broke in pieces the bronze serpent that Moses had made, for until those days the people of Israel had burned incense to it; it was called Nehush'tan. 5 He trusted in the LORD the God of Israel; so that there was none like him among all the kings of Judah after him, nor among those who were before him . . . 7 And the LORD was with him; wherever he went forth, he prospered. He rebelled against the king of Assyria, and would not serve him. 8 He smote the Philistines as far as Gaza and its territory, from watchtower to fortified city.

9 In the fourth year of King Hezeki'ah . . . Shalmane'ser king of Assyria came up against Samar'ia and besieged it 10 and at the end of three years he took it. In the sixth year of Hezeki'ah . . . Samar'ia was taken.

* * *

13 In the fourteenth year of King Hezeki'ah, Sennach'erib king of Assyria came up against all the fortified cities of Judah and took them. 14 And Hezeki'ah king of Judah sent to the king of Assyria at Lachish, saying, "I have done wrong; withdraw from me; whatever you impose on me I will bear." And the king of Assyria required of Hezeki'ah king of Judah three hundred talents of silver and thirty talents of gold. 15 And Hezeki'ah gave him all the silver that was found in the house of the LORD, and in the treasuries of the king's house. 16 At that time Hezeki'ah stripped the gold from the doors of the temple of the LORD, and from the doorposts which Hezeki'ah king of Judah had overlaid and gave it to the king of Assyria. 17 And the king of Assyria sent the Tartan, the Rab'saris, and the Rab'shakeh with a great army from Lachish to King Hezeki'ah at Jerusalem. And they went up and came to Jerusalem. When they arrived, they came and stood by the conduit of the upper pool, which is on the highway to the Fuller's Field. 18 And when they called for the king, there came out to them Eli'akim the son of Hilki'ah, who was over the household, and Shebnah the secretary, and Jo'ah the son of Asaph, the recorder.

19 And the Rab'shakeh said to them, "Say to Hezeki'ah, 'Thus says the great king, the king of Assyria: On what do you rest this confidence of yours? 20 Do you think that mere words are strategy and power for war? On whom do you now rely, that you have rebelled against me? 21 Behold, you are relying now on Egypt, that broken reed of a staff, which will pierce the hand of any man who leans on it. Such is Pharaoh king of Egypt to all who rely on him. 22 But if you say to me, "We rely on the LORD our God," is it not he whose high places and altars Hezeki'ah has removed, saying

to Judah and to Jerusalem, "You shall worship before this altar in Jerusalem"? 23 Come now, make a wager with my master the king of Assyria: I will give you two thousand horses, if you are able on your part to set riders upon them. 24 How then can you repulse a single captain among the least of my master's servants, when you rely on Egypt for chariots and for horsemen? 25 Moreover, is it without the LORD that I have come up against this place to destroy it? The LORD said to me, Go up against this land, and destroy it.'"

26 Then Eli'akim the son of Hilki'ah, and Shebnah, and Jo'ah, said to the Rab'shakeh, "Pray, speak to your servants in the Aramaic language, for we understand it; do not speak to us in the language of Judah within the hearing of the people who are on the wall." 27 But the Rab'shakeh said to them, "Has my master sent me to speak these words to your master and to you, and not to the men sitting on the wall, who are doomed with you to eat their own dung and to drink their own urine?"

28 Then the Rab'shakeh stood and called out in a loud voice in the language of Judah: "Hear the word of the great king, the king of Assyria! 29 Thus says the king: 'Do not let Hezeki'ah deceive you, for he will not be able to deliver you out of my hand. 30 Do not let Hezeki'ah make you to rely on the LORD by saying, The LORD will surely deliver us, and this city will not be given into the hand of the king of Assyria.' 31 Do not listen to Hezeki'ah; for thus says the king of Assyria: 'Make your peace with me and come out to me; then every one of you will eat of his own vine, and every one of his own fig tree, and every one of you will drink the water of his own cistern; 32 until I come and take you away to a land like your own land, a land of grain and wine, a land of bread and vineyards, a land of olive trees and honey, that you may live, and not die. And do not listen to Hezeki'ah when he misleads you by saying, The LORD will deliver us. 33 Has any of the gods of the nations ever delivered his land out of the hand of the king of Assyria? 34 Where are the gods of Hamath and Arpad? Where are the gods of Sepharva'im, Hena, and Ivvah? Have they delivered Samar'ia out of my hand? 35 Who among all the gods of the countries have delivered their countries out of my hand, that the LORD should deliver Jerusalem out of my hand?'"

36 But the people were silent and answered him not a word, for the king's command was, "Do not answer him." 37 Then Eli'akim the son of Hilki'ah, who was over the household, and Shebna the secretary, and Jo'ah the son of Asaph, the recorder, came to Hezeki'ah with their clothes rent, and told him the words of the Rab'shakeh.

Ch. 19 When King Hezeki'ah heard it, he rent his clothes, and covered himself with sackcloth, and went into the house of the LORD . . . 5 When the servants of King Hezeki'ah came to Isaiah, 6 Isaiah said to them, "Say to your master, 'Thus says the LORD: Do not be afraid because of the words that you have heard, with which the servants of the king of Assyria have reviled me. 7 Behold, I will put a spirit in him, so that he shall hear a rumor and return to his own land; and I will cause him to fall by the sword in his own land.'" . . .

v. 35 . . . [Later] the angel of the LORD went forth, and slew a hundred and eighty-five thousand in the camp of the Assyrians; and when men arose early in the morning, behold, these were all dead bodies. 36 Then Sennach'erib king of Assyria departed, and went home, and dwelt at Nin'eveh. 37 And as he was worshiping in the house of Nisroch his god, Adram'melech and Share'zer, his sons, slew him with the sword, and escaped into the land of Ararat. And Esarhad'don his son reigned in his stead.

Questions

1. How does each text represent its king? The king's relationship with the divine? What does this suggest about Neo-Assyrian and Jewish models of rulers and their authority to rule, c. 700 BCE?

2. In 2 Kings and on the Taylor prism, what are some of the details of the negotiations between the Neo-Assyrians and Hezekiah, and what do those details suggest about Neo-Assyrian power? About Hezekiah's power? In 2 Kings, how do the Neo-Assyrian negotiators use their own linguistic skills to their advantage? What do these and other details suggest about international relations among the Neo-Assyrians, the Egyptians, the people of Judah, and others?

3. How does the outcome of the dispute between Hezekiah and Sennacherib end in 2 Kings? How does it end on Sennacherib's Taylor

prism? How do such issues as genre and audience account for the differing outcome in the two reports?

Cyrus the Great, The Decree for the Return of the Jews (c. 538 BCE)

The following documents give two perspectives on the return of the Jews to the land of Israel after their exile in Babylon. Cyrus "the Great" was the founder of the Achaeminid dynasty of the Persian Empire. From 550 BCE he conquered most of the Near East, as well as much of central Asia, creating the largest empire that had yet existed. The ancient sources present him as a ruler who was religiously tolerant and welcomed by the peoples he conquered. The biblical book of Ezra describes the return of the Jews to Jerusalem and their rebuilding of the temple. It was probably compiled in the fourth century BCE by an unknown author.

I am Cyrus, King of the world, the great King, the mighty King, King of Babylon, King of Sumer and Akkad, King of the four quarters of the world, son of Cambyses, the great King, King of Anshan, grandson of Cyrus, the great King, King of Anshan, great-grandson of Teispes, the great King, King of Anshan; an everlasting seed of royalty, whose government Bel and Nabu love, whose reign in the goodness of their hearts they desire. When I entered in peace into Babylon, with joy and rejoicing I took up my lordly dwelling in the royal palace, Marduk, the great lord, moved the understanding heart of the people of Babylon to me, while I daily sought his worship. * * *

[As to the region from as far as] Ashur and Susa, Agade, Eshnunak, Zamban, Meturnu, Deri, to the border of Gutium, the cities beyond the Tigris, whose sites had been founded of old—the gods who dwelt in them I returned to their places, and caused them to settle in their eternal shrines. All their people I assembled and returned them to their dwellings. And the gods of Sumer and Akkad, whom Nabuna'id, to the anger of the lord of the gods, had brought into Babylon, at the command of Marduk, the great lord, I caused in peace to dwell in their abodes, the dwellings in which their hearts delighted.

EZRA I

1 * * * Then in the first year that Cyrus was king of Persia, the Lord kept his promise by having Cyrus send this official message to all parts of his kingdom: 2–3 I am King Cyrus of Persia.

The Lord God of heaven, who is also the God of Israel, has made me the ruler of all nations on earth. And he has chosen me to build a temple for him in Jerusalem, which is in Judah. The Lord God will watch over and encourage any of his people who want to go back to Jerusalem and help build the temple.

4 Everyone else must provide what is needed. They must give money, supplies, and animals, as well as gifts for rebuilding God's temple.

5 Many people felt that the Lord God wanted them to help rebuild his temple, and they made plans to go to Jerusalem. Among them were priests, Levites, and leaders of the tribes of Judah and Benjamin. 6 The others helped by giving silver articles, gold, personal possessions, cattle, and other valuable gifts, as well as offerings for the temple.

7 King Cyrus gave back the things that Nebuchadnezzar had taken from the Lord's temple in Jerusalem and had put in the temple of his own gods. 8 Cyrus placed Mithredath, his chief treasurer, in charge of these things. Mithredath counted them and gave a list to Sheshbazzar, the governor of Judah.

SOURCE: *The Sacred Books and Early Literature of the East,* edited by Charles F. Horne (New York: Parke, Austin and Lipscomb, 1917), pp. 461–62, and Ezra 1.1–8, Contemporary English Version, American Bible Society.

Questions

1. What does Cyrus see as the basis of his legitimacy?

2. What is Cyrus' strategy for dealing with his conquered peoples?

3. How does the author of Ezra interpret Cyrus' decision to let the Jews return to the land of Israel?

Herodotus, Persians Debate Governance (c. 522 BCE)

Herodotus (c. 484–c. 425 BCE) is regarded in the West as the father of history and of anthropology. His curiosity about the origins of the Greco-Persian wars (490, 480–479 BCE) resulted in *The Histories*, a researched, documented, structured account of the past. Although he calls some of his informants "liars" and scholars today believe that Herodotus himself elaborated his material, the work nevertheless remains an important source for an otherwise poorly documented period, and particularly valuable for understanding how Greeks understood other cultures.

The Histories is roughly structured by the reigns of four Persian kings: Cyrus, Cambyses, Darius, and Xerxes. Although it purports to explain a period of Persian conquest and consolidation followed by imperial downfall, much of the book is "digressions," stories and descriptions of other peoples that Herodotus gathered by traveling around the Mediterranean.

In this passage Herodotus portrays a debate about appropriate forms of governance. In the preceding passage (not shown), seven Persian conspirators had unseated a usurper. In the wake of their victory, they made a conscious decision about how to rule.

---

80. And now when five days were gone, and the hubbub had settled down, the conspirators met together to consult about the situation of affairs. At this meeting speeches were made, to which

SOURCE: George Rawlinson, *The History of Herodotus* (New York: D. Appleton & Company, 1866), vol. 2, pp. 393–95.

many of the Greeks give no credence, but they were made neverthe-less. Otanes [who led the fight against the Magian usurper Gaumâta] recommended that the management of public affairs should be entrusted to the whole nation. "To me," he said, "it seems advisable, that we should no longer have a single man to rule over us—the rule of one is neither good nor pleasant. Ye cannot have forgotten to what lengths Cambyses went in his haughty tyranny, and the haughti-ness of the Magi ye have yourselves experienced. How indeed is it possible that monarchy should be a well-adjusted thing, when it allows a man to do as he likes without being answerable? Such licence is enough to stir strange and unwonted thoughts in the heart of the worthiest of men. Give a person this power, and straightway his manifold good things puff him up with pride, while envy is so natural to human kind that it cannot but arise in him. But pride and envy together include all wickedness; both leading on to deeds of savage violence. True it is that kings, possessing as they do all that heart can desire, ought to be void of envy, but the contrary is seen in their conduct towards the citizens. They are jealous of the most virtuous among their subjects, and wish their death; while they take delight in the meanest and basest, being ever ready to listen to the tales of slanderers. A king, besides, is beyond all other men inconsistent with himself. Pay him court in moderation, and he is angry because you do not show him more profound respect— show him profound respect, and he is offended again, because (as he says) you fawn on him. But the worst of all is, that he sets aside the laws of the land, puts men to death without trial, and subjects women to violence. The rule of the many, on the other hand, has, in the first place, the fairest of names, to wit, *isonomy;* and further it is free from all those outrages which a king is wont to commit. There, places are given by lot, the magistrate is answerable for what he does, and measures rest with the commonalty. I vote, therefore, that we do away with monarchy, and raise the people to power. For the people are all in all."

81. Such were the sentiments of Otanes. Megabyzus [an impor-tant military commander and one of the conspirators] spoke next, and advised the setting up of an oligarchy:—"In all that Otanes has said to persuade you to put down monarchy," he observed, "I fully

concur; but his recommendation that we should call the people to power seems to me not the best advice. For there is nothing so void of understanding, nothing so full of wantonness as the unwieldy rabble. It were folly not to be borne for men, while seeking to escape the wantonness of a tyrant, to give themselves up to the wantonness of a rude unbridled mob. The tyrant, in all his doings, at least knows what he is about, but a mob is altogether devoid of knowledge; for how should there be any knowledge in a rabble, untaught, and with no natural sense of what is right and fit? It rushes wildly into state affairs with all the fury of a stream swollen in the winter, and confuses everything. Let the enemies of the Persians be ruled by democracies; but let us choose out from the citizens a certain number of the worthiest, and put the government into their hands. For thus both we ourselves shall be among the governors, and power being entrusted to the best men, it is likely that the best counsels will prevail in the state."

82. This was the advice which Megabyzus gave, and after him Darius came forward, and spoke as follows:—"All that Megabyzus said against democracy was well said, I think; but about oligarchy he did not speak advisedly; for take these three forms of government, democracy, oligarchy, and monarchy, and let them each be at their best, I maintain that monarchy far surpasses the other two. What government can possibly be better than that of the very best man in the whole state? The counsels of such a man are like himself, and so he governs the mass of the people to their heart's content; while at the same time his measures against evil-doers are kept more secret than in other states. Contrariwise, in oligarchies, where men vie with each other in the service of the commonwealth, fierce enmities are apt to arise between man and man, each wishing to be leader, and to carry his own measures; whence violent quarrels come, which lead to open strife, often ending in bloodshed. Then monarchy is sure to follow; and this too shows how far that rule surpasses all others. Again, in a democracy, it is impossible but that there will be malpractices: these malpractices, however, do not lead to enmities, but to close friendships, which are formed among those engaged in them, who must hold well together to carry on their villainies. And so things go on until a man stands

forth as champion of the commonalty, and puts down the evil-doers. Straightway the author of so great a service is admired by all, and from being admired soon comes to be appointed king; so that here too it is plain that monarchy is the best government. Lastly, to sum up all in a word, whence, I ask, was it that we got the freedom which we enjoy?—did democracy give it us, or oligarchy, or a monarch? As a single man recovered our freedom for us, [Cyrus the Great, r. 559–529] my sentence is that we keep to the rule of one. Even apart from this, we ought not to change the laws of our forefathers when they work fairly; for to do so, is not well."

83. Such were the three opinions brought forward at this meeting; the four other Persians voted in favour of the last.

Questions

1. What are the benefits and drawbacks of each of the three forms of governance debated by Persian leaders in the period immediately before the reign of Darius I?

2. How would the Persians taking part in this debate have known about these various forms of government?

3. Darius claims that a monarchy is best able to provide stability and put down "evil doers." Years later, he erected the Behistun inscription to commemorate his accomplishments and remind people of royal power. Does the inscription bear out the views on monarchy attributed to him by Herodotus? Why or why not?

Thucydides, "Melian Dialogue" (416/15 BCE)

Thucydides was a general and politician who lived during the Peloponnesian War, which was fought from 431 to 404 BCE between Athens and its allies and Sparta and Corinth and their allies. An active participant in, and recorder of, the events of what he called "the greatest war of all," Thucydides was, with Herodotus, another of the first true historians of the Western tradition, conscious of the nature of his sources and their impact on his reporting. For instance, reflecting on the nature of building and city planning at Sparta compared with Athens, Thucydides wrote that "future generations would, as time passed, find it difficult to believe that [Sparta] had really been as powerful as it was represented to be . . . since the city is not regularly planned and contains no temples or monuments of great magnificence," but "one would conjecture from what met the eye that [Athens] had been twice as powerful as in fact it is" [I.10]. Despite his more critical use of sources, Thucydides included in his history several speeches and debates he did not witness (including the "Melian Dialogue," excerpted below). Commenting on his own approach, Thucydides famously wrote: "My method has been, while keeping as closely as possible to the general sense of the words that were actually used, to make the speakers say what, in my opinion, was called for by each situation" [I.22].

During the Peloponnesian War, the two sides were fighting over the nature of Athenian power. The democratic city-state of Athens rose to prominence through its administration of the Delian League, an organization that had been formed to consolidate the resources of Greek city-states to fight against the Persians who had already invaded Greece twice (c. 490 and 480 BCE). The Delian League transformed into the Athenian Empire once the Persian threat waned in the mid-fifth century BCE. The transformation from League to Empire was brutal, and some states did not consent to Athens's forced "tributes." An example of the disastrous results of such resistance were recorded in the "Melian Dialogue", excerpted below, a debate between the governing body of the Greek island city-state of Melos and Athenian representatives sent to encourage their compliance with Athenian demands.

———————

84. The Athenians next made an expedition against the island of Melos with thirty ships of their own, six Chian, and two Lesbian, 1,200 hoplites and 300 archers besides twenty mounted archers of their own, and about 1500 hoplites furnished by their allies in the islands. The Melians are colonists of the Lacedaemonians who would not submit to Athens like the other islanders. At

SOURCE: Thucydides, *History of the Peloponnesian War,* translated into English with introduction, marginal analysis, and index by B. Jowett, edited by A. P. Peabody (Boston: D. Lothrop & Co., 1883), pp. 398–402, 404–7.

first they were neutral and took no part. But when the Athenians tried to coerce them by ravaging their lands, they were driven into open hostilities. The generals, Cleomedes the son of Lycomedes and Tisias the son of Tisimachus, encamped with the Athenian forces on the island. But before they did the country any harm they sent envoys to negotiate with the Melians. Instead of bringing these envoys before the people, the Melians desired them to explain their errand to the magistrates and to the chief men. . . .

* * *

89. Athenians: Well, then, we Athenians will use no fine words; we will not go out of our way to prove at length that we have a right to rule, because we overthrew the Persians; or that we attack you now because we are suffering any injury at your hands. We should not convince you if we did; nor must you expect to convince us by arguing that, although a colony of the Lacedaemonians, you have taken no part in their expeditions, or that you have never done us any wrong. But you and we should say what we really think, and aim only at what is possible, for we both alike know that into the discussion of human affairs the question of justice only enters where the pressure of necessity is equal, and that the powerful exact what they can, and the weak grant what they must.

90. Melians: . . . Your interest in this principle is quite as great as ours, inasmuch as you, if you fall, will incur the heaviest vengeance, and will be the most terrible example to mankind.

91. Athenians: The fall of our empire, if it should fall, is not an event to which we look forward with dismay; for ruling states such as Lacedaemon are not cruel to their vanquished enemies. And we are fighting not so much against the Lacedaemonians, as against our own subjects who may some day rise up and overcome their former masters. But this is a danger which you may leave to us. And we will now endeavour to show that we have come in the interests of our empire, and that in what we are about to say we are only seeking the preservation of your city. For we want to make you ours with the least trouble to ourselves, and it is for the interests of us both that you should not be destroyed.

92. Melians: It may be your interest to be our masters, but how can it be ours to be your slaves?

93. Athenians: To you the gain will be that by submission you will avert the worst; and we shall be all the richer for your preservation.

94. Melians: But must we be your enemies? Will you not receive us as friends if we are neutral and remain at peace with you?

95. Athenians: No, your enmity is not half so mischievous to us as your friendship; for the one is in the eyes of our subjects an argument of our power, the other of our weakness . . .

* * *

98. Melians: . . . are you not strengthening the enemies whom you already have, and bringing upon you others who, if they could help, would never dream of being your enemies at all?

99. Athenians: We do not consider our really dangerous enemies to be any of the peoples inhabiting the mainland who, secure in their freedom, may defer indefinitely any measures of precaution which they take against us, but islanders who, like you, happen to be under no control, and all who may be already irritated by the necessity of submission to our empire—these are our real enemies, for they are the most reckless and most likely to bring themselves as well as us into a danger which they cannot but foresee.

100. Melians: Surely then, if you and your subjects will brave all this risk, you to preserve your empire and they to be quit of it, how base and cowardly would it be in us, who retain our freedom, not to do and suffer anything rather than be your slaves.

101. Athenians: Not so, if you calmly reflect: for you are not fighting against equals to whom you cannot yield without disgrace, but you are taking counsel whether or no you shall resist an overwhelming force. The question is not one of honour but of prudence.

* * *

111. Athenians: Help may come from Lacedaemon to you as it has come to others, and should you ever have actual experience of it, then you will know that never once have the Athenians retired from a siege through fear of a foe elsewhere. You told us that the

safety of your city would be your first care, but we remark that, in this long discussion, not a word has been uttered by you which would give a reasonable man expectation of deliverance. Your strongest grounds are hopes deferred, and what power you have is not to be compared with that which is already arrayed against you. . . . you ought to see that there can be no disgrace in yielding to a great city which invites you to become her ally on reasonable terms, keeping your own land, and merely paying tribute; and that you will certainly gain no honour if, having to choose between two alternatives, safety and war, you obstinately prefer the worse. To maintain our rights against equals, to be politic with superiors, and to be moderate towards inferiors is the path of safety. Reflect once more when we have withdrawn, and say to yourselves over and over again that you are deliberating about your one and only country, which may be saved or may be destroyed by a single decision.

112. The Athenians left the conference: the Melians, after consulting among themselves, resolved to persevere in their refusal, and answered as follows, "Men of Athens, our resolution is unchanged; and we will not in a moment surrender that liberty which our city, founded 700 years ago, still enjoys; we will trust to the good-fortune which, by the favour of the gods, has hitherto preserved us, and for human help to the Lacedaemonians, and endeavour to save ourselves. We are ready however to be your friends, and the enemies neither of you nor of the Lacedaemonians, and we ask you to leave our country when you have made such a peace as may appear to be in the interest of both parties."

113. Such was the answer of the Melians; the Athenians, as they quitted the conference, spoke as follows, "Well, we must say, judging from the decision at which you have arrived, that you are the only men who deem the future to be more certain than the present, and regard things unseen as already realised in your fond anticipation, and that the more you cast yourselves upon the Lacedaemonians and fortune, and hope, and trust them, the more complete will be your ruin."

114. The Athenian envoys returned to the army; and the generals, when they found that the Melians would not yield, immediately commenced hostilities. They surrounded the town of Melos with a

wall, dividing the work among the several contingents. They then left troops of their own and of their allies to keep guard both by land and by sea, and retired with the greater part of their army; the remainder carried on the blockade. . . . [Later] the Melians took that part of the Athenian wall which looked towards the agora by a night assault, killed a few men, and brought in as much corn and other necessaries as they could; they then retreated and remained inactive. After this the Athenians set a better watch. So the summer ended . . .

* * *

116. In the following winter . . . the Melians took another part of the Athenian wall; for the fortifications were insufficiently guarded. Whereupon the Athenians sent fresh troops, under the command of Philocrates the son of Demeas. The place was now closely invested, and there was treachery among the citizens themselves. So the Melians were induced to surrender at discretion. The Athenians thereupon put to death all who were of military age, and made slaves of the women and children. They then colonized the island, sending thither 500 settlers of their own.

Questions

1. On what principles and with what rationales do the Athenians and the Melians base their positions in the argument? With which side do you agree and why?

2. How does the situation between the Athenians and the Melians resolve? What does this resolution suggest about the nature of Athenian imperialism and the fifth-century democracy for which Athens is so famed?

3. Episodes like this one are often used by modern commentators to discuss the fundamental nature of imperialism. What are the problems with such parallels? To what extent do such parallels work?

Guanzi, How to Rule (completed c. 122 BCE)

Guan Zhong or Guanzi (725–645 BCE) could not have written the *Guanzi*, an extended set of instructions for rulers. It was probably written by many authors over four or five centuries, and perhaps not completed until 122 BCE. But Guan Zhong—a very successful prime minister of the North Chinese state of Qi (in modern Shandong)—did pursue policies like those described in the *Guanzi*: bypassing the aristocracy to tax and rule peasants directly, creating state monopolies of strategic goods, aiding agriculture, and so on. In this selection, he emphasizes limiting luxuries and giving priority to food production and military power.

[III]

On entering the capital (*guo*) and towns (*vi*), examine the residences and observe the chariots, horses, and clothing to ascertain whether a state is wasteful or frugal. * * *

Therefore it is said: "If the ruler on high has no stockpiles of provisions but his residences are splendid, if the households of the common people [also] have no stockpiles but their clothing is highly ornate, if those who ride in chariots make an elaborate display and those walking about are dressed in variegated colors, if basic commodities are scarce but nonessential items are plentiful— these are the practices of a wasteful state."

When the state is wasteful, it exhausts its resources. When its resources are exhausted, its people are impoverished. When the people are impoverished, wicked ideas arise. When wicked ideas arise, there are evil and cunning acts. Thus the origin of wickedness and evil lies in scarcity and insufficiency. The origin of scarcity and insufficiency lies in wastefulness. The origin of wastefulness lies in not setting proper limits.

SOURCE: *Guanzi: Political, Economic, and Philosophical Essays from Early China: A Study*, translated by W. Allyn Rickett (Princeton, N.J.: Princeton University Press, 1985), vol. 1, pp. 228–30.

Therefore it is said: "It is vital for the state to be judicious in setting limits, frugal in dress, economical in the use of resources, and to prohibit extravagance."

* * *

[IV]

Take note of extensive hunger, calculate the amount of military and labor service, observe [the number of] pleasure pavilions, and measure the state's expenditures to ascertain whether a state rests on a solid basis or not. In general, it takes an area of land fifty *li* square to feed ten thousand households. If the number is less than ten thousand, the people may spread [freely] into the mountains and marshlands. If it is more, they may [be required to] leave them. If the fields are fully developed yet the people have no stockpiles of provisions, it is because the area of the state is too small and food-producing land is spread too thin. If the fields are only half cultivated yet the people have surplus food and grain is plentiful, it is because the area of the state is large and food-producing land is ample. If the area is large yet the fields are not developed, it is because the prince likes possessions and his ministers like profit. If the developed land covers a wide area yet the people do not have enough, it is because levies exacted by the sovereign are heavy and the reserves [of the people] are drained away.

Therefore it is said: "If one-tenth [of the people] become soldiers and three-tenths do not engage in productive work, one-third of the crop will be lost. If one-third of the crop is lost and no reserves have been previously set aside, the roads will be filled with the corpses of displaced persons. If one-tenth [of the people] become soldiers and are not released within three years, and if there was no excess food [to begin with], the people will sell their children."

Even though the mountains and forests be near at hand and the grass and trees lush, proper limits must be set on residences and the proper times set for the closing and opening [of mountains and forests]. Why is this? The answer is that large trees cannot be felled, lifted, or transported by an individual acting alone, nor can they be used for the thin walls [of small houses].

Therefore it is said: "Even though the mountains and forests be extensive and the grass and trees lush, proper times must be set for the closing and opening [of the mountains and forests]."

Even though the state be overflowing [with riches] and possess an abundance of gold and jade, there must be proper limits set on residences. Even though rivers and lakes be extensive, pools and marshes widespread, and fish and turtles plentiful, there must be regulations on the use of nets and lines. Boats and nets cannot be the only resources for there to be success. It is wrong to be partial toward grass and trees or favor fish and turtles, and it is inadmissible to subvert people from the production of grain.

Therefore it is said: "When the former kings prohibited work in the mountains and marshlands, it was to expand [the efforts of] the people in the production of grain."

Unless the people have grain, they will have nothing to eat. Unless there is land, [grain] will not be produced. Unless there are people, [the land] will not be worked. Unless people have the energy to work, there will be no way to acquire the resources [required by the state]. What the world produces emanates from the expenditure of energy. Such energy emanates from hard physical labor. For this reason, if the ruler on high is unrestrained in the use of resources, it means the people will have no rest in their expenditure of energy.

Therefore it is said: "If pleasure pavilions are [so numerous that they stand] in sight of each other, those above and below will harbor resentments against each other."

If the people have no surplus stores, prohibitions will certainly not be obeyed. If the masses become refugees and die of starvation, battles will certainly not be won * * * danger and destruction will follow.

Questions

1. What reasons does Guanzi give for the ruler to focus on grain supplies?

2. Guanzi says repeatedly that rulers should limit people's use of forests, ponds, and other nonagricultural lands. Why? What do these reasons suggest about his views of what elites will do if they are not controlled? Peasants? People in general?

3. Compare Guanzi's attitude toward farming, civilization and state interests with that of Mencius (Mencius, On the Legendary Sage Kings, in Chapter 2). What are the differences and how might you account for them?

Chapter *5*

WORLDS TURNED INSIDE OUT, 1000–350 BCE

Zoroaster, Yasna 30.1–11 from the Gathas (1000–600 BCE)

Zoroaster, also called Zarathustra, was the legendary founder of the religion that came to be known as Zoroastrianism. Exactly where and when Zoroaster lived is not certain, but he appears to have lived in Southwest Asia sometime between 1000 and 600 BCE. As with the words associated with so many founders of "axial age" traditions, the poetic verses of Gathas that articulate Zoroaster's innovative thoughts reached their current form long after his lifetime. Despite the complexity of their textual transmission, the hymns offer a vivid expression of the tenets of Zoroastrianism. One of the remarkable features of Zoroastrianism is its distinct dualism, a battle between light and dark, truth and lie, right and wrong, embodied by Ahura Mazda and his cosmic rival Ahriman, respectively. Zoroastrianism exerted a profound influence on the Indo-Iranian-speaking, nomadic Persians who migrated westward out of the Iranian plateau and ultimately unified a multicultural empire reaching from northern Greece in the west to the Indus Valley in the east.

30.1
Now I will speak, O proselytes, of what ye may bring to the
    attention even of one who knows,

SOURCE: M. L. West, *Hymns of Zoroaster: A New Translation of the Most Ancient Sacred Texts of Iran* (London: I. B. Tauris, 2010), pp. 51, 53, 55.

133

praises for the Lord and Good Thought's acts of worship
well considered, and for Right; the gladness beheld by the daylight.

2
Hear with your ears the best message, behold with lucid mind the
  two choices in the decision
each man makes for his own person
before the great Supplication, as ye look ahead to the declaration
  to Him.

3
They are the two walls, the twins who in the beginning made
  themselves heard through dreaming,
those two kinds of thought, of speech, of deed, the better and the
  evil;
and between them well-doers discriminate rightly, but ill-doers
  do not.

4
Once those two Wills join battle, a man adopts
life or non-life, the way of existence that will be his at the last:
  that of the wrongful the worst kind, but for the righteous one,
  best thought.

5
Of those two Wills, the wrongful one chooses to do the worst things,
but the most Bounteous Will (chooses) Right, he who clothes
  himself in adamant;
as do those who committedly please the Lord with genuine
  actions, the Mindful One.

6
Between those two very Daevas fail to discriminate rightly,
  because delusion
comes over them as they deliberate, when they choose worst
  thought;

they scurry together to the violence with which mortals blight the
    world.

7

But suppose one comes with dominion for Him, with good
    thought and right,
then vitality informs the body, piety the soul;
their ringleader Thou wilt have as if in irons:

8

and when the requital comes for their misdeeds,
for Thee, Mindful One, together with Good Thought, will be
    found dominion
to proclaim to those, Lord, who deliver Wrong into the hands of
    Right.

9

May we be the ones who will make this world splendid,
Mindful One and Ye Lords, bringers of change, and Right, as our
    minds come together where insight is fluctuating.

10

For then destruction will come down upon Wrong's prosperity,
and the swiftest (steeds) will be yoked from their fair dwelling of
    Good Thought,
of the Mindful One, and of Right, and they will be winners in
    good repute.

11

When ye grasp those rules that the Mindful One lays down, O
    mortals,
through success and failure, and the lasting harm that is for the
    wrongful
as furtherance is for the righteous, then thereafter desire will be
    fulfilled.

Questions

1. The opening verse here speaks directly to "proselytes"; but who exactly are these converts/believers that comprise the audience of this hymn? How can you tell? How does identifying the intended audience shape your interpretation of the text?

2. What are the "two Wills" and what range of behaviors do they govern? How would an individual's choice of one Will over the other have an impact on her or his broader community?

3. Yasna 30.9 proclaims: "May we be the ones who will make this world splendid." To what extent would the ideas in this text apply in a pastoral nomadic world? In a more settled, urban community? Why would such flexibility matter for the worlds the Persians brought together?

Confucius, Analects (fifth century BCE)

Confucius (551–479 BCE) was a minor aristocrat in one of the small states struggling for survival in China's Warring States period, brought on by the decline of the Zhou dynasty. Concerned about what he perceived as a decline in social order and ethical conduct, he offered advice to rulers and instruction to young men on both public and private behavior.

The *Analects* were assembled by his students some time after his death, and are thought to contain the basics of his philosophical teachings. In these selections, Confucius deals with the virtues of reciprocity, humaneness, and filial piety, which he saw as the essential bases for both a proper personal life and an ordered society. Spelling has been updated in the following excerpt to reflect modern orthography.

SOURCE: *Sources of Chinese Tradition*, compiled by Wm. Theodore de Bary et al. (New York: Columbia University Press, 1960), vol. 1, pp. 25–28.

The Unitary Principle: Reciprocity or Humanity

* * *

39. Confucius said: "Shen! My teaching contains one principle that runs through it all." "Yes," replied Zeng Zi. When Confucius had left the room the disciples asked: "What did he mean?" Zeng Zi replied: "Our Master's teaching is simply this: loyalty and reciprocity."

40. Zi Gong asked: "Is there any one word that can serve as a principle for the conduct of life?" Confucius said: "Perhaps the word 'reciprocity': Do not do to others what you would not want others to do to you."

41. Confucius said: "Perfect indeed is the virtue which is according to the Mean. For long people have seldom had the capacity for it."

* * *

43. Zhonggong asked about humanity. Confucius said: "Behave when away from home as though you were in the presence of an important guest. Deal with the common people as though you were officiating at an important sacrifice. Do not do to others what you would not want others to do to you. Then there will be no dissatisfaction either in the state or at home."

44. Confucius said: * * * "The humane man, desiring to be established himself, seeks to establish others; desiring himself to succeed, he helps others to succeed. To judge others by what one knows of oneself is the method of achieving humanity."

45. Fan Chi asked about humanity. Confucius said: "Love men."

46. Zi Zhang asked Confucius about humanity. Confucius said: "To be able to practice five virtues everywhere in the world constitutes humanity." Zi Zhang begged to know what these were. Confucius said: "Courtesy, magnanimity, good faith, diligence, and kindness. He who is courteous is not humiliated, he who is magnanimous wins the multitude, he who is of good faith is trusted by the people, he who is diligent attains his objective, and he who is kind can get service from the people."

47. Confucius said: "Without humanity a man cannot long endure adversity, nor can he long enjoy prosperity. The humane rest in humanity; the wise find it beneficial."

48. Confucius said: "Only the humane man can love men and can hate men."

49. Someone inquired: "What do you think of 'requiting injury with kindness'?" Confucius said: "How will you then requite kindness? Requite injury with justice, and kindness with kindness."

* * *

Filial Piety

56. Zi You asked about filial piety. Confucius said: "Nowadays a filial son is just a man who keeps his parents in food. But even dogs or horses are given food. If there is no feeling of reverence, wherein lies the difference?"

* * *

58. Confucius said: "In serving his parents, a son may gently remonstrate with them. If he sees that they are not inclined to follow his suggestion, he should resume his reverential attitude but not abandon his purpose. If he is belabored, he will not complain."

59. The Duke of She observed to Confucius: "Among us there was an upright man called Gong who was so upright that when his father appropriated a sheep, he bore witness against him." Confucius said: "The upright men among us are not like that. A father will screen his son and a son his father—yet uprightness is to be found in that."

60. Zai Wo questioned the three years' mourning and thought one year was long enough: "If the gentlemen for three years abstain from the practice of ritual, ritual will decay; if for three years they make no music, music will go to ruin. In one year the old crops are exhausted and the new crops have come up, the friction-sticks have made the several seasonal fires—one year should be enough." Confucius said: "Would you then feel at ease in eating polished rice and wearing fineries?" "Quite at ease," was the reply. Confucius continued: "If you would really feel at ease, then do so. When a gentleman

is in mourning, he does not relish good food if he eats it, does not enjoy music if he hears it, and does not feel at ease in a comfortable dwelling. Hence he abstains from these things. But now since you would feel at ease, then you can have them." When Zai Wo had gone out, Confucius said: "What lack of humanity in Yu Zai Wo! Only when a child is three years old does it leave its parents' arms. The three years' mourning is the universal observance in the world. And Yu—did he not enjoy the loving care of his parents for three years?"

Questions

1. What is reciprocity, and how does it differ from treating everyone equally? What is humaneness (humanity), and how does it differ from selflessness?

2. What is the point of the anecdote about the Duke of She? Why does Confucius want to base social order on putting family loyalty above obedience to the law?

3. In the last anecdote, Confucius clearly thinks Zai Wo's values are fundamentally wrong. Why, then, doesn't he argue with him?

Mencius, Humane Government (c. 371–289 BCE)

Mencius (c. 371–289 BCE) was recognized in his lifetime as a very important Confucian thinker, though it took over 1,000 years before his interpretation was accepted as *the* orthodox repository of the Confucian Way, marginalizing Xunzi's (c. 312–230 BCE) more hard-nosed views. These passages portray Mencius at his usual occupation: visiting kings and nobles, and trying to persuade them that attending to the welfare of commoners was not only a moral duty, but the most practical way to succeed as a ruler amid intense, often violent competition.

SOURCE: *Sources of Chinese Tradition,* compiled by Wm. Theodore de Bary et al. (New York: Columbia University Press, 1960), vol. 1, pp. 92–94.

Mencius went to see King Hui of Liang. The king said: "You have not considered a thousand *li* too far to come, and must therefore have something of profit to offer my kingdom?" Mencius replied: "Why must you speak of profit? What I have to offer is humanity and righteousness, nothing more. If a king says, 'What will profit my kingdom?' the high officials will say, 'What will profit our families?' and the lower officials and commoners will say, 'What will profit ourselves?' Superiors and inferiors will try to seize profit one from another, and the state will be endangered. * * * Let your Majesty speak only of humanity and righteousness. Why must you speak of profit?"

Mencius said: "It was by virtue of humanity that the Three Dynasties won the empire, and by virtue of the want of humanity that they lost it. States rise and fall for the same reason. Devoid of humanity, the emperor would be unable to safeguard the four seas, a feudal lord would be unable to safeguard the altars of land and grain [i.e., his state], a minister would be unable to safeguard the ancestral temple [i.e., his clan-family], and the individual would be unable to safeguard his four limbs. Now people hate destruction and yet indulge in want of humanity—this is as if one hates to get drunk and yet forces oneself to drink wine."

Mencius said: "An overlord is he who employs force under a cloak of humanity. To be an overlord one has to be in possession of a large state. A king, on the other hand, is he who gives expression to his humanity through virtuous conduct. To be a true king, one does not have to have a large state. Tang [founder of the Shang dynasty] had only a territory of seventy *li* and King Wen [founder of the Zhou] only a hundred. When men are subdued by force, it is not that they submit from their hearts but only that their strength is unavailing. When men are won by virtue, then their hearts are gladdened and their submission is sincere, as the seventy disciples were won by the Master, Confucius.

* * *

Mencius said: "It was because Jie and Zhou lost the people that they lost the empire, and it was because they lost the hearts of the people that they lost the people. Here is the way to win the empire:

win the people and you win the empire. Here is the way to win the people: win their hearts and you win the people. Here is the way to win their hearts: give them and share with them what they like, and do not do to them what they do not like. The people turn to a humane ruler as water flows downward or beasts take to wilderness."

* * *

Mencius said to King Xuan of Qi: * * * "Only the true scholar is capable of maintaining, without certain means of livelihood, a steadfast heart. As for the multitude, if they have no certain means of livelihood, they surely cannot maintain a steadfast heart. Without a steadfast heart, they are likely to abandon themselves to any and all manner of depravity. If you wait till they have lapsed into crime and then mete out punishment, it is like placing traps for the people. If a humane ruler is on the throne how can he permit such a thing as placing traps for the people? Therefore, when an intelligent ruler regulates the livelihood of the people, he makes sure that they will have enough to serve their parents on the one hand and to support their wives and children on the other, so that in good years all may eat their fill and in bad years no one need die of starvation. Thus only will he urge them to walk the path of virtue, and the people will follow him effortlessly. But as the people's livelihood is ordered at present, they do not have enough to serve their parents on the one hand or to support their wives and children on the other. * * * Such being the case, they are only anxiously trying to stay alive. What leisure have they for cultivating decorum and righteousness?

"If your Majesty wishes to practice humane government, would it not be well to go back to the root of the matter?

"Let the five *mu* of land surrounding the farmer's cottage be planted with mulberry trees, and persons over fifty may all be clothed in silk. Let poultry, dogs, and swine be kept and bred in season, and those over seventy may all be provided with meat. Let the cultivation of the hundred-*mu* farm not be interfered with, and a family of eight mouths need not go hungry. Let attention be paid to teaching in schools and let the people be taught the principles of filial piety and brotherly respect, and white-headed old men will not be seen carrying loads on the road. When the aged wear silk and eat meat and the common people are free from hunger and cold, never has the lord of such a people failed to become king."

Questions

1. Why does Mencius claim that it is self-defeating for a ruler (or anyone else) to focus on his own self-interest?

2. How does Mencius expect people to respond to humane government? What does this assume about human nature?

3. What relationships does Mencius see between popular material welfare, personal virtue, and political loyalty? What economic policies does he favor?

Aristotle, Politica (384–322 BCE)

Aristotle (384–322 BCE), a pupil of Plato and tutor of Alexander the Great, is one of the foremost philosophers in the Western tradition. His ideas greatly influenced Islamic philosophy, Latin Christian theology, and science throughout Southwest Asia, North Africa, and Europe. He wrote over 400 works on a great variety of topics, including philosophy, natural history, poetics, rhetoric, ethics, and politics. The following selection is from his *Politica*, a treatise on the science of politics. For Aristotle man was by nature a social animal, one who had to live in a community in order to live the good life.

I.2 He who thus considers things in their first growth and origin, whether a state or anything else, will obtain the clearest view of them. In the first place there must be a union of those who cannot exist without each other; for example, of male and female, that the race may continue; and this is a union which is formed, not of deliberate purpose, but because, in common with other animals and with

SOURCE: *The Politics of Aristotle*, translated by B. Jowett (Oxford: Clarendon Press, 1885), vol. 1, pp. 2–3, 6–10.

plants, mankind have a natural desire to leave behind them an image of themselves. And there must be a union of natural ruler and subject, that both may be preserved. For he who can foresee with his mind is by nature intended to be lord and master, and he who can work with his body is a subject, and by nature a slave; hence master and slave have the same interest. Nature, however, has distinguished between the female and the slave. For she is not niggardly, like the smith who fashions the Delphian knife for many uses; she makes each thing for a single use, and every instrument is best made when intended for one and not for many uses. But among barbarians no distinction is made between women and slaves, because there is no natural ruler among them: they are a community of slaves, male and female. Wherefore the poets say,—

"It is meet that Hellenes should rule over barbarians;"

as if they thought that the barbarian and the slave were by nature one.

Out of these two relationships between man and woman, master and slave, the family first arises, and Hesiod is right when he says,—

"First house and wife and an ox for the plough,"

for the ox is the poor man's slave. The family is the association established by nature for the supply of men's everyday wants, and the members of it are called by Charondas "companions of the cupboard" and by Epimenides the Cretan, "companions of the manger." But when several families are united, and the association aims at something more than the supply of daily needs, then comes into existence the village. And the most natural form of the village appears to be that of a colony from the family, composed of the children and grandchildren, who are said to be "suckled with the same milk." And this is the reason why Hellenic states were originally governed by kings; because the Hellenes were under royal rule before they came together, as the barbarians still are. Every family is ruled by the eldest, and therefore in the colonies of the family the kingly form of government prevailed because they were of the same blood. As Homer says

"Each one gives law to his children and to his wives"

For they lived dispersedly, as was the manner in ancient times. Wherefore men say that the Gods have a king, because they themselves either are or were in ancient times under the rule of a king. For they imagine, not only the forms of the Gods, but their ways of life to be like their own.

* * *

I.4 Property is a part of the household, and therefore the art of acquiring property is a part of the art of managing the household; for no man can live well, or indeed live at all, unless he be provided with necessaries. And as in the arts which have a definite sphere the workers must have their own proper instruments for the accomplishment of their work, so it is in the management of a household. Now, instruments are of various sorts; some are living, others lifeless; in the rudder, the pilot of a ship has a lifeless, in the look-out man, a living instrument; for in the arts the servant is a kind of instrument. Thus, too, a possession is an instrument for maintaining life. And so, in the arrangement of the family, a slave is a living possession, and property a number of such instruments; and the servant is himself an instrument, which takes precedence of all other instruments. For if every instrument could accomplish its own work, obeying or anticipating the will of others, like the statues of Daedalus, or the tripods of Hephaestus, which, says the poet,

"of their own accord entered the assembly of the Gods;"

if, in like manner, the shuttle would weave and the plectrum touch the lyre without a hand to guide them, chief workmen would not want servants, nor masters slaves. * * *

I.5 But is there any one thus intended by nature to be a slave, and for whom such a condition is expedient and right, or rather is not all slavery a violation of nature?

There is no difficulty in answering this question, on grounds both of reason and of fact. For that some should rule, and others be ruled is a thing, not only necessary, but expedient; from the hour of their birth, some are marked out for subjection, others for rule.

* * * And it is clear that the rule of the soul over the body, and of the mind and the rational element over the passionate is natural and expedient; whereas the equality of the two or the rule of the inferior is always hurtful. The same holds good of animals as well as of men; for tame animals have a better nature than wild, and all tame animals are better off when they are ruled by man; for then they are preserved. Again, the male is by nature superior, and the female inferior; and the one rules, and the other is ruled; this principle, of necessity, extends to all mankind. Where then there is such a difference as that between soul and body, or between men and animals (as in the case of those whose business is to use their body, and who can do nothing better), the lower sort are by nature slaves, and it is better for them as for all inferiors that they should be under the rule of a master. For he who can be, and therefore is another's, and he who participates in reason enough to apprehend, but not to have, reason, is a slave by nature. Whereas the lower animals cannot even apprehend reason; they obey their instincts. And indeed the use made of slaves and of tame animals is not very different; for both with their bodies minister to the needs of life. Nature would like to distinguish between the bodies of freemen and slaves, making the one strong for servile labour, the other upright, and although useless for such services, useful for political life in the arts both of war and peace. But this does not hold universally: for some slaves have the souls and others have the bodies of freemen. And doubtless if men differed from one another in the mere forms of their bodies as much as the statues of the Gods do from men, all would acknowledge that the inferior class should be slaves of the superior. And if there is a difference in the body, how much more in the soul? [B]ut the beauty of the body is seen, whereas the beauty of the soul is not seen. It is clear, then, that some men are by nature free, and others slaves, and that for these latter slavery is both expedient and right.

I.6 But that those who take the opposite view have in a certain way right on their side, may be easily seen. For the words slavery and slave are used in two senses. There is a slave or slavery by law as well as by nature. The law of which I speak is a sort of convention, according to which whatever is taken in war is supposed to belong to the victors. But this right many jurists impeach, as they would an orator who brought forward an unconstitutional measure: they detest the notion that, because one man has the power of doing violence and is superior in brute strength, another shall be his slave and subject. Even among philosophers there is a difference of opinion. The origin of the dispute, and the reason why the arguments cross, is as follows: Virtue, when furnished with means, may be deemed to have the greatest power of doing violence: and as superior power is only found where there is superior excellence of some kind, power is thought to imply virtue. But does it likewise imply justice?—that is the question. And, in order to make a distinction between them, some assert that justice is benevolence: to which others reply that justice is nothing more than the rule of a superior. If the two views are regarded as antagonistic and exclusive [i.e., if the notion that justice is benevolence excludes the idea of a just rule of a superior], the alternative [viz. that no one should rule over others] has no force or plausibility, because it implies that not even the superior in virtue ought to rule, or be master. Some, clinging, as they think, to a principle of justice (for law and custom are a sort of justice), assume that slavery in war is justified by law, but they are not consistent. For what if the cause of the war be unjust? No one would ever say that he is a slave who is unworthy to be a slave. Were this the case, men of the highest rank would be slaves and the children of slaves if they or their parents chance to have been taken captive and sold. Wherefore Hellenes do not like to call themselves slaves, but confine the term to barbarians. Yet, in using this language, they really mean the natural slave of whom we spoke at first; for it must be admitted that some are slaves everywhere, others nowhere.

Questions

1. For Aristotle, what is the basis of political authority?

2. How does Aristotle understand the development of political society?

3. How does Aristotle justify slavery?

Aristotle, On the Constitution of Carthage (384–322 BCE)

Aristotle (384–322 BCE), like Herodotus (see Herodotus, Persians Debate Governance, in Chapter 4), displayed a deep interest in understanding his own society and engagement with Greece's neighbors, trading partners, and political rivals. In a quest for more harmonious social and political organization, Aristotle collected evidence about institutional structures from Greek city-states and beyond. One of the places that interested Aristotle was Carthage. Originally a Phoenician colony, it became a major trading port and leading power in the Mediterranean. Aristotle found much to admire in the civic administration of Carthage, as well as cautionary lessons about policies to be avoided.

The Carthaginian constitution resembles the Spartan and Cretan: all three are like one another, but unlike any others. The Carthaginian, though containing an element of democracy, has lasted well, and has never degenerated into a tyranny. At Carthage there are clubs which have common tables: these answer to the Spartan pheiditia. There is also a magistracy of 104, which answers to the Ephoralty, but unlike the Ephors, the Carthaginian magistrates are elected for merit. Like the Spartans they have Kings and a Council of Elders, but, unlike the Spartan, their Kings are elected for merit, and are not always of the same family.

The deviations of Carthage from the perfect state are the same as in most other states. The deviations from aristocracy and polity incline both to democracy and to oligarchy. For instance, the people discuss and determine any matter which has been brought before them by the Kings and Elders (this is not the case at Sparta and Crete); and when the Kings and Elders are not unanimous, the people may decide whether the matter shall be brought forward or not. These are democratical features. But the election of the magistrates by co-optation and their great power after they have ceased to hold

---

SOURCE: *The Politics of Aristotle*, translated by B. Jowett (Oxford: Clarendon Press, 1885), vol. 1, pp. xlvi–xlvii.

office are oligarchical features. The inclination to oligarchy is further shown in the regard which is paid in all elections, to wealth. (On this point however the majority of mankind would agree with the Carthaginians.) Once more, the appointment to offices without salary, the election by vote and not by lot, and the practice of having all suits tried by certain magistrates, and not some by one and some by another, are characteristic of aristocracy. The constitution of Carthage therefore is neither a pure aristocracy nor an oligarchy, but a third form which includes both, and has regard both to merit and wealth. (1) The over-estimation of wealth leads to the sale of offices, which is a great evil. True, the rulers must have the leisure which wealth alone can supply, but office should be the reward of merit, and therefore the legislator should find some other way of making a provision for the ruling class. The sale of offices is a gross abuse, and is a bad example to the people, who always imitate their rulers. (2) It is not a good principle that one man should hold several offices. In a large state they should be distributed as much as possible. (3) The Carthaginians remedy the evils of their government by sending out colonies. The accident of their wealth and position enables them to avail themselves of this outlet; but the safety of the state should not depend upon accidents.

Questions

1. What elements of Carthaginian government does Aristotle admire? Why?

2. In Aristotle's view, what is significant about the connection between wealth and leadership roles?

3. What could explain Aristotle's interest in comparative politics?

The Buddha, Sermons and Teachings (fourth century BCE to first century BCE)

Siddhartha Gautama (c. 563–c. 483 BCE), sometimes called Shakyamnuni Buddha or simply "the Buddha," was the son of the king of a small North Indian state. Accordingly, he grew up in luxury, but at age twenty-nine a series of encounters with suffering people changed his life. Escaping his father's palace (leaving his wife and newborn son), Siddhartha spent six years mastering the teachings of holy ascetics, who insisted that only those who made themselves suffer physically could attain spiritual truth. Ultimately, he rejected this idea. After forty-nine days of meditation, he came to understand the truth (*dharma*). While he initially doubted that humans could understand this truth, he decided that some could. He then spent the rest of his life traveling and preaching, attracting many followers.

The material world, according to the Buddha, is an illusion, and misery results from attachment to the things of this world: thus not only hatred and greed, but even such seemingly positive emotions as love for one's family, are traps that bind a person to this hopeless world. Yet, as this sermon emphasizes, going to the opposite extreme by mortifying the flesh is still relying on the physical world for enlightenment rather than transcending that world.

The records of the Buddha's life and teachings were first transmitted orally, and written down much later, some time before the end of the first century BCE. Still most scholars believe that accounts of his teachings, such as this sermon, are reasonably accurate. There is, of course, much greater disagreement over the miraculous events included in his life story.

The five bhikshus [ascetics] saw their old teacher approach and agreed among themselves not to salute him, nor to address him as a master, but by his name only. "For," so they said, "he has broken his vow and has abandoned holiness. He is no bhikshu but Gautama, and Gautama has become a man who lives in abundance and indulges in the pleasures of worldliness."

But when the Blessed One approached in a dignified manner, they involuntarily rose from their seats and greeted him in spite of their resolution. Still they called him by his name and addressed him as "friend."

When they had thus received the Blessed One, he said: "Do not call the Tathâgata ["one who has come and gone"] by his name nor

SOURCE: Paul Carus, *The Gospel of Buddha: According to Old Records*, 5th ed. (Chicago: Open Court Publishing Company, 1897), pp. 38–42. [Editorial insertions appear in square brackets—*Ed.*]

address him 'friend,' for he is Buddha, the Holy One. Buddha looks equally with a kind heart on all living beings and they therefore call him 'Father.' To disrespect a father is wrong; to despise him, is sin.

"The Tathâgata," Buddha continued, "does not seek salvation in austerities, but for that reason you must not think that he indulges in worldly pleasures, nor does he live in abundance. The Tathâgata has found the middle path.

"Neither abstinence from fish or flesh, nor going naked, nor shaving the head, nor wearing matted hair, nor dressing in a rough garment, nor covering oneself with dirt, nor sacrificing to Agni, will cleanse a man who is not free from delusions.

"Reading the Vêdas, making offerings to priests, or sacrifices to the gods, self-mortification by heat or cold, and many such penances performed for the sake of immortality, these do not cleanse the man who is not free from delusions.

"Anger, drunkenness, obstinacy, bigotry, deception, envy, self-praise, disparaging others, superciliousness, and evil intentions constitute uncleanness; not verily the eating of flesh.

"Let me teach you, O bhikshus, the middle path, which keeps aloof from both extremes. By suffering, the emaciated devotee produces confusion and sickly thoughts in his mind. Mortification is not conducive even to worldly knowledge; how much less to a triumph over the senses!

"He who fills his lamp with water will not dispel the darkness, and he who tries to light a fire with rotten wood will fail.

"Mortifications are painful, vain, and profitless. And how can any one be free from self by leading a wretched life if he does not succeed in quenching the fires of lust.

"All mortification is vain so long as self remains, so long as self continues to lust after either worldly or heavenly pleasures. But he in whom self has become extinct is free from lust; he will desire neither worldly nor heavenly pleasures, and the satisfaction of his natural wants will not defile him. Let him eat and drink according to the needs of the body.

*　*　*

"On the other hand, sensuality of all kind is enervating. The sensual man is a slave of his passions, and pleasure-seeking is degrading and vulgar.

"But to satisfy the necessities of life is not evil. To keep the body in good health is a duty, for otherwise we shall not be able to trim the lamp of wisdom, and keep our mind strong and clear.

"This is the middle path, O bhikshus, that keeps aloof from both extremes."

And the Blessed One spoke kindly to his disciples, pitying them for their errors, and pointing out the uselessness of their endeavors, and the ice of ill-will that chilled their hearts melted away under the gentle warmth of the Master's persuasion.

* * *

"He who recognises the existence of suffering, its cause, its remedy, and its cessation has fathomed the four noble truths. He will walk in the right path.

"Right views will be the torch to light his way. Right aims will be his guide. Right words will be his dwelling-place on the road. His gait will be straight, for it is right behavior. His refreshments will be the right way of earning his livelihood. Right efforts will be his steps: right thoughts his breath; and peace will follow in his footprints."

And the Blessed One explained the instability of the ego.

"Whatsoever is originated will be dissolved again. All worry about the self is vain; the ego is like a mirage, and all the tribulations that touch it will pass away. They will vanish like a nightmare when the sleeper awakes.

"He who has awakened is freed from fear; he has become Buddha; he knows the vanity of all his cares, his ambitions, and also of his pains.

"It easily happens that a man, when taking a bath, steps upon a wet rope and imagines that it is a snake. Horror will overcome him, and he will shake from fear, anticipating in his mind all the agonies caused by the serpent's venomous bite. What a relief does this man experience when he sees that the rope is no snake. The cause of his fright lies in his error, his ignorance, his illusion. If the true nature of the rope is recognised, his tranquility of mind will come back to him; he will feel relieved; he will be joyful and happy.

"This is the state of mind of one who has recognised that there is no self, that the cause of all his troubles, cares, and vanities is a mirage, a shadow, a dream.

"Happy is he who has overcome all selfishness; happy is he who has attained peace; happy is he who has found the truth.

* * *

"Have confidence in the truth, although you may not be able to comprehend it, although you may suppose its sweetness to be bitter, although you may shrink from it at first. Trust in the truth.

"The truth is best as it is. No one can alter it; neither can any one improve it. Have faith in the truth and live it.

* * *

"Self is a fever; self is a transient vision, a dream; but truth is wholesome, truth is sublime, truth is everlasting. There is no immortality except in truth. For truth alone abideth forever."

Questions

1. Why do the bhikshus (ascetic monks) have doubts about greeting Gautama (Gotama)? How does he respond to their doubts about him?

2. What is the middle path? Why is it better than extreme self-denial?

3. What does the story about the rope mean? How should one live in the world after recognizing that the self is illusory?

Chapter 6

SHRINKING THE AFRO-EURASIAN WORLD, 350–100 BCE

Arthashastra, Duties of a King
(c. fourth century BCE)

The Arthashastra (roughly translated as "the science of politics") has often been attributed to Chānaka (c. 350–283 BCE), a prime minister during the Mauryan Empire. At its greatest extent the empire covered most of contemporary India, Pakistan, and Bangladesh, plus bits of Afghanistan. Other scholars think it was probably not compiled until some time after 100 CE, but concede that it is based on earlier materials of some sort. It appears to have been heavily studied prior to the twelfth century CE, but it later became lost, and was not rediscovered until the early twentieth century. Today it has a new life, not only as an important guide to South Asian statecraft in earlier times, but also as an advice book for businessmen. The same thing has happened to classic texts from other traditions, such as Sunzi's *Art of War*.

The text is very broad-ranging, covering issues ranging from war making to law enforcement, the conservation of forests, economic policy, the use of spies, and the education of future leaders. Scholars often note the treatise's emphasis on unsentimental realism, both in dealing with other states and with the ruler's own people, including its support for the use of violence in many contexts. But as the excerpt below shows, it also insists that the ruler discipline himself strictly, and pay attention to the welfare of his subjects, providing support of various kinds when his people need it.

Only if a king is himself energetically active, do his officers follow him energetically. If he is sluggish, they too remain sluggish. And, besides, they eat up his works. He is thereby easily overpowered by his enemies. Therefore, he should ever dedicate himself energetically to activity.

He should divide the day as well as the night into eight parts. * * * During the first one-eighth part of the day, he should listen to reports pertaining to the organization of law and order and to income and expenditure. During the second, he should attend to the affairs of the urban and the rural population. During the third, he should take his bath and meal and devote himself to study. During the fourth, he should receive gold and the departmental heads. During the fifth, he should hold consultations with the council of ministers through correspondence and also keep himself informed of the secret reports brought by spies. During the sixth, he should devote himself freely to amusement or listen to the counsel of the ministers. During the seventh, he should inspect the military formations of elephants, cavalry, chariots, and infantry. During the eighth, he, together with the commander-in-chief of the army, should make plans for campaigns of conquest. When the day has come to an end he should offer the evening prayers.

During the first one-eighth part of the night, he should meet the officers of the secret service. During the second, he should take his bath and meals and also devote himself to study. During the third, at the sounding of the trumpets, he should enter the bed chamber and should sleep through the fourth and fifth. Waking up at the sounding of the trumpets, he should, during the sixth part, ponder over the teachings of the sciences and his urgent duties for the day. During the seventh, he should hold consultations and send out the officers of the secret service for their operations. During the eighth, accompanied by sacrificial priests, preceptors, and the chaplain, he should receive benedictions; he should also have interviews with the physician, the kitchen-superintendent, and the astrologer. Thereafter, he should circumambulate by the right a cow with a calf and an ox

---

SOURCE: *Sources of Indian Tradition*, edited by Ainslie T. Embree (New York: Columbia University Press, 1988), vol. 1, pp. 241–43, 248–49.

and then proceed to the reception hall. Or he should divide the day and the night into parts in accordance with his own capacities and thereby attend to his duties.

When he has gone to the reception hall, he should not allow such persons, as have come for business, to remain sticking to the doors of the hall [i.e., waiting in vain]. For, a king, with whom it is difficult for the people to have an audience, is made to confuse between right action and wrong action by his close entourage. Thereby he suffers from the disaffection of his own subjects or falls prey to the enemy. Therefore he should attend to the affairs relating to gods, hermitages, heretics, learned brāhmans, cattle, and holy places as also those of minors, the aged, the sick, those in difficulty, the helpless, and women—in the order of their enumeration or in accordance with the importance or the urgency of the affairs.

A king should attend to all urgent business, he should not put it off. For what has been thus put off becomes either difficult or altogether impossible to accomplish.

* * *

In the happiness of the subjects lies the happiness of the king; in their welfare, his own welfare. The welfare of the king does not lie in the fulfillment of what is dear to him; whatever is dear to the subjects constitutes his welfare.

* * *

[In foreign affairs observe] the sixfold policy. The teacher says: "Peace, war, marking time, attack, seeking refuge, and duplicity. * * *" "There are only two forms of policy," says Vātavyādhi, "for the sixfold policy is actually accomplished through peace and war." Kautilya says: "The forms of policy are, verily, six in number, for conditions are different in different cases."

Of these six forms: binding through pledges means peace; offensive operation means war; apparent indifference means marking time; strengthening one's position means attack; giving oneself to another [as a subordinate ally or vassal] means seeking refuge; keeping oneself engaged simultaneously in peace and war with the same state means duplicity. These are the six forms of policy.

When one king [the would-be conqueror] is weaker than the other [i.e., his immediate neighbor, the enemy], he should make peace with him. When he is stronger than the other, he should make war with him. When he thinks: "The other is not capable of putting me down nor am I capable of putting him down," he should mark time. When he possesses an excess of the necessary means, he should attack. When he is devoid of strength, he should seek refuge with another. When his end can be achieved only through the help of an ally, he should practice duplicity.

Questions

1. What does this recommended schedule for a king suggest about his priorities? What sorts of things does a king need to know?

2. What are the possible failures of leadership that the author seems most concerned to prevent?

3. What are the things that the king is told to consider when making policy toward neighboring states? What does this suggest about the political environment of the time?

The Jataka or Stories of the Buddha's Former Births (c. 300 BCE)

The Jataka tales, written down around 300 BCE, tell stories involving Buddha in various incarnations. They were originally said to be a prose commentary that helped explain a series of difficult poems in the Buddhist canon, but many also draw on earlier Hindu legends. They are still immensely popular today among both Hindus and Buddhists, especially as a way of introducing various moral lessons for children.

Most of the tales have the same basic pattern seen in this one. Buddha tells a story about a person or animal who accomplished something difficult through wisdom and/or virtue, sometimes contrasting this with the failure of someone less admirable. He then informs his audience that he was one of the characters in the tale, and that one of the people in attendance was one of the others, often likening that person's current striving for spiritual enlightenment to their earlier efforts to reach some earthly goal.

Once on a time when Brahmadatta was reigning in Benares in Kāsi, the Bodhisatta was born into the Treasurer's family, and growing up, was made Treasurer, being called Treasurer Little. A wise and clever man was he, with a keen eye for signs and omens. One day on his way to wait upon the king, he came on a dead mouse lying on the road; and, taking note of the position of the stars at that moment, he said, "Any decent young fellow with his wits about him has only to pick that mouse up, and he might start a business and keep a wife."

His words were overheard by a young man of good family but reduced circumstances, who said to himself, "That's a man who has always got a reason for what he says." And accordingly he picked up the mouse, which he sold for a farthing at a tavern for their cat.

With the farthing he got molasses and took drinking water in a water-pot. Coming on flower-gatherers returning from the forest, he gave each a tiny quantity of the molasses and ladled the water out to them. Each of them gave him a handful of flowers, with the proceeds of which, next day, he came back again to the flower grounds provided with more molasses and a pot of water. That day the flower-gatherers, before they went, gave him flowering plants with half the flowers left on them; and thus in a little while he obtained eight pennies.

Later, one rainy and windy day, the wind blew down a quantity of rotten branches and boughs and leaves in the king's pleasaunce [pleasure garden], and the gardener did not see how to clear them away. Then up came the young man with an offer to remove the lot, if the wood and leaves might be his. The gardener closed with the offer on the spot. Then this apt pupil of Treasurer Little repaired to the children's playground and in a very little while had got them by bribes of molasses to collect every stick and leaf in the place into a

---

SOURCE: *The Jataka or Stories of the Buddha's Former Births*, edited by E. B. Cowell, translated by Robert Chalmers (Cambridge: Cambridge University Press, 1855), vol. 1, pp. 19–20.

heap at the entrance to the pleasaunce. Just then the king's potter was on the look out for fuel to fire bowls for the palace, and coming on this heap, took the lot off his hands. The sale of his wood brought in sixteen pennies to this pupil of Treasurer Little, as well as five bowls and other vessels. Having now twenty-four pennies in all, a plan occurred to him. He went to the vicinity of the city-gate with a jar full of water and supplied 500 mowers with water to drink. Said they, "You've done us a good turn, friend. What can we do for you?" "Oh, I'll tell you when I want your aid," said he; and as he went about, he struck up an intimacy with a land-trader and a sea-trader. Said the former to him, "To-morrow there will come to town a horse-dealer with 500 horses to sell." On hearing this piece of news, he said to the mowers, "I want each of you to-day to give me a bundle of grass and not to sell your own grass till mine is sold." "Certainly," said they, and delivered the 500 bundles of grass at his house. Unable to get grass for his horses elsewhere, the dealer purchased our friend's grass for a thousand pieces. Only a few days later his sea-trading friend brought him news of the arrival of a large ship in port; and another plan struck him. He hired for eight pence a well appointed carriage which plied for hire by the hour, and went in great style down to the port. Having bought the ship on credit and deposited his signet-ring as security, he had a pavilion pitched hard by and said to his people as he took his seat inside, "When merchants are being [shown] in, let them be passed on by three successive ushers into my presence." Hearing that a ship had arrived in port, about a hundred merchants came down to buy the cargo; only to be told that they could not have it as a great merchant had already made a payment on account. So away they all went to the young man; and the footmen duly announced them by three successive ushers, as had been arranged before-hand. Each man of the hundred severally gave him a thousand pieces to buy a share in the ship and then a further thousand each to buy him out altogether. So it was with 200,000 pieces that this pupil of Treasurer Little returned to Benares.

[Wanting to show] his gratitude, he went with one hundred thousand pieces to call on Treasurer Little. "How did you come by all this wealth?" asked the Treasurer. "In four short months, simply by following your advice," replied the young man; and he told him the whole story, starting with the dead mouse. Thought Lord High Treasurer Little, on hearing all this, "I must see that a young fellow of these parts does not fall into anybody else's hands." So he married him to his own grown-up daughter and settled all the family estates on the young man. And at the Treasurer's death, he became Treasurer in that city. And the Bodhisatta passed away to fare according to his deserts.

Questions

1. What are the different strategies that the young man uses to increase his wealth? What role does luck (or heavenly favor) play in his successes?

2. What character traits do these different episodes illustrate? Does the tale seem to regard some of them as more important or more admirable than others? Explain.

3. Why do you think that this tale revolves around a merchant hero's pursuit of wealth (this is also true of other Jataka tales)? Does this suggest anything to you about the religion?

Aśoka, Three Edicts (ruled 269–231 BCE)

Aśoka (ruled 269–231 BCE) was the third king of the Mauryan dynasty; he ruled the empire at its height and his territories extended across most of South Asia. Aśoka ruled an ethnically, linguistically, and religiously diverse population. Although he was a devoted follower of the Buddha, his rule was effective in part because of the tolerance he showed to other religions. He had inscriptions carved onto pillars, boulders, and cave walls, written in various local languages. More than thirty-three remain, distributed throughout modern-day India, Pakistan, and Nepal. They are the first concrete evidence of Buddhism. Many of the inscriptions address recurrent themes of Aśoka's conversion to Buddhism, his efforts to spread the religion, his religious and moral ideas, and his ideas of social and animal welfare.

Excerpts from three different edicts show Aśoka's concerns with just governance, social welfare, and the connection between material and moral well-being. In addition to acknowledging the diversity of people under his rule, Aśoka makes clear his standards of fair administration. He also explicitly asks for obedience in return for tolerance and justice.

FROM THE KALINGA EDICT

By order of the Beloved of the Gods. Addressed to the officers in charge of Tosali. * * * Let us win the affection of all men. All men are my children, and as I wish all welfare and happiness in this world and the next for my own children, so do I wish it for all men. But you do not realize what this entails—here and there an officer may understand in part, but not entirely.

Often a man is imprisoned and tortured unjustly, and then he is liberated for no [apparent] reason. Many other people suffer also [as a result of this injustice]. Therefore it is desirable that you should practice impartiality, but it cannot be attained if you are inclined to habits of jealousy, irritability, harshness, hastiness, obstinacy, laziness, or lassitude. I desire you not to have these habits. The basis of all this is the constant avoidance of irritability and hastiness in your business. * * *

This inscription has been engraved in order that the officials of the city should always see to it that no one is ever imprisoned or tortured without good cause. To ensure this I shall send out every five years on a tour of inspection officers who are not fierce or harsh. * * * The prince at Ujjain shall do the same not more than every three years, and likewise at Taxila.

FROM THE FOURTH PILLAR EDICT

My governors are placed in charge of hundreds of thousands of people. Under my authority they have power to judge and to punish, that they calmly and fearlessly carry out their duties, and that they may bring welfare and happiness to the people of the provinces and

---

SOURCE: *Sources of Indian Tradition*, edited by Ainslee T. Embree (New York: Columbia University Press, 1988), vol. 1, pp. 145–46, 148–49.

be of help to them. They will know what brings joy and what brings sorrow, and, conformably to righteousness, they will instruct the people of the provinces that they may be happy in this world and the next. * * * And as when one entrusts a child to a skilled nurse one is confident that * * * she will care for it well, so have I appointed my governors for the welfare and happiness of the people. That they may fearlessly carry out their duties I have given them power to judge and to inflict punishment on their own initiative. I wish that there should be uniformity of justice and punishment.

FROM THE SEVENTH PILLAR EDICT

In the past, kings sought to make the people progress in righteousness, but they did not progress. * * * And I asked myself how I might uplift them through progress in righteousness. * * * Thus I decided to have them instructed in righteousness, and to issue ordinances of righteousness, so that by hearing them the people might conform, advance in the progress of righteousness, and themselves make great progress. * * * For that purpose many officials are employed among the people to instruct them in righteousness and to explain it to them. * * *

Moreover I have had banyan trees planted on the roads to give shade to man and beast; I have planted mango groves, and I have had ponds dug and shelters erected along the roads at every eight kos. Everywhere I have had wells dug for the benefit of man and beast. But his benefit is but small, for in many ways the kings of olden time have worked for the welfare of the world; but what I have done has been done that men may conform to righteousness.

All the good deeds that I have done have been accepted and followed by the people. And so obedience to mother and father, obedience to teachers, respect for the aged, kindliness to brāhmans and ascetics, to the poor and weak, and to slaves and servants, have increased and will continue to increase. * * * And this progress of righteousness among men has taken place in two manners, by enforcing conformity to righteousness, and by exhortation. I have enforced the law against killing certain animals and many others, but the greatest progress of righteousness among men comes from exhortation in favor of noninjury to life and abstention from killing living beings.

I have done this that it may endure * * * as long as the moon and sun and that my sons and my great-grandsons may support it; for by supporting it they will gain both this world and the next.

Questions

1. Both the Kalinga and the Fourth Pillar edicts emphasize ideas of uniform rather than arbitrary punishments. Why would this idea be important to Aśoka?

2. The exercise of state power in the Fourth Pillar and Seventh Pillar edicts is described in familial terms, using metaphors of child care and parental obedience. How do such descriptions of obedience have particular relevance in a multicultural empire?

3. Does Aśoka appeal to moral or religious values in his discussions of governance? Why or why not?

Arrian, Alexander Adopts Persian Ways (324 BCE)

Arrian was born in Hellenistic-influenced Asia Minor and wrote in Greek. He composed works with a global perspective, including a *Periplus of the Black Sea,* comparable with *The Periplus of the Erythraean Sea,* which is excerpted later in this chapter; a history of the Parthians, who were a significant political and military rival of Rome in Southwest Asia during his lifetime; and a history of India. Arrian was a general, philosopher, governor, and historian whose prime of life spanned the reigns of the Roman emperors Trajan (r. 98–117 CE), Hadrian (r. 117–138 CE), and Antoninus Pius (r. 138–161 CE). Trajan and Hadrian are both credited with foreign expansion and military campaigns, although it was Trajan's expansion eastward to the Tigris and Euphrates in Mesopotamia at the end of his life and Trajan's personal identification with, and aspiration to, the exploits of Alexander the Great (356–323 BCE) that made his contemporary Arrian's interest in Alexander and India so timely.

Arrian is probably best known for his *Anabasis of Alexander,* a history of Alexander the Great's campaigns in the east. Although Arrian was writing several centuries after Alexander's campaigns, he drew on eyewitness reports from Alexander's generals Ptolemy and Aristobulus, among others, to compose his narrative. Due to his troops' unwillingness to go any further at the Hyphasis River in 326 BCE, Alexander had turned back from his campaigns in India, and after a difficult march he and what remained of his troops returned to the capital cities of the Persians they had conquered years before. This passage describes various unusual policies Alexander set into effect upon reaching the Persian capital at Susa in 324 BCE. Shortly thereafter, Alexander and his forces set out for Babylon, where he died within the year.

IV. At this time Alexander dispatched Atropates to his satrapy, after he had himself proceeded to Susa. There he arrested Abulites and his son Oxathres, since he had abused his office as governor of the Susians, and put them to death. For there had been many irregularities on the part of those rulers of countries which Alexander had captured in war; whether towards temples, tombs, or the subjects themselves, since the King had been a long time on his Indian expedition, and there seemed little likelihood of his returning safe from so many tribes and so many fighting elephants, doomed to perish beyond the Indus, Hydaspes, Acesines, and Hyphasis. The disasters too which he suffered in Gadrosia all the more encouraged the satraps on this side to scout any idea of his return. Not but what Alexander himself is said to have grown at this time more ready to listen to any accusations, as if they were wholly reliable, and to punish severely those who were convicted even of slight errors, because he felt they might, in the same frame of mind, commit heavier crimes.

SOURCE: Arrian, *Anabasis of Alexander,* Vol. II.4–6, translated by E. Iliff Robson (Cambridge, MA: Harvard University Press, 1933, repr. 1958), pp. 213, 215, 217, 219, 221.

Then he held also weddings at Susa, both his own and for his Companions; he married Dareius' eldest daughter Barsine, and, as Aristobulus says, another wife besides, the youngest daughter of Ochus, Parysatis. He had already taken to wife Roxane, the daughter of Oxyartes the Bactrian. To Hephaestion he gave Drypetis, also a daughter of Dareius, sister to his own wife, for he desired that Hephaestion's children should be his own nephews and nieces; to Craterus, Amastrine daughter of Oxyartes, Dareius' brother; to Perdiccas a daughter of Atropates, the satrap of Media; to Ptolemaeus the officer of the bodyguard and Eumenes the royal secretary, the daughters of Artabazus, Artacama to Ptolemaeus, Artonis to Eumenes; to Nearchus the daughter of Barsine and Mentor; to Seleucus the daughter of Spitamenes the Bactrian, and similarly to the other Companions the noblest daughters of Persians and Medes, to the number of eighty. These weddings were solemnized in the Persian fashion; chairs were placed for the bridegrooms in order; then after the health-drinkings the brides came in, and each sat down by the side of her bridegroom; they took them by the hand and kissed them, the King setting the example; for all the weddings took place together. In this, if ever, Alexander was thought to have shown a spirit of condescension and comradeship. Then the bridegrooms having received their brides led them back to their homes, and to all Alexander gave dowries. Alexander also ordered the names of any other Macedonians who had married Asian women to be registered. They proved to be more than ten thousand, and to all Alexander gave wedding gifts.

V. This seemed a convenient moment to clear up all debts of the army, and Alexander ordered a list to be made of all debts, with a promise of settlement. At first only a few entered their names on the list, being nervous lest Alexander had merely tried an experiment to see who had not lived on their pay and who had been living extravagantly; but when Alexander learnt that most of the soldiers were not sending in their names, but concealing their bonds, he reproved the suspicions of the troops; the King, he said, must always speak truth to his subjects, and the subjects must never suppose that their King speaks anything but truth. So he had banking tables set up in the camp, with money thereon, and told the accountants charged with the distribution to cancel the debts to all who produced any bond, without so much as registering the names. So they came to believe that Alexander spoke truth, and they were more gratified by the concealment of their names than by the cancellation of the debts. This gift of his to the army is said to have amounted to twenty thousand talents.

He gave also various other gifts, according to the repute in which anyone was held, or to valour shown conspicuously in dangers. He also decorated with golden crowns those distinguished for bravery—Peucestas, first, who saved his life; then Leonnatus, who did likewise, and also for his risks run in India and his victory among the Orians, and because he faced, with the forces remaining to him, the rebel Oreitans and their neighbours, and beat them in the battle; and also for all his other dispositions which he had satisfactorily made among the Orians. Then, besides, he decorated Nearchus for his coasting voyage from India by way of the ocean; for Nearchus also had now arrived at Susa; and next, Onesicritus, the helmsman of the royal ship; also Hephaestion and the rest of the bodyguards.

VI. Then there came to him also the governors of the new cities which he had founded, and of the provinces he had captured besides, bringing about thirty thousand youths, all of the same age, whom Alexander called his "Successors," all dressed in Macedonian dress and trained to warlike exercises on the Macedonian system. Their arrival is said to have annoyed the Macedonians, as if Alexander was contriving every means of dispensing with Macedonians in future; in fact they had been greatly pained to see Alexander wearing the Median robes, and his Persian marriage ceremonies had not given satisfaction to most of them; indeed, not even to some of the bridegrooms, though they had been highly honoured by their being thus raised to a level with the King. Then they were indignant that Pencestas the satrap of Persia was aping Persian ways both in dress and speech, and more, that Alexander seemed to like his Oriental habits; then again, Bactrian, Sogdian, and Arachotian cavalry, and Zarangians, Areians, Parthyaeans, and of the Persians those called the Evacae, were brigaded with the Companions' Cavalry, that is, those who seemed conspicuous for handsomeness or some other excellence. Then, too, apart from these, a fifth cavalry regiment was added, not entirely Oriental, but the whole cavalry force being increased, some of the Orientals were specially picked for it; into the special squadron were enrolled Cophen the son of Artabazus and Hydarnes and Artiboles sons of Mazaeus, Sisines and Phradasmenes, sons of Phrataphernes the satrap of Parthyaea and Hyrcania, and Histanes son of Oxyartes and brother of Roxane, Alexander's wife. Autobares also, and his brother Mithrobaeus; and as commander over all these was appointed Hystaspes the Bactrian, and they were given Macedonian spears instead of the Oriental javelins. All this caused indignation to the Macedonians, as giving an idea that Alexander's heart was growing entirely Orientalized, and that he paid little consideration to Macedonian customs and Macedonians themselves.

Questions

1. What do you think Alexander was trying to accomplish in marrying his Companions and troops to Persian brides "in the Persian fashion"? In forgiving the debts of his soldiers? To what extent was he successful in his aims?

2. How do you think the 10,000 Persian wives married to Macedonian soldiers and 30,000 adolescent boys trained in the Macedonian way felt about their treatment by Alexander? What evidence is there in the passage for how the Macedonian soldiers felt about these developments?

3. Alexander's campaigns were instrumental in paving the way for the spread of Hellenism in the East, through Persia, Bactria, and beyond. What do Alexander's troops think of his "Medizing," or adoption of Persian ways? What do Alexander's actions and the other Greeks' responses to those actions suggest about the directional nature of Hellenism?

Livy, Cato Speaks Against the Repeal of the Oppian Law (195 BCE)

Marcus Porcius Cato (234–149 BCE) is perhaps best known for his oft-repeated phrase, "Carthago delenda est" (Carthage must be destroyed!). Cato's political career thrived in the wake of the second Punic war (218–202 BCE). That war between Rome and Carthage, the rivals for hegemony in the western Mediterranean, had brought a harsh two decades of conflict to the Italic and Iberian peninsulas and to North Africa. The onset of this war had been so harsh for Rome that in the immediate aftermath of Rome's first losses to Hannibal in Italy, Romans had passed a law called the Lex Oppia (215 BCE), which decreed: "no woman should possess more than a half ounce of gold, or wear party-colored clothing, or ride in a horse-drawn vehicle in a city or town or within a mile therefrom, unless taking part in a public religious act" (Livy, *History of Rome* XXXIV.1). The arguable goal of the law was to direct as much money as possible toward the war effort against Carthage and to promote mourning for Rome's losses. After the second Punic war ended in 202 BCE, however, a victorious Rome turned to the east and began expanding toward Greece and beyond. Hellenistic influences and wealth streamed into Roman markets.

It was in this postwar, open-market context that some politicians suggested a repeal of the Oppian law (in 195 BCE) and its limits on women's ownership of property and display of wealth. In what would seem to be a contrast to his brutally imperialist desire for Carthage's destruction, in the passage here from Livy's *History of Rome,* Cato appears isolationist in his concern about the influence of foreign ideas on Roman ways. Livy wrote his *History of Rome* at the beginning of the reign of the first emperor Augustus (r. 27 BCE–14 CE), whose rule ushered in what would come to be known as the *Pax Romana.* This Augustan "peace" brought a great deal of openness and exchange to the Mediterranean. Augustus was married to a powerful woman named Livia, whose influence was resented by many. Cato's speech as recounted by Livy nearly 200 years later likely carried a double meaning for those hearing them. Cato's words offered a criticism of women's involvement in politics and concern about the foreign influences that Roman imperialism brought to the heart of empire that spoke both to Cato's and Livy's day.

2. Citizens of Rome, if each one of us had set himself to retain the rights and the dignity of a husband over his own wife, we should have less trouble with women as a whole sex. As things are, our liberty, overthrown in the home by female indiscipline, is now being crushed and trodden underfoot here too, in the Forum. It is because we have not kept them under control individually that we are now terrorized by them collectively . . .

For myself, it was with something like a blush of shame that I made my way just now to the Forum through the midst of an army of women. Had I not been restrained by my respect for the dignity and modesty of some individual women . . . I should have said: "What sort of behaviour is this? Are you in the habit of running out into the streets, blocking the roads, and addressing other women's husbands? Couldn't you have made the very same request of your own husbands at home? Or are you more alluring in the street than in the home, more attractive to other women's husbands than to your own? And yet, even at home, if modesty restrained matrons within the limits of their own rights, it would not become you to be concerned about the question of what laws should be passed or repealed in this place."

Our ancestors refused to allow any woman to transact even private business without a guardian to represent her; women had to be under the control of fathers, brothers, or husbands. But we (heaven preserve us!) are now allowing them even to take part in politics, and actually to appear in the Forum and to be present at our meetings and assemblies! What are they now doing in the streets and at the street corners? Are they not simply canvassing for the proposal of the tribunes, and voting for the repeal of the law? Give a free rein to their undisciplined nature, to this untamed animal, and then expect them to set a limit to their own license! Unless you impose that limit, this is the least of the restraints imposed on women by custom or by law which they resent. What they are longing for is complete liberty, or rather—if we want to speak the truth—complete license.

SOURCE: Livy, *Rome and the Mediterranean,* Book XXXIV. 2–4 of *History of Rome,* translated by Henry Bettenson, (New York: Penguin, 1976), pp. 142–146.

3. Indeed, if they carry this point, what will they not attempt? Run over all the laws relating to women whereby your ancestors curbed their license and brought them into subjection to their husbands. Even with all these bonds you can scarcely restrain them. And what will happen if you allow them to seize these bonds, to wrest them from your hands one by one, and finally to attain equality with their husbands? Do you imagine that you will find them endurable? The very moment they begin to be your equals, they will be your superiors. Good heavens! They object to the passing of a new measure against them; they complain that this is not law but rank injustice. . . . [T]hey intend that by the abolition of this one law you should weaken the force of all the others. If every individual is to destroy and demolish any law which hinders him in his particular interests, what use will it be for the whole citizen body to pass measures which will soon be repealed by those whom they directed?

I should like to be told what it is that has led these matrons to rush out into the streets in a tumult, scarcely refraining from entering the Forum and attending a public meeting. It is to plead that their fathers, their husbands, their sons, their brothers, may be ransomed from Hannibal? Such a disaster to our country is far away—and may it always be so! . . . And what excuse, that can be spoken without shame, is offered for this present feminine insurrection? "We want to gleam with purple and gold," says one of them "and to ride in our carriages on festal days and on ordinary days: we want to ride through Rome as if in triumph over the law which has been vanquished and repealed, and over those votes of yours which we have captured and wrested from you; we want no limit to our spending and our extravagance."

4. You have often heard my complaints about the excessive spending of the women, and of the men, magistrates as well as private citizens, about the sorry state of our commonwealth because of two opposing vices, avarice, and extravagance—plagues which have been the destruction of all great empires. As the fortune of our commonwealth grows better and happier day by day, and as our empire increases—and already we have crossed into Greece and Asia (regions full of all kinds of sensual allurements) and are even laying hands on the treasures of kings—I am the more alarmed lest

these things should capture us instead of our capturing them; those statues brought from Syracuse, believe me, were hostile standards brought against this city. And now I hear far too many people praising the ornaments of Corinth and Athens, and jeering at the terracotta antefixes of the Roman gods. . . .

It is within memory of our fathers that Pyrrhus, through his agent Cineas, tried to win over with gifts the minds not only of our men but of our women as well. The Lex Oppia had not then been passed to restrain female extravagance; and yet no woman accepted these gifts. What do you suppose was the reason for this? . . . [T]here was no extravagance to be restrained. Diseases must be known before their cures are found; by the same token, appetites come into being before the laws to limit their exercise. . . . And so it is not in the least surprising that no Oppian law, or any other law, was required to set limits on female expenditure at a time when they refused gifts of gold and purple offered without their asking. If Cineas were going round the city today with those gifts, he would find women standing in the streets to accept them.

. . . Is your wish, citizens, to start such a competition between your wives, so that the rich will desire to possess what no other woman can possess; while the poor will stretch themselves beyond their means, to avoid being looked down on for their poverty? Let them once begin to be ashamed of what should cause no shame, and they will not be ashamed of what is truly shameful. The woman who can buy these things with her own money, will buy them; the woman who cannot, will entreat her husband to buy them. Pity the poor husband, if he yields! Pity him if he refuses, since what he does not give himself he will see given by another man! At the present time they are making requests of other women's husbands, in public, and (what is more important) they are asking for legislation and for votes; and from some men they get what they want. Against your own interests and the interests of your property and your children, you, my friend, are open to their entreaties; and when once the law has ceased to put a limit on your wife's spending, you yourself will never do it.

. . . My opinion is that the Lex Oppia should on no account be repealed; and I pray the blessing of all the gods on your decision.

Questions

1. What is it about women's involvement in the political process to repeal the Oppian law that appears to bother Cato?

2. Toward the end of his speech, Cato claims that "avarice and extravagance [are] plagues which have been the destruction of all great empires." What do Greek city-states (Syracuse, Corinth, and Athens), Asia (meaning modern Turkey), and an agent of the Greek king Pyrrhus of Epirus (famous for his "Pyrrhic victory" against Rome in southern Italy in 275 BCE) have to do with this claim? What does implicating these regions in his claim about the fall of empires suggest about Cato's view of Hellenism and Greek influence on the West?

3. What is at the root of Cato's concern about women, wealth, and power? Based on this passage and the fact that the Oppian law was successfully repealed, to what extent was Cato's opinion shared by others?

1 Maccabees, Resisting Hellenism (167 BCE)

Hellenism is the term used to describe the common Greek culture—language, literature, laws, building, beliefs, and aesthetics—that spread into, and beyond, the regions conquered by Alexander in the late fourth century BCE. In much the same way as modern-day globalization and the spread of "Western" ideas are openly welcomed by some and violently resisted by others, Hellenism met with mixed response in the regions into which it spread in the centuries after Alexander's death (d. 323 BCE). The shores of the Eastern Mediterranean were a particularly fierce battleground for this culture war. The passage that follows is drawn from the opening of 1 Maccabees. While scholars argue about the original language in which 1 Maccabees was composed, the earliest surviving versions are preserved, ironically, in Greek. Written in close proximity to the events described, 1 Maccabees holds a varied place in several modern faith traditions. For instance, it is a foundational historical text for Judaism; it is in the canon of biblical literature for Catholicism; and it is an important noncanonical text for Protestants. The text takes its name from the word *Maccabeus*, which by some etymologies means "the hammer." This was the surname or epithet (nickname) of Judas, the ultimate leader of the revolt against the Hellenistic Seleucid king

Antiochus Epiphanes (r. 175–164 BCE). This passage describes the beginning of the series of events that are remembered in the Jewish observance of Hanukkah.

––––––––––––––––

1 MAC.1

[7] And after Alexander [the Great] had reigned twelve years, he died (323 BCE).

[8] Then his officers began to rule, each in his own place.

[9] They all put on crowns after his death, and so did their sons after them for many years; and they caused many evils on the earth.

[10] From them came forth a sinful root, Antiochus Epiphanes, son of Antiochus the king. . . .

[11] In those days lawless men came forth from Israel, and misled many, saying, "Let us go and make a covenant with the Gentiles round about us, for since we separated from them many evils have come upon us."

[12] This proposal pleased them,

[13] and some of the people eagerly went to the king [Antiochus]. He authorized them to observe the ordinances of the Gentiles.

[14] So they built a gymnasium in Jerusalem, according to Gentile custom,

[15] and removed the marks of circumcision, and abandoned the holy covenant. They joined with the Gentiles and sold themselves to do evil.

[16] When Antiochus saw that his kingdom was established, he determined to become king of the land of Egypt, that he might reign over both kingdoms . . .

* * *

[20] After subduing Egypt, Antiochus returned in the one hundred and forty-third year. He went up against Israel and came to Jerusalem with a strong force.

––––––––––––––––

SOURCE: 1 Maccabees 1:7–2:28, Revised Standard Version Bible, National Council of the Churches of Christ, 1952.

[21] He arrogantly entered the sanctuary and took the golden altar, the lampstand for the light, and all its utensils.

[22] He took also the table for the bread of the Presence, the cups for drink offerings, the bowls, the golden censers, the curtain, the crowns, and the gold decoration on the front of the temple; he stripped it all off.

[23] He took the silver and the gold, and the costly vessels; he took also the hidden treasures which he found.

[24] Taking them all, he departed to his own land. He committed deeds of murder, and spoke with great arrogance.

[25] Israel mourned deeply in every community,
[26] rulers and elders groaned,
maidens and young men became faint,
the beauty of women faded . . .

*　　*　　*

[29] Two years later the king sent to the cities of Judah a chief collector of tribute, and he came to Jerusalem with a large force.

[30] Deceitfully he spoke peaceable words to them, and they believed him; but he suddenly fell upon the city, dealt it a severe blow, and destroyed many people of Israel.

[31] He plundered the city, burned it with fire, and tore down its houses and its surrounding walls.

[32] And they took captive the women and children, and seized the cattle.

[33] Then they fortified the city of David with a great strong wall and strong towers, and it became their citadel.

[34] And they stationed there a sinful people, lawless men. These strengthened their position . . .

*　　*　　*

[37] On every side of the sanctuary they shed innocent blood; they even defiled the sanctuary.
[38] Because of them the residents of Jerusalem fled . . .
[39] Her sanctuary became desolate as a desert . . .

*　　*　　*

[41] Then the king wrote to his whole kingdom that all should be one people,

[42] and that each should give up his customs.

[43] All the Gentiles accepted the command of the king. Many even from Israel gladly adopted his religion; they sacrificed to idols and profaned the sabbath.

[44] And the king sent letters by messengers to Jerusalem and the cities of Judah; he directed them to follow customs strange to the land,

[45] to forbid burnt offerings and sacrifices and drink offerings in the sanctuary, to profane sabbaths and feasts,

[46] to defile the sanctuary and the priests,

[47] to build altars and sacred precincts and shrines for idols, to sacrifice swine and unclean animals,

[48] and to leave their sons uncircumcised. They were to make themselves abominable by everything unclean and profane,

[49] so that they should forget the law and change all the ordinances.

[50] "And whoever does not obey the command of the king shall die."

[51] In such words he wrote to his whole kingdom. And he appointed inspectors over all the people and commanded the cities of Judah to offer sacrifice, city by city.

[52] Many of the people, everyone who forsook the law [i.e., Jewish law], joined them, and they did evil in the land;

[53] they drove Israel into hiding in every place of refuge they had.

[54] Now on the fifteenth day of Chislev, in the one hundred and forty-fifth year, they erected a desolating sacrilege upon the altar of burnt offering. They also built altars in the surrounding cities of Judah,

[55] and burned incense at the doors of the houses and in the streets.

[56] The books of the law which they found they tore to pieces and burned with fire.

[57] Where the book of the covenant was found in the possession of any one, or if any one adhered to the law, the decree of the king condemned him to death.

[58] They kept using violence against Israel, against those found month after month in the cities.

[59] And on the twenty-fifth day of the month they offered sacrifice on the altar which was upon the altar of burnt offering.

[60] According to the decree, they put to death the women who had their children circumcised,

[61] and their families and those who circumcised them; and they hung the infants from their mothers' necks.

[62] But many in Israel stood firm . . .

[63] They chose to die rather than to be defiled by food or to profane the holy covenant; and they did die.

[64] And very great wrath came upon Israel.

1MAC.2

[1] In those days Mattathias the son of John, son of Simeon, a priest of the sons of Joarib, moved from Jerusalem and settled in Modein.

[2] He had five sons, John surnamed Gaddi,

[3] Simon called Thassi,

[4] Judas called Maccabeus,

[5] Eleazar called Avaran, and Jonathan called Apphus.

[6] He saw the blasphemies being committed in Judah and Jerusalem,

[7] and said, "Alas! Why was I born to see this,
the ruin of my people, the ruin of the holy city,
and to dwell there when it was given over to the enemy,
the sanctuary given over to aliens?

[8] Her temple has become like a man without honor;

[9] her glorious vessels have been carried into captivity.
Her babes have been killed in her streets,
her youths by the sword of the foe.

[10] What nation has not inherited her palaces
and has not seized her spoils?

[11] All her adornment has been taken away;
no longer free, she has become a slave.

[12] And behold, our holy place, our beauty,
and our glory have been laid waste;
the Gentiles have profaned it.

[13] Why should we live any longer?"

[14] And Mattathias and his sons rent their clothes, put on sackcloth, and mourned greatly.

[15] Then the king's officers who were enforcing the apostasy came to the city of Modein to make them offer sacrifice . . .

* * *

[17] Then the king's officers spoke to Mattathias as follows: "You are a leader, honored and great in this city, and supported by sons and brothers.

[18] Now be the first to come and do what the king commands, as all the Gentiles and the men of Judah and those that are left in Jerusalem have done. Then you and your sons will be numbered among the friends of the king, and you and your sons will be honored with silver and gold and many gifts."

[19] But Mattathias answered and said in a loud voice: "Even if all the nations that live under the rule of the king obey him, and have chosen to do his commandments, departing each one from the religion of his fathers,

[20] yet I and my sons and my brothers will live by the covenant of our fathers.

[21] Far be it from us to desert the law and the ordinances.

[22] We will not obey the king's words by turning aside from our religion to the right hand or to the left."

[23] When he had finished speaking these words, a Jew came forward in the sight of all to offer sacrifice upon the altar in Modein, according to the king's command.

[24] When Mattathias saw it, he burned with zeal and his heart was stirred. He gave vent to righteous anger; he ran and killed him upon the altar.

[25] At the same time he killed the king's officer who was forcing them to sacrifice, and he tore down the altar.

[26] Thus he burned with zeal for the law . . .

[27] Then Mattathias cried out in the city with a loud voice, saying: "Let every one who is zealous for the law and supports the covenant come out with me!"

[28] And he and his sons fled to the hills and left all that they had in the city.

Questions

1. How does the passage describe Greek rule from Alexander the Great to Antiochus Epiphanes? What measures does Antiochus take in asserting his power over, and introducing Greek ways to, the region? To what extent do his policies change over time?

2. What is the local response to Antiochus's rule? In what ways do some locals accept Greek power and Hellenistic ideas and practices? In what ways is there resistance?

3. How does this text, together with the others in this chapter, challenge the notion of a welcome spread of Hellenism in the wake of Alexander and his successors?

The Periplus of the Erythraean Sea
(first century CE)

A periplus consisted of sailing directions that listed ports and coastal landmarks, with the approximate distance between them, to help navigate along a shoreline. These Greek documents were familiar to merchants and travelers in the ancient Mediterranean world; some passages in the histories of Herodotus and Thucydides appear to draw from such descriptions. *The Periplus of the Erythraean* [Red] *Sea* describes travel from the Egyptian port of Berenice to locations in the Red Sea, along the east coast of Africa (Azania in the text), into the Persian Gulf and across to India. The document was likely written by a resident of Alexandria sometime in the first century CE. Given the extent of the details provided, the author probably had firsthand knowledge of many of the ports. The text is an important source for understanding what the ancient Mediterranean societies knew about far-distant trading opportunities. While some of the locations described in the text can be correlated to present-day towns or archaeological sites (for example, Adulis, the port city of the Axum kingdom in present-day Eretria, or the Ganges River in India), other place names have several possible locations.

The text gives topographical descriptions, tides, detailed lists of trade goods imported and exported at specific ports, descriptions of local political relationships, and occasional commentary on the local inhabitants.

2. On the right-hand coast next below Berenice is the country of the Berbers. Along the shore are the Fish-Eaters, living in scattered caves in the narrow valleys. Further inland are the Berbers, and beyond them the Wild-flesh-Eaters and Calf-Eaters, each tribe governed by its chief; and behind them, further inland, in the country toward the west, there lies a city called Meroe.

3. Below the Calf-Eaters there is a little market-town on the shore after sailing about four thousand stadia from Berenice, called Ptolemais of the Hunts, from which the hunters started for the interior under the dynasty of the Ptolemies. This market-town has the true land-tortoise in small quantity; it is white and smaller in the shells. And here also is found a little ivory, like that of Adulis. But the place has no harbor and is reached only by small boats.

4. Below * * * is Adulis, a port established by law, lying at the inner end of a bay that runs in toward the south. Before the harbor lies the so-called Mountain Island, about two hundred stadia seaward from the very head of the bay, with the shores of the mainland close to it on both sides. Ships bound for this port now anchor here because of attacks from the land. They used formerly to anchor at the very head of the bay, by an island called Diodorus, close to the shore, which could be reached on foot from the land; by which means the barbarous natives attacked the island. Opposite Mountain Island, on the mainland twenty stadia from shore, lies Adulis, a fair-sized village, from which there is a three-days' journey to Coloe, an inland town and the first market for ivory. From that place to the city of the people called Auxumites there is a five days' journey more; to that place all the ivory is brought from the country beyond the Nile through the district called Cyeneum, and thence to Adulis. Practically the whole number of elephants and rhinoceros that are killed live in the places inland, although at rare intervals they are hunted on the seacoast even near Adulis. Before the harbor of that market-town, out at sea on the right hand, there lie a great many little sandy islands called Alalæi, yielding tortoise-shell, which is brought to market there by the Fish-Eaters.

SOURCE: *The Periplus of the Erythraean Sea*, translated by Wilfred H. Schoff (London: Longmans, Green, and Co., 1912), pp. 22–23, 27–30, 34, 40–43.

5. And about eight hundred stadia beyond there is another very deep bay, with a great mound of sand piled up at the right of the entrance; at the bottom of which the opsian stone is found, and this is the only place where it is produced. These places, from the Calf-Eaters to the other Berber country, are governed by Zoscales; who is miserly in his ways and always striving for more, but otherwise upright, and acquainted with Greek literature.

6. There are imported into these places, undressed cloth made in Egypt for the Berbers; robes from Arsinoe; cloaks of poor quality dyed in colors; double-fringed linen mantles; many articles of flint glass, and others of murrhine, made in Diospolis; and brass, which is used for ornament and in cut pieces instead of coin; sheets of soft copper, used for cooking-utensils and cut up for bracelets and anklets for the women; iron, which is made into spears used against the elephants and other wild beasts, and in their wars. Besides these, small axes are imported, and adzes and swords; copper drinking-cups, round and large; a little coin for those coming to the market; wine of Laodicea and Italy, not much; olive oil, not much; for the king, gold and silver plate made after the fashion of the country, and for clothing, military cloaks, and thin coats of skin, of no great value. Likewise from the district of Ariaca across this sea, there are imported Indian iron, and steel, and Indian cotton cloth; the broad cloth called *monachê* and that called *sagmatogênê*, and girdles, and coats of skin and mallow-colored cloth, and a few muslins, and colored lac. There are exported from these places ivory, and tortoise-shell and rhinoceros-horn.

* * *

15. Beyond Opone, the shore trending more toward the south, first there are the small and great bluffs of Azania; this coast is destitute of harbors, but there are places where ships can lie at anchor, the shore being abrupt; and this course is of six days, the direction being south-west. Then come the small and great beach for another six days' course * * * beyond which, a little to the south of south-west, after two courses of a day and night along the Ausanitic coast, is the island Menuthias, about three hundred stadia from the mainland, low and wooded, in which there are rivers and many

kinds of birds and the mountain-tortoise. There are no wild beasts except the crocodiles; but there they do not attack men. In this place there are sewed boats, and canoes hollowed from single logs, which they use for fishing and catching tortoise. In this island they also catch them in a peculiar way, in wicker baskets, which they fasten across the channel-opening between the breakers.

16. Two days' sail beyond, there lies the very last market-town of the continent of Azania, which is called Rhapta [perhaps near the mouth of the Rufiji River, Tanzania]; which has its name from the sewed boats (*rhaptôn ploiariôn*) already mentioned; in which there is ivory in great quantity, and tortoise-shell. Along this coast live men of piratical habits, very great in stature, and under separate chiefs for each place. The Mapharitic chief governs it under some ancient right that subjects it to the sovereignty of the state that is become first in Arabia. And the people of Muza now hold it under his authority, and send thither many large ships; using Arab captains and agents, who are familiar with the natives and intermarry with them, and who know the whole coast and understand the language.

* * *

20. [In Arabia,] different tribes inhabit the country, differing in their speech, some partially, and some altogether. The land next the sea is similarly dotted here and there with caves of the Fish-Eaters, but the country inland is peopled by rascally men speaking two languages, who live in villages and nomadic camps, by whom those sailing off the middle course are plundered, and those surviving shipwrecks are taken for slaves. And so they too are continually taken prisoners by the chiefs and kings of Arabia; and they are called Carnaites. Navigation is dangerous along this whole coast of Arabia, which is without harbors, with bad anchorages, foul, inaccessible because of breakers and rocks, and terrible in every way. Therefore we hold our course down the middle of the gulf and pass on as fast as possible by the country of Arabia until we come to the Burnt Island; directly below which there are regions of peaceful people, nomadic, pasturers of cattle, sheep and camels.

* * *

31. It happens that just as Azania is subject to Charibael and the Chief of Mapharitis, this island is subject to the King of the Frankincense Country. Trade is also carried on there by some people from Muza and by those who chance to call there on the voyage from Damirica and Barygaza; they bring in rice and wheat and Indian cloth, and a few female slaves; and they take for their exchange cargoes, a great quantity of tortoise-shell. Now the island is farmed out under the Kings and is garrisoned.

* * *

45. Now the whole country of India has very many rivers, and very great ebb and flow of the tides; increasing at the new moon, and at the full moon for three days, and falling off during the intervening days of the moon. But about Barygaza it is much greater, so that the bottom is suddenly seen, and now parts of the dry land are sea, and now it is dry where ships were sailing just before; and the rivers, under the inrush of the flood tide, when the whole force of the sea is directed against them, are driven upwards more strongly against their natural current, for many stadia.

46. For this reason entrance and departure of vessels is very dangerous to those who are inexperienced or who come to this market-town for the first time. For the rush of waters at the incoming tide is irresistible, and the anchors cannot hold against it; so that large ships are caught up by the force of it, turned broadside on through the speed of the current, and so driven on the shoals and wrecked; and smaller boats are overturned; and those that have been turned aside among the channels by the receding waters at the ebb, are left on their sides, and if not held on an even keel by props, the flood tide comes upon them suddenly and under the first head of the current they are filled with water. For there is so great force in the rush of the sea at the new moon, especially during the flood tide at night, that if you begin the entrance at the moment when the waters are still, on the instant there is borne to you at the mouth of the river, a noise like the cries of an army heard from afar; and very soon the sea itself comes rushing in over the shoals with a hoarse roar.

* * *

49. There are imported into this market-town, wine, Italian pre-ferred, also Laodicean and Arabian; copper, tin, and lead; coral and topaz; thin clothing and inferior sorts of all kinds; bright-colored girdles a cubit wide; storax, sweet clover, flint glass, realgar, anti-mony, gold and silver coin, on which there is a profit when exchanged for the money of the country; and ointment, but not very costly and not much. And for the King there are brought into those places very costly vessels of silver, singing boys, beautiful maidens for the harem, fine wines, thin clothing of the finest weaves, and the choic-est ointments. There are exported from these places spikenard, cos-tus, bdellium, ivory, agate and carnelian, lycium, cotton cloth of all kinds, silk cloth, mallow cloth, yarn, long pepper and such other things as are brought here from the various market-towns. Those bound for this market-town from Egypt make the voyage favorably about the month of July, that is Epiphi.

50. Beyond Barygaza the adjoining coast extends in a straight line from north to south; and so this region is called Dachinabades, for *dachanos* in the language of the natives means "south." The inland country back from the coast toward the east comprises many desert regions and great mountains; and all kinds of wild beasts—leopards, tigers, elephants, enormous serpents, hyenas, and baboons of many sorts; and many populous nations, as far as the Ganges.

Questions

1. Based on these excerpts, what topics seem most important to the per-son who wrote this periplus? Why?

2. Scholars continue to debate whether this is a firsthand account of these voyages, or a collection of reports. Which passages in the text make you think the author visited these ports? Which passages sup-port the notion that this document is secondhand reporting?

3. How do the descriptions of distant lands and people in the *Periplus* com-pare to such descriptions in other ancient texts?

Chapter 7

HAN DYNASTY CHINA AND IMPERIAL ROME, 300 BCE–300 CE

Pliny the Elder, The Seres (c. 77 CE)

Gaius Plinius Secundus (23 CE–79 CE), called Pliny the Elder since his nephew was a well-known lawyer and writer, was a military commander of the Roman Empire, equally well-remembered for his scholarship as for his military accomplishments and political connections. His major surviving work is *The Natural History*, an encyclopedia published c. 77 CE. It still serves as a model for the genre, achieving breadth and accuracy (in its day); validating the need for references; and providing an index. *The Natural History* investigates the diversity of human societies, plants, animals, and the physical world, making claims to encompass the entire field of ancient knowledge (Herodotus and Thucydides also made universalist claims to knowledge). Pliny's descriptions served as the basis for many subsequent European descriptions of Asia well into the modern era.

"The Seres" chapter of *The Natural History* refers to various groups of people of central, east, and south Asia, some of whom were, in fact, drawn from Greek mythology. Other groups were among those Pliny refers to elsewhere as the "fabulous Indian races." Pliny famously describes silk cultivation and production—and the reasons behind Rome's demand for silk.

After we have passed the Caspian Sea and the Scythian Ocean, our course takes an easterly direction, such being the turn here taken by the line of the coast. The first portion of these shores, after we pass the Scythian Promontory, is totally uninhabitable, owing to the snow, and the regions adjoining are uncultivated, in consequence of the savage state of the nations which dwell there. Here are the abodes of the Scythian Anthropophagi [described earlier by Herodotus], who feed on human flesh. Hence it is that all around them consists of vast deserts, inhabited by multitudes of wild beasts, which are continually lying in wait, ready to fall upon human beings just as savage as themselves. After leaving these, we again come to a nation of the Scythians, and then again to desert tracts tenanted by wild beasts, until we reach a chain of mountains which runs up to the sea, and bears the name of Tabis. It is not, however, before we have traversed very nearly one half of the coast that looks towards the north-east, that we find it occupied by inhabitants.

The first people that are known of here are the Seres, so famous for the wool that is found in their forests. After steeping it in water, they comb off a white down that adheres to the leaves; and then to the females of our part of the world they give the twofold task of unravelling their textures, and of weaving the threads afresh. So manifold is the labour, and so distant are the regions which are thus ransacked to supply a dress through which our ladies may in public display their charms. The Seres are of inoffensive manners, but, bearing a strong resemblance therein to all savage nations, they shun all intercourse with the rest of mankind, and await the approach of those who wish to traffic with them. The first river that is known in their territory is the Psitharas, next to that the Cambari, and the third the Laros; after which we come to the Promontory of Chryse, the Gulf of Cynaba, the river Atianos, and the nation of the Attacori on the gulf of that name, a people protected by their sunny hills from all noxious blasts, and living in a climate of the same temperature as that of the Hyperhorei. Amometus has written a work entirely devoted to the history of these people, just as Hecatæus has done in his treatise on the Hyperborei. After the

SOURCE: "The Seres," in *The Natural History of Pliny*, translated by John Bostock and H. T. Riley (London: George Bell and Sons, 1855), vol. 2, pp. 35–38.

Attacori, we find the nations of the Phruri and the Tochari, and, in the interior, the Casiri, a people of India, who look toward the Scythians, and feed on human flesh. Here are also numerous wandering Nomad tribes of India. There are some authors who state that in a north-easterly direction these nations touch upon the Cicones and the Brysari.

Questions

1. What was the role of silk in connecting Rome to Asia? What does Pliny think about Roman demand for silk?

2. Why might Pliny have described Anthropophagi as cannibals? Do you think this description is accurate or exaggerated? Why?

3. Pliny describes Seres, peoples who lived in the area that is now northwestern China, as being disconnected from "the rest of mankind." If they had been entirely isolated, however, they could not have traded their silk. Why might Pliny have described them as so cut off from mankind?

Diodorus Siculus, On the Slave Revolt in Sicily (136–132 BCE)

The domination of the Mediterranean by Rome in the second century BCE transformed Roman society. Victorious Roman wars produced a massive flow of slaves into Italy. Small-scale farming was replaced by large aristocratic estates worked by slave labor. Between the 130s BCE and the 70s BCE three massive slave rebellions took place. The first of these occurred in Sicily between 136 and 132 BCE. Rebellious slaves under the leadership of Eunus from Apamea in Syria, their elected king, successfully resisted the Romans for several years. The following account of this "First Servile War" comes from the *Library* of Diodorus Siculus. Diodorus was a Greek-speaking inhabitant of Sicily who composed his work before 30 BCE.

––––––––––––––––

The Sicilians, having shot up in prosperity and acquired great wealth, began to purchase a vast number of slaves, to whose bodies, as they were brought in droves from the slave markets, they at once applied marks and brands. The young men they used as cowherds, the others in such ways as they happened to be useful. But they treated them with a heavy hand in their service, and granted them the most meagre care, the bare minimum for food and clothing. As a result most of them made their livelihood by brigandage, and there was bloodshed everywhere, since the brigands were like scattered bands of soldiers.

* * *

There was a certain Syrian slave, belonging to Antigenes of Enna; he was an Apamean by birth and had an aptitude for magic and the working of wonders. He claimed to foretell the future, * * * he not only gave oracles by means of dreams, but even made a pretence of having waking visions of the gods and of hearing the future from their own lips. * * * [H]is reputation advanced apace. Finally, through some device, while in a state of divine possession, he would produce fire and flame from his mouth, and thus rave oracularly about things to come. For he would place fire, and fuel to maintain it, in a nut—or something similar—that was pierced on both sides; then, placing it in his mouth and blowing on it, he kindled now sparks, and now a flame. Prior to the revolt he used to say that the Syrian goddess appeared to him, saying that he should be king, and he repeated this, not only to others, but even to his own master. Since his claims were treated as a joke, Antigenes, taken by his hocus-pocus, would introduce Eunus (for that was the wonder-worker's name) at his dinner parties, and cross-question him about his kingship and how he would treat each of the men present. And since he gave a full account of everything without hesitation, explaining with what moderation he would treat the masters and in sum making a colourful tale of his quackery, the guests were always stirred to laughter. * * * The beginning of the whole revolt took place as follows.

SOURCE: *Diodorus of Sicily*, translated by Francis R. Walton (Cambridge: Harvard University Press, 1967), vol. xii, pp. 57–71.

There was a certain Damophilus of Enna, a man of great wealth but insolent of manner; he had abused his slaves to excess, and his wife Megallis vied even with her husband in punishing the slaves and in her general inhumanity towards them. The slaves, reduced by this degrading treatment to the level of brutes, conspired to revolt and to murder their masters. Going to Eunus they asked him whether their resolve had the favour of the gods. He, resorting to his usual mummery, promised them the favour of the gods, and soon persuaded them to act at once. Immediately, therefore, they brought together four hundred of their fellow slaves and, having armed themselves in such ways as opportunity permitted, they fell upon the city of Enna, with Eunus at their head and working his miracle of the flames of fire for their benefit. When they found their way into the houses they shed much blood, sparing not even suckling babes. * * * By now a great multitude of slaves from the city had joined them, who, after first demonstrating against their own masters their utter ruthlessness, then turned to the slaughter of others. When Eunus and his men learned that Damophilus and his wife were in the garden that lay near the city, they sent some of their band and dragged them off. * * * Only in the case of the couple's daughter were the slaves seen to show consideration throughout, and this was because of her kindly nature, in that to the extent of her power she was always compassionate and ready to succour the slaves. Thereby it was demonstrated that the others were treated as they were, not because of some "natural savagery of slaves," but rather in revenge for wrongs previously received. The men appointed to the task, having dragged Damophilus and Megallis into the city * * * brought them to the theatre, where the crowd of rebels had assembled. But when Damophilus attempted to devise a plea to get them off safe and was winning over many of the crowd with his words, Hermeias and Zeuxis, men bitterly disposed towards him, denounced him as a cheat, and without waiting for a formal trial by the assembly the one ran him through the chest with a sword, the other chopped off his head with an axe. Thereupon Eunus was chosen king. * * *

* * * [H]e called an assembly and put to death all the citizenry of Enna except for those who were skilled in the manufacture of arms: these he put in chains and assigned them to this task. He

gave Megallis to the maidservants to deal with as they might wish; they subjected her to torture and threw her over a precipice. * * * Having set a diadem upon his head, and arrayed himself in full royal style, he proclaimed his wife queen, * * * and appointed to the royal council such men as seemed to be gifted with superior intelligence, among them one Achaeus, * * * a man who excelled both at planning and in action. In three days Eunus had armed, as best he could, more than six thousand men, besides others in his train who had only axes and hatchets, or slings, or sickles, or fire-hardened stakes, or even kitchen spits; and he went about ravaging the countryside. Then, since he kept recruiting untold numbers of slaves, he ventured even to do battle with Roman generals, and on joining combat repeatedly overcame them with his superior numbers, for he now had more than ten thousand soldiers.

* * *

* * * Cities were captured with all their inhabitants, and many armies were cut to pieces by the rebels, until Rupilius, the Roman commander, recovered Tauromenium for the Romans by placing it under strict siege and confining the rebels under conditions of unspeakable duress and famine: conditions such that, beginning by eating the children, they progressed to the women, and did not altogether abstain even from eating one another. * * * Finally, after Sarapion, a Syrian, had betrayed the citadel, the general laid hands on all the runaway slaves in the city, whom, after torture, he threw over a cliff. From there he advanced to Enna, which he put under siege in much the same manner, bringing the rebels into extreme straits and frustrating their hopes. * * * Rupilius captured this city also by betrayal, since its strength was impregnable to force of arms. Eunus, taking with him his bodyguards, a thousand strong, fled in unmanly fashion to a certain precipitous region. The men with him, however, aware that their dreaded fate was inevitable, * * * killed one another with the sword, by beheading. Eunus, the wonderworker and king, who through cowardice had sought refuge in certain caves, was dragged out with four others, a cook, a baker, the man who massaged him at his bath, and a fourth, whose duty it had been to amuse him at drinking parties. Remanded to prison, where

his flesh disintegrated into a mass of lice, he met such an end as befitted his knavery, and died at Morgantina.

Questions

1. How do the rebellious slaves organize themselves? What problems do they encounter in resisting the Roman forces?

2. What can we conclude about relationships between slaves and masters from Diodorus's description of the rebellion and its origins?

3. Does Diodorus believe that the slaves' rebellion is justified?

The Debate on Salt and Iron (81 BCE)

This excerpt is a famous example of a frequent practice in ancient China: debates on political, religious, or other policies held before a ruler. In the text below, two groups that we would call Confucian and Legalist debate economic policy. The Confucian literati advocate a state with low taxes and limited regulatory and military ambitions; the Legalist officials support much greater state activism. The recently deceased Legalist emperor, Han Wudi, had expanded deep into central Asia—succeeding militarily, but placing a considerable strain on the imperial finances. Iron, used for both weapons and plows, and salt—a necessity produced in just a few places, and thus highly profitable—were hotly debated, but so were other topics. Afterward, some of the monopolies were abolished—even though, in this record of the debate, the Confucians seem to wind up on the defensive.

In the sixth year of the era Shiyuan [81 BCE], an imperial edict was issued directing the chancellor and the imperial secretaries to confer with the worthies and literati who had been recommended

SOURCE: *Sources of Chinese Tradition*, 2nd ed., compiled by Wm. Theodore de Bary and Irene Bloom et al. (New York: Columbia University Press, 1999), vol. 1, pp. 360–63.

to the government and to inquire into the grievances and hardships of the people.

The literati responded: We have heard that the way to govern men is to prevent evil and error at their source, to broaden the beginnings of morality, to discourage secondary occupations, and open the way for the exercise of humaneness and rightness. Never should material profit appear as a motive of government. Only then can moral instruction succeed and the customs of the people be reformed. But now in the provinces the salt, iron, and liquor monopolies, and the system of equitable marketing have been established to compete with the people for profit, dispelling rustic generosity and teaching the people greed. Therefore those who pursue primary occupations [farming] have grown few and those following secondary occupations [trading] numerous. As artifice increases, basic simplicity declines; and as the secondary occupations flourish, those that are primary suffer. When the secondary is practiced the people grow decadent, but when the primary is practiced they are simple and sincere. When the people are sincere then there will be sufficient wealth and goods, but when they become extravagant then famine and cold will follow. We recommend that the salt, iron, and liquor monopolies and the system of equitable marketing be abolished so that primary pursuits may be advanced and secondary ones suppressed. This will have the advantage of increasing the profitableness of agriculture.

His Lordship [the Imperial Secretary Sang Hongyang] replied: The Xiongnu have frequently revolted against our sovereignty and pillaged our borders. If we are to defend ourselves, then it means the hardships of war for the soldiers of China, but if we do not defend ourselves properly, then their incursions cannot be stopped. The former emperor [Wu] took pity upon the people of the border areas who for so long had suffered disaster and hardship and had been carried off as captives. Therefore he set up defense stations, established a system of warning beacons, and garrisoned the outlying areas to ensure their protection. But the resources of these areas were insufficient, and so he established the salt, iron, and liquor monopolies and the system of equitable marketing in order to raise more funds for expenditures at the borders. Now our critics, who desire that these measures be abolished, would empty the treasuries and deplete the funds used for defense. They would have the men who are defending our passes and patrolling our walls suffer hunger and cold. How else can we provide for them? Abolition of these measures is not expedient!

His Lordship stated: In former times the peers residing in the provinces sent in their respective products as tribute, but there was much confusion and trouble in transporting them and the goods were often of such poor quality that they were not worth the cost of transportation. For this reason transportation offices have been set up in each district to handle delivery and shipping and to facilitate the presentation of tribute from outlying areas. Therefore the system is called "equitable marketing." Warehouses have been opened in the capital for the storing of goods, buying when prices are low and selling when they are high. Thereby the government suffers no loss and the merchants cannot speculate for profit. Therefore this is called the "balanced level" [stabilization]. With the balanced level the people are protected from unemployment, and with equitable marketing the burden of labor service is equalized. Thus these measures are designed to ensure an equal distribution of goods and to benefit the people and are not intended to open the way to profit or provide the people with a ladder to crime.

The literati replied: In ancient times taxes and levies took from the people what they were skilled in producing and did not demand what they were poor at. Thus the husbandmen sent in their harvests and the weaving women their goods. Nowadays the government disregards what people have and requires of them what they have not, so that they are forced to sell their goods at a cheap price in order to meet the demands from above. * * * The farmers suffer double hardships and the weaving women are taxed twice. We have not seen that this kind of marketing is "equitable." The government officials go about recklessly opening closed doors and buying everything at will so they can corner all the goods. With goods cornered prices soar, and when prices soar the merchants make their own deals for profit. The officials wink at powerful racketeers, and the rich merchants hoard commodities and wait for an emergency. With slick merchants and corrupt officials buying cheap and selling dear we have not seen that your level is "balanced." The system of equitable marketing of ancient times was designed to equalize the burden of labor upon the people and facilitate the transporting of tribute. It did not mean dealing in all kinds of commodities for the sake of profit.

THE LITERATI ATTACK LEGALIST PHILOSOPHY

The literati spoke: He who is good with a chisel can shape a round hole without difficulty; he who is good at laying foundations can build to a great height without danger of collapse. The statesman Yi Yin made the ways of Yao and Shun the foundation of the Yin dynasty, and its heirs succeeded to the throne for a hundred generations without break. But Shang Yang made heavy penalties and harsh laws the foundation of the Qin state and with the Second Emperor it was destroyed. Not satisfied with the severity of the laws, he instituted the system of mutual responsibility, made it a crime to criticize the government, and increased corporal punishments until the people were so terrified they did not know where to put their hands and feet. Not content with the manifold taxes and levies, he prohibited the people from using the resources of forests and rivers and made a hundred-fold profit on the storage of commodities, while the people were given no chance to voice the slightest objection. Such worship of profit and slight of what is right, such exaltation of power and achievement, lent, it is true, to expansion of land and acquisition of territory. Yet it was like pouring more water upon people who are already suffering from flood and only increasing their distress. You see how Shang Yang opened the way to imperial rule for the Qin, but you fail to see how he also opened for the Qin the road to ruin!

CONFUCIAN LITERATI RIDICULED

His Excellency spoke: * * * Now we have with us over sixty worthy men and literati who cherish the ways of the Six Confucian Arts, fleet in thought and exhaustive in argument. It is proper, gentlemen, that you should pour forth your light and dispel our ignorance. And yet you put all your faith in the past and turn your backs upon the present, tell us of antiquity and give no thought to the state of the times. Perhaps we are not capable of recognizing true scholars. Yet do you really presume with your fancy phrases and attacks upon men of ability to pervert the truth in this manner?

See them [the Confucians] now present us with nothingness and consider it substance, with emptiness and call it plenty! In their coarse gowns and worn shoes they walk gravely along, sunk in meditation as though they had lost something. These are not men who can do great deeds and win fame. They do not even rise above the vulgar masses.

Questions

1. What problems do the literati blame on state monopolies? What benefits do the officials attribute to them?

2. How does each side defend its policies?

3. Our passage ends with the officials criticizing the literati, not just their proposals. Why is this significant? Why might a pro-literati chronicler have included this?

Josephus on the Roman Army (c. 70 CE)

For several hundred years, Rome's army was made up of a citizen militia. As early as the start of the Republic in 509 BCE, men aged fifteen and older were organized in an assembly called the *comitia centuriata*. Assigned to groups based on property owning and wealth, this was the citizenry assembled to vote, particularly for consuls (essentially their war leaders), and to fight the very wars whose waging they approved. Men voted as a group with the same men they would stand shoulder-to-shoulder with in battle. Around 100 BCE, social and political pressures on the domestic front and foreign threats in Gaul, North Africa, and the East led to various reforms that resulted in the formation of a standing professional army. This shift toward a standing army contributed to the political chaos of the last century of Rome's Republic, as troops loyal to rival faction leaders fought in brutal civil wars. The shift also made possible the dramatic expansion and consolidation of Rome's power across the Mediterranean in the early Empire, especially the first and second centuries CE. One of the regions in which this military was most active in asserting Rome's might was the eastern shores of the Mediterranean. In the passage excerpted here, the former Jewish military commander Josephus describes the army of his land's conqueror. Josephus lived in the first century CE and had fought against the Roman occupation of Judea in the 60s CE. After his surrender to the future emperor Vespasian, who at the time was commanding the legions in the east for the emperor Nero, Josephus wrote his *History of the Jewish War* in which he recounted the events that led to the Jewish revolt (66–70 CE) as well as Rome's brutally methodical and disciplined quelling of that revolt.

Anyone who will take a look at the organization of [the Roman] army in general will recognize that they hold their wide-flung empire as the prize of valour, not the gift of fortune. They do not wait for war to begin before handling their arms, nor do they sit idle in peacetime and take action only when the emergency comes—but as if born ready armed they never have a truce from training or wait for war to be declared. Their battle-drills are no different from the real thing; every man works as hard at his daily training as if he was on active service. That is why they stand up so easily to the strain of battle: no indiscipline dislodges them from their regular formation, no panic incapacitates them, no toil wears them out; so victory over men not so trained follows as a matter of course. It would not be far from the truth to call their drills bloodless battles, their battles bloody drills.

They never give the enemy a chance to catch them off their guard; for whenever they invade hostile territory they rigidly refuse battle till they have fortified their camp. This they do not construct haphazardly or unevenly, nor do they tackle the job with all their man-power or without organized squads; if the ground is uneven it is thoroughly levelled, then the site is marked out as a rectangle. To this end the army is followed by a large number of engineers with all the tools needed for building. The inside is divided up ready for the huts.

SOURCE: Josephus, *History of the Jewish War,* 3.71–109, translated by G. A. Williamson (New York: Penguin Books, 1970), pp. 194–97.

From outside the perimeter looks like a wall and is equipped with towers evenly spaced. In the gaps between the towers they mount spear-throwers, catapults, stone-throwers, and every type of ordnance, all ready to be discharged. Four gates are constructed, one in each length of wall, practicable for the entry of baggage-animals and wide enough for armed sorties, if called for. The camp is divided up by streets accurately marked out; in the middle are erected the officers'-huts, and in the middle of these the commander's headquarters, which resembles a shrine. It all seems like a mushroom town with market-place, workmen's quarters, and orderly-rooms where junior and senior officers can settle disputes as they arise. The erection of the outer wall and the buildings inside is accomplished faster than thought, thanks to the number and skill of the workers. If necessary a ditch is dug all round, six feet deep and the same width.

The fortifications completed, the men go to their own quarters unit by unit in a quiet and orderly manner. All other duties are carried out with attention to discipline and security, wood, food, and water as required being brought in by the units detailed. They do not have supper or breakfast just when they fancy at their individual discretion, but all together. Times for sleep, guard-duty, and reveille are announced by trumpet-calls, and nothing whatever is done without orders. At dawn the private soldiers report by units to their centurions, the centurions go to their tribunes to salute them, and the tribunes accompany all their superior officers to headquarters, where the commander-in-chief, in accordance with routine, gives them the password and other orders to communicate to their subordinates. They act in the same orderly way on the battlefield, changing direction promptly as required, and whether attacking or retreating move as one man.

When camp is to be struck, the trumpet sounds and every man springs to his duty. Following tile signal huts are instantly dismantled and all preparations made for departure. The trumpet then sounds "Stand by to march!" At once they load the mules and wagons with the baggage and take their places like runners lined up and hardly able to wait for the starter's signal. Then they fire the camp, which they can easily reconstruct if required, lest it might some day be useful to the enemy. For the third time the trumpets give the same signal for departure, to urge on those who for any reason have been loitering, so that not a man may be missing from his place. Then the announcer, standing on the right of the supreme commander, asks three times in their native language whether they are ready for war. They three times shout loudly and with enthusiasm "Ready," hardly waiting for the question, and filled with a kind of martial fervour they raise their right arms as they shout. Then they step off, all marching silently and in good order, as on active service every man keeping his place in the column.

The infantry are armed with breastplate and helmet and carry a blade on each side; of these by far the longer is the one on the left, the other being no more than nine inches long. The general's bodyguard of picked infantry carry lance and buckler, the other units javelin and long shield, together with saw and basket, axe and pick, as well as strap, reaphook, chain, and three days' rations, so that there is not much difference between a foot-soldier and a pack-mule! The cavalryman carries a long sword on his right hip and an enormous pike in his hand, a shield slanted across his horse's flank, and in a quiver slung alongside three or more darts, broad-pointed and as big as spears. Helmets and breast-plates of infantry pattern are worn by all arms. Equipment is exactly the same for the general's mounted bodyguard as for the other cavalry units. Lots are always drawn for the legion that is to head the column. So much for Roman routine on the march and in quarters, and for the variety of equipment.

In battle nothing is done without plan or on the spur of the moment; careful thought precedes action of any kind, and to the decisions reached all actions must conform. As a result they meet with very few setbacks, and if anything does go wrong, the setbacks are easily cancelled out. They regard successes due to luck as less desirable than a planned but unsuccessful stroke, because victories that come of themselves tempt men to leave things to chance, but forethought, in spite of occasional failures, is good practice in avoiding the same mistake. Good things that come of themselves bring no credit to the recipient, but unfortunate accidents that upset calculations have at least this comfort in them, that plans were properly laid.

Military exercises give the Roman soldier not only tough bodies but determined spirits too. Training methods are partly based on fear; for military law demands the death penalty not only for leaving a post but even for trivial misdemeanours; and the generals inspire more fear than the law, since by rewarding good soldiers they avoid seeming harsh towards the men they punish. So complete is their submission to their superiors that in peace they are a credit to Rome and in the field the whole army is a single body; so knit together are their ranks, so flexible their manoeuvres, so ready their ears for orders, their eyes for signals, their hands for the tasks to be done. Thus it is that they are as quick to act as they are slow to give way, and never was there an engagement in which they were worsted by numbers, tactical skill, or unfavourable ground—or even by fortune, which is less within their grasp than is victory. When planning goes before action, and the plans are followed by so effective an army, who can wonder that in the east the Euphrates, in the west the ocean, in the south the richest plains of Africa, and in the north the Danube and the Rhine are the limits of the Empire? One might say with truth that the conquests are less remarkable than the conquerors.

The purpose of the foregoing account has been less to eulogize the Romans than to console their defeated enemies and to deter any who may be thinking of revolt; and possibly those of an enquiring frame of mind who have not studied the matter may find it useful to get an insight into the Roman military set-up. This is all that I propose to say on the subject.

Questions

1. What range of professional skills, apart from fighting, does the Roman military require?

2. How is a Roman soldier equipped and trained? What lessons does Josephus draw from this equipment and training?

3. What reasons does Josephus offer to explain the ability of the Roman army to achieve and maintain Empire? Based on this Josephus reading, what might you hypothesize are the benefits of a standing army, over a citizen militia, when attempting to achieve and maintain Empire?

Sima Guang (eleventh century CE), Han Battle Tactics in 184 CE

Sima Guang composed his monumental history, the *Comprehensive Mirror for Aid in Government,* in the eleventh century CE, during the early Song dynasty. Assigned its title by the emperor who sponsored the work, Sima Guang's history recounted events from the beginning of the Warring States period (403 BCE) through the Five Dynasties period (960 CE). Sima Guang drew upon contemporary accounts of the events described, such as Fan Yeh's fifth-century *Hou Han Shu* (History of the Later Han) and Chen Shu's third-century *Sanguo Zhi* (Record of the Three Kingdoms), in order to construct his narrative. As one might expect from the title given to his work, Sima Guang highlighted the moral lessons of the events; yet he was also careful to preserve the historicity of the events described. While it may seem flawed to explore a source written several hundred years after the Han instead of a contemporary one, the translator of Sima Guang's work, Rafe de Crespigny, explains the relevance of the text best when he writes: "Here, in convenient arrangement, with perfect classical style, is one of the great works of Chinese historical writing, and in this form, based upon the earliest sources, it is the best and most detailed account of the last years of Han" (Crespigny 1989, p. xxii).

The passage excerpted here recounts a pivotal moment at the start of the Yellow Turban Rebellion in 184 CE, when imperial forces led by Zhu Jun besieged Yellow Turban rebels, led first by Zhao Hong and then by Han Zhong in Wan city (modern Nanyang, in Henan province). While the Han military leaders are successful in quelling this first pulse of rebellion in 184, the widespread damage caused by the Yellow Turban rebels contributed ultimately to the fall of the Han dynasty in 220 CE.

The remnants of Zhang Mancheng's party [i.e., the Yellow Turban rebels] elected Zhao Hong as their leader, and their strength again

---

SOURCE: *Emperor Huan and Emperor Ling: Being the Chronicle of Later Han for the Years 157 to 189 AD as Recorded in Chapters 54 to 59 of the Zizhi tongjian of Sima Guang,* translated by Rafe de Crespigny (Canberra: Australian National University, 1989), pp. 188–89.
[Editorial insertions appear in square brackets—*Ed.*]

increased until they numbered more than a hundred thousand. They occupied Wan city. Zhu Jun and other local commanders under the Inspector of Jing province, Xu Qiu, collected forces together and besieged the rebels. They had attacked the place from the sixth month to the eight[h] month without success.

Some senior officials at the capital memorialised that Zhu Jun should be recalled, but the Minister of Works Zhang Wen wrote in to the emperor, "In ancient times, Qin used Bo Qi and Yan gave office to Yue Yi. Both of them spent years doing nothing, but when it came to the end their enemies were defeated. Zhu Jun has already had considerable success in Yingchuan, and now he is leading his army against the south and his plans are settled. All the military writers caution against changing generals in the middle of a campaign. We may wait for days o[r] even months, but in the end he will produce results." So the emperor kept Zhu Jun in his command, and then Zhu Jun attacked Zhao Hong and cut off his head.

The rebel leader Han Zhong re-occupied Wan and opposed Zhu Jun once more. Zhu Jun sent in an attack, with battle-cries and drums, from the southwest and all the enemy went to deal with it. Zhu Jun himself led picked troops secretly to the northeast, and they climbed the wall and got into the city. Han Zhong then retreated to hold the citadel, and he was now frightened and asked to surrender. All the officers thought they should accept his plea, but Zhu Jun said, "In warfare, things may look the same but be quite different in reality. In ancient times, when the Xiang family opposed the Qin dynasty [from 209–206 BCE], the people had no recognised ruler, and so it was necessary to offer rewards in order to encourage new recruits. At the present day, all the world is united in our empire, and it is only the Yellow Turbans who make rebellion. If we accept their surrender, it will be no encouragement to people that they should practise virtue; but if we kill them it will be sufficient warning to everyone that they should avoid evil conduct. If we take them in now, we will be opening the way to ideas of rebellion: when bandits see advantage they will come forward to attack us, and when they feel they are in difficulties they will simply ask to surrender. The enemies of the state everywhere will become bolder and more dangerous. This would not be a good plan." So he continued to press his attacks, but after several battles he had still not captured the fortress.

Zhu Jun climbed a hill of earth to look over the scene, and he turned to his Major Zhang Chao and said, "I have it! The enemy have a tight siege-ring around them, and inside their camp they must be quite desperate. They have asked to surrender and it has been refused, they want to break out but they find it impossible. So they know they must fight to the death. Ten thousand men with one idea in their minds would be too much to handle, and now we've got a hundred thousand to deal with! The best thing to do is to break off the siege and combine our forces to enter the city. When Han Zhong sees that the siege has opened he will certainly come out, and when he comes out of his defences he will become less vigilant. That is the easy way to destroy him." So they opened the siege, and Han Zhong did come out to fight. Zhu Jun attacked him and completely defeated him and they took more than ten thousand heads.

Qin Jie, the Grand Administrator of Nanyang, killed Han Zhong, and the remaining rebels chose Sun Xia as their leader. He went back to camp in Wan, and Zhu Jun pressed his attacks still more fiercely.

The Major Sun Jian led his troops and was the first to climb the walls. On the day guisi [11 Jan 185] they stormed Wan city. Sun Xia fled, Zhu Jun chased him as far as the Jing Hills of Xi'e [north of present-day Nanyang in Henan], and he defeated him once more and cut off another ten thousand heads.

At this, the Yellow Turbans were defeated and scattered. The remainder of them were dealt with by the provincial and command-ery [i.e., local] governments. Thousands of people were executed in a single commandery.

Questions

1. What are the battle tactics of the Han generals? How do the engage-ments resolve? What impact do you think these resolutions had on the Yellow Turban rebels?

2. What evidence do you see of internal disagreement among the Han leaders?

3. Given the didactic aim of Sima Guang's *Comprehensive Mirror,* what lessons "for Aid in Government" do you think he was trying to highlight in the retelling of these events from the first year of the Yellow Turban Rebellion?

Keeping the Records of the Military (Rome in 81 CE and Han in 3/2 BCE)

The following set of documents offers a glimpse into the management of both the Roman and the Han military and the empires they served. The "pay-record" of Quintus Iulius Proculus, a Roman legionary, was preserved on papyrus in Egypt. The text dates to within about a decade of Josephus's description of the Roman military in the excerpt from *History of the Jewish War* (this chapter). The papyrus lists what appears to be Proculus's pay (installments of 247.5 drachma), out of which three separate sets of debits are taken, each recorded in a different handwriting. Given that Proculus was just one legionary (of 5,000) from one legion (of as many as 30 legions) for one year (across the hundreds of years of Empire), there must have been millions of these pay records kept by the Roman military (Fink 1971, p. 242). The Han document comes from the years 3/2 BCE at a garrison settlement at Mu-durbeljin, on the north western frontier of the Han Empire. This document was preserved on twenty-two thin wooden strips, probably of tamarisk, each written in the same hand. Each strip noted the monthly rations (computed in units of shih=c. 20 liters) disbursed to an individual soldier. Some of the strips have a check mark, presumably made by the recipient, to indicate the ration was received. As with the Roman records, these strips offer a mere glimpse of Han recordkeeping: a month's ration for seventeen troops of the estimated 3,250 troops likely posted along the defenses of the 1000 km frontier from Tun-huang to Shuo-fang in a given year [for troop estimates, see Loewe, Vol. 1 (1967), 90–91]. The number of ration records kept, not to mention the rations doled out, by the Han Dynasty is staggering.

SOURCE: Robert O. Fink, *Roman Military Records on Papyrus* (Cleveland, OH: Case Western Reserve Press, 1971), pp. 248–49, and Michael Loewe, *Records of Han Administration,* (London: Cambridge University Press, 1967), vol. 2, pp. 77, 79, 81.

ROMAN MILITARY RECORDS, A.D. 81

Q. Iulius Proculus, born at Damascus,
received the first pay of the third year of the Emperor,
    247 ½ drachmas out of which

5	hay money (?)	10 drachmas
	for food	80 drachmas
	boots, socks	12 drachmas
	camp Saturnalia	20 drachmas
	. . . . r . . . torium	60 drachmas
10	spent	182 drachmas
	deposited the balance	65 ½ drachmas
	and had from before	136 drachmas
	total	201 ½ drachmas

received the second pay of the same year, 247 ½ drachmas
15   out of which

	hay money (?)	10 drachmas
	for food	80 drachmas
	boots, socks	12 drachmas
	to the standards	4 drachmas
20	spent	106 drachmas
	deposited the balance	141 ½ drachmas
	and had from before	201 ½ drachmas
	entire total	343 drachmas

received the third pay of the same year, 247 ½ drachmas
25   out of which

	hay money (?)	10 drachmas
	for food	80 drachmas
	boots, socks	12 drachmas
	for clothing	145 ½ drachmas
30	spent	247 ½ drachmas
	has on deposit	343 drachmas

HAN MILITARY RECORDS

1 List of names and allowances of food for officers and men, twelfth month . . . year of Chien [p'ing].

2 T'ien Chung, ling-shih; food allowance for the twelfth month 3 .3 shih; received in person on keng-shen, eleventh month.

3 Chang Ching, private soldier, defence forces; salt .03 shih; food allowance for the twelfth month 3 .3 shih; received in person on keng-shen, eleventh month.

4 Li Chiu, private soldier, defence forces; salt .03 shih; food allowance for the twelfth month 3 .3 shih; received in person on keng-shen, eleventh month.

5 . . . [salt] .03 shih; food allowance for the twelfth month 3 .3 shih; received in person on keng-shen, eleventh month.

6 . . . food allowance for the twelfth month 3 .3 shih; received in person on keng-shen, eleventh month.

7 Wang Ch'ang, private [no. 7?] sui; food allowance for the twelfth month 3 .3 shih; received by Feng Hsi, private, on ping-yin, eleventh month. [Check mark]

8 Cheng Feng, ling-shih; food allowance for the twelfth month 3 .3 shih . . . on ping-yin, eleventh month.

9 . . . [3.] 3 shih; received in person by Pa on wu-ch'en, eleventh month.

10 Shih Tz'u, private soldier, defence forces; salt .03 shih; food allowance for the twelfth month 3 .3 shih . . . eleventh month.

11 Chang P'ing, private . . . hu sui; salt .03 shih; food allowance for the twelfth month . . .

12 T'ien Hsüan . . . food allowance for the twelfth month 3 .3 shih; received by private Kan Yu on kuei-yu, twelfth month. [Check mark]

13 List of names and allowances of food for officers and men, Wan-sui sector, fifth month, fifth year of Chien-p'ing. [2 B.C.]

14 Wang Wang, OC . . . sui; food allowance for the fifth month 3 .3 shih; received by private Ts'ao Fang on chia-wu, fourth month. [Check mark]

15 . . . food allowance for the fifth month 3 .3 shih; received by private Hsü Shou on chia-wu, fourth month. [Check mark]

16 . . . food allowance for the fifth month 3 .3 shih; received by private Kan Yu on wu-hsü, fourth month. [Check mark]

17 Sun T'ung, private, [Shang-kuan?] sui; food allowance for the second month 3 .3 shih; received in person on i-yu, first month.

18 List of names and allowances of food for officers and men of the [hou]-kuan, twelfth month, fifth year of Chien-p'ing. [2 B.C.]

19 Foregoing four officers: unhusked millet consumed 13 .3 shih . . .

20 In all seventeen officers and men; total of salt consumed .39 shih; unhusked millet consumed 56 .6 shih.

21 Ssu-ma Lo, private, Chih-hu sui.

Questions

1. What sorts of items are listed on each document? How often, and by what means, do the items appear to be disbursed?

2. What do these documents suggest about the economics, and even the composition, of each military force?

3. What do these documents suggest about the record keeping of each military force? Why would the Roman and Han administrations keep such documentation?

Chapter 8

THE RISE OF UNIVERSAL RELIGIONS, 300–600 CE

Eusebius, The Conversion of Constantine to Christianity (fourth century CE)

One of the pivotal moments in the history of Christianity was the conversion of the Roman Emperor Constantine (c. 274–337 CE) to Christianity. Christianity became, first, the empire's favored religion, then its official religion, and finally the only legal religion (apart from Judaism, which had a tolerated inferior status). This description of Constantine's final conversion comes from Eusebius of Caesarea's *Life of Constantine*. Eusebius (c. 260–339 CE) was bishop of Caesarea, a town north of the modern Jaffa and Tel Aviv in Israel. He was a prominent figure in the ecclesiastical politics of the eastern half of the Roman Empire, and a man who knew the Emperor Constantine personally. In the passage below, Eusebius depicts Constantine on the eve of a battle with a pagan rival for control of the western half of the Roman Empire. The text suggests that at this point Constantine was already beginning to think of himself as a Christian. Eusebius's *Life* is a mixture of eulogy and hagiography, and avoids discussing anything negative about the emperor. The reliability of the text, and even its authorship by Eusebius, have been questioned by some historians.

SOURCE: Eusebius Pamphilus, *The Life of the Blessed Emperor Constantine, in Four Books, from 306 to 337 A.D.* (London: Samuel Bagster and Sons, 1845), pp. 25–30.

CHAPTER XXVII.

*   *   *

Being convinced, however, that he needed some more powerful aid than his military forces could afford him, on account of the wicked and magical enchantments which were so diligently practised by the tyrant, [Constantine] began to seek for Divine assistance; deeming the possession of arms and a numerous soldiery of secondary importance, but trusting that the co-operation of a Deity would be his security against defeat or misfortune. He considered, therefore, on what God he might rely for protection and assistance. While engaged in this inquiry, the thought occurred to him, that, of the many emperors who had preceded him, those who had rested their hopes in a multitude of gods, and served them with sacrifices and offerings, had in the first place been deceived by flattering predictions, and oracles which promised them all prosperity, and at last had met with an unhappy end, while not one of their gods had stood by to warn them of the impending wrath of Heaven. On the other hand he recollected that his father, who had pursued an entirely opposite course, who had condemned their error, and honoured the one Supreme God during his whole life, had found Him to be the Saviour and Protector of his empire, and the Giver of every good thing. Reflecting on this, and well weighing the fact that they who had trusted in many gods had also fallen by manifold forms of death, without leaving behind them either family or offspring, stock, name, or memorial among men: and considering further that those who had already taken arms against the tyrant, and had marched to the battle field under the protection of a multitude of gods, had met with a dishonourable end (for one of them had shamefully retreated from the contest without a blow, and the other, being slain in the midst of his own troops, had become as it were the mere sport of death); reviewing, I say, all these considerations, he judged it to be folly indeed to join in the idle worship of those who were no gods, and, after such convincing evidence, to wander from the truth; and therefore felt it incumbent on him to honour no other than the God of his father.

Chapter XXVIII.

* * *

Accordingly he called on Him with earnest prayer and supplications that He would reveal to him who He was, and stretch forth His right hand to help him in his present difficulties. And while he was thus praying with fervent entreaty, a most marvellous sign appeared to him from heaven, the account of which it might have been difficult to receive with credit, had it been related by any other person. But since the victorious emperor himself long afterwards declared it to the writer of this history, when he was honoured with his acquaintance and society, and confirmed his statement by an oath, who could hesitate to accredit the relation, especially since the testimony of after-time has established its truth? He said that about mid-day, when the sun was beginning to decline, he saw with his own eyes the trophy of a cross of light in the heavens, above the sun, and bearing the inscription, Conquer by this. At this sight he himself was struck with amazement, and his whole army also, which happened to be following him on some expedition, and witnessed the miracle.

Chapter XXIX.

* * *

He said, moreover, that he doubted within himself what the import of this apparition could be. And while he continued to ponder and reason on its meaning, night imperceptibly drew on; and in his sleep the Christ of God appeared to him with the same sign which he had seen in the heavens, and commanded him to procure a standard made in the likeness of that sign, and to use it as a safeguard in all engagements with his enemies.

Chapter XXX.

* * *

At dawn of day he arose, and communicated the secret to his friends: and then, calling together the workers in gold and precious stones, he sat in the midst of them, and described to them the figure of the sign he had seen, bidding them represent it in gold and precious stones. And this representation I myself have had an opportunity of seeing.

CHAPTER XXXI.

* * *

Now it was made in the following manner. A long spear, overlaid with gold, formed the figure of the cross by means of a piece transversely laid over it. On the top of the whole was fixed a crown, formed by the intertexture of gold and precious stones; and on this, two letters indicating the name of Christ, symbolized the Saviour's title by means of its first characters, the letter P [*rho*] being intersected by X [*chi*, together χρ are the first two letters of Christ in Greek] exactly in its centre: and these letters the emperor was in the habit of wearing on his helmet at a later period. From the transverse piece which crossed the spear was suspended a kind of streamer of purple cloth, covered with a profuse embroidery of most brilliant precious stones; and which, being also richly interlaced with gold, presented an indescribable degree of beauty to the beholder. This banner was of a square form, and the upright staff, which in its full extent was of great length, bore a golden half-length portrait of the pious emperor and his children on its upper part, beneath the trophy of the cross, and immediately above the embroidered streamer.

The emperor constantly made use of this salutary sign as a safeguard against every adverse and hostile power, and commanded that others similar to it should be carried at the head of all his armies.

CHAPTER XXXII.

These things were done shortly afterwards. But at the time above specified, being struck with amazement at the extraordinary vision, and resolving to worship no other God save Him who had appeared to him, he sent for those who were acquainted with the mysteries of His doctrines, and inquired who that God was, and what was intended by the sign of the vision he had seen.

They affirmed that He was God, the only begotten Son of the one and only God: that the sign which had appeared was the symbol of immortality, and the trophy of that victory over death which He had gained in time past when sojourning on earth. They taught him also the causes of His advent, and explained to him the true account of His incarnation. Thus he sought instruction in these matters, but was still impressed with wonder at the divine manifestation which had been presented to his sight. Comparing, therefore, the heavenly vision with the interpretation given, he found his judgment confirmed; and, in the persuasion that the knowledge of these things had been imparted to him by Divine teaching, he determined thenceforth to devote himself to the perusal of the Inspired writings.

Moreover, he made the priests of God his counsellors, and deemed it incumbent on him to honour the God who had appeared to him with all devotion. And after this, being fortified by well-grounded hopes in Him, he undertook to quench the fury of the fire of tyranny.

Questions

1. What is the process by which Constantine decided to convert? What roles did "reason" and revelation play in his decision?

2. How did Constantine conceive of religion? What effects does correct belief have in this world? How are politics related to religion in the emperor's mind?

3. What was the role of Christian believers in the emperor's conversion?

Priscus, The Court of Attila (449 CE)

For almost two thousand years the pastoral nomads of Inner Asia presented a major challenge to the settled peoples on whose frontiers they lived. The Huns, a federation of nomadic peoples, originating in central Asia, played a major role in the events that marked the disintegration of the Roman Empire. In the late 300s CE they entered the southern Russia steppe and drove the Goths over the Danube into the

Roman Empire. They alternately raided the empire and served as mercenaries in its armies. Their political and military strength was at its peak during the reign of Attila (434–453 CE), who regularly raided the Roman Empire. He defeated the East Roman emperor and received tribute from him. In 451 CE he invaded Gaul; in 452 CE he devastated much of Italy. After his death, however, the Hunnic empire quickly disintegrated. Priscus, the author of the selection below, was an East Roman imperial servant and historian. In 449 CE he took part in an embassy sent from Constantinople to negotiate with Attila. He wrote in a classicizing style and therefore referred to the Huns as Scythians, a nomadic people described by Herodotus in the fifth century BCE.

The next morning, at dawn of day, Maximin sent me to Onegesius, with presents offered by himself as well as those which the Emperor had sent, and I was to find out whether he would have an interview with Maximin and at what time. When I arrived at the house, along with the attendants who carried the gifts, I found the doors closed, and had to wait until some one should come out and announce our arrival. As I waited and walked up and down in front of the enclosure which surrounded the house, a man, whom from his Scythian dress I took for a barbarian, came up and addressed me in Greek, with the word Χαῖρε, "Hail!" I was surprised at a Scythian speaking Greek. For the subjects of the Huns, swept together from various lands, speak, besides their own barbarous tongues, either Hunnic or Gothic, or—as many as have commercial dealings with the western Romans—Latin; but none of them easily speak Greek, except captives from the Thracian or Illyrian sea-coast; and these last are easily known to any stranger by their torn garments and the squalor of their heads, as men who have met with a reverse. This man, on the contrary, resembled a well-to-do Scythian, being well dressed, and having his hair cut in a circle after Scythian fashion. Having returned his salutation, I asked him

SOURCE: J. B. Bury, *History of the Later Roman Empire from the Death of Theodosius I to the Death of Justinian* (New York: Dover Publications, 1958), vol. 1, pp. 283–85.

who he was and whence he had come into a foreign land and adopted Scythian life. When he asked me why I wanted to know, I told him that his Hellenic speech had prompted my curiosity. Then he smiled and said that he was born a Greek and had gone as a merchant to Viminacium, on the Danube, where he had stayed a long time, and married a very rich wife. But the city fell a prey to the barbarians, and he was [stripped] of his prosperity, and on account of his riches was allotted to Onegesius in the division of the spoil, as it was the custom among the Scythians for the chiefs to reserve for themselves the rich prisoners. Having fought bravely against the Romans and the Acatiri, he had paid the spoils he won to his master, and so obtained freedom. He then married a barbarian wife and had children, and had the privilege of eating at the table of Onegesius.

He considered his new life among the Scythians better than his old life among the Romans, and the reasons he gave were as follows: "After war the Scythians live in inactivity, enjoying what they have got, and not at all, or very little, harassed. The Romans, on the other hand, are in the first place very liable to perish in war, as they have to rest their hopes of safety on others, and are not allowed, on account of their *tyrants*, to use arms. And those who use them are injured by the cowardice of their generals, who cannot support the conduct of war. But the condition of the subjects in time of peace is far more grievous than the evils of war, for the exaction of the taxes is very severe, and unprincipled men inflict injuries on others, because the laws are practically not valid against all classes. A transgressor who belongs to the wealthy classes is not punished for his injustice, while a poor man, who does not understand business, undergoes the legal penalty, that is if he does not depart this life before the trial, so long is the course of lawsuits protracted, and so much money is expended on them. The climax of the misery is to have to pay in order to obtain justice. For no one will give a court to the injured man unless he pay a sum of money to the judge and the judge's clerks."

In reply to this attack on the Empire, I asked him to be good enough to listen with patience to the other side of the question. "The creators of the Roman republic," I said, "who were wise and good men, in order to prevent things from being done at haphazard, made one class of men guardians of the laws, and appointed another class to the profession of arms, who were to have no other object than to be always ready for battle, and to go forth to war without dread, as though to their ordinary exercise, having by practice exhausted all their fear beforehand. Others again were assigned to attend to the cultivation of the ground, to support both themselves and those who fight in their defence, by contributing the military corn-supply. * * * To those who protect the interests of the litigants a sum of money is paid by the latter, just as a payment is made by the farmers to the soldiers. Is it not fair to support him who assists and requite him for his kindness? The support of the horse benefits the horseman. * * * Those who spend money on a suit and lose it in the end cannot fairly put it down to anything but the injustice of their case. And as to the long time spent on lawsuits, that is due to concern for justice, that judges may not fail in passing correct judgments, by having to give sentence offhand; it is better that they should reflect, and conclude the case more tardily, than that by judging in a hurry they should both injure man and transgress against the Deity, the institutor of justice. * * * The Romans treat their servants better than the king of the Scythians treats his subjects. They deal with them as fathers or teachers, admonishing them to abstain from evil and follow the lines of conduct which they have esteemed honourable; they reprove them for their errors like their own children. They are not allowed, like the Scythians, to inflict death on them. They have numerous ways of conferring freedom; they can manumit not only during life, but also by their wills, and the testamentary wishes of a Roman in regard to his property are law."

My interlocutor shed tears, and confessed that the laws and constitution of the Romans were fair, but deplored that the governors, not possessing the spirit of former generations, were ruining the State.

Questions

1. What can be inferred from this passage about the organization of the Huns under Attila?

2. How does the Greek-speaking man whom Priscus meets argue that life among the Huns is better than among the Romans?

3. How does Priscus counter this and argue for the superiority of Roman ways?

Salvian of Marseilles, On the Governance of God (fifth century CE)

The fifth century CE was a very difficult time for the peoples of the western half of the Roman Empire. Imperial governing institutions weakened, the economy went into decline, and various "barbarian" peoples, most speaking Germanic languages, crossed the Roman frontiers and created kingdoms within former Roman provinces, including in North Africa. Making sense of the empire's troubles posed a major challenge to its inhabitants. One of these was Salvian of Marseilles (c. 400–480 CE). He was born in Trier in modern Germany, not far from the Roman frontier with the German barbarians. In the fourth century Trier had been a major administrative center and a frequent residence for Roman emperors. Salvian eventually moved to Marseilles, an ancient port city on the Mediterranean, where he served as priest. There he wrote *The Governance of God*, in which he argued that the disasters of the fifth century were God's punishment of the Romans for their sins.

CRIMES OF THE RICH AND POWERFUL

As regards people in high places, of what does their dignity consist but in confiscating the property of the cities? As regards some whose names I do not mention, what is a prefecture, but a kind of plunder? There is no greater pillaging of the poor than that done by those in power. For this, office is bought by the few to be paid for by ravaging the many. What can be more disgraceful and wicked than

SOURCE: *From Roman to Merovingian Gaul: A Reader*, edited and translated by Alexander Callander Murray (Peterborough: Broadview Press, 2000), pp. 113–17.

this? The poor pay the purchase price for positions which they themselves do not buy. They are ignorant of the bargain, but know the amount paid. The world is turned upside down that the light of a few may become illustrious. The elevation of one man is the downfall of all the others. The cities of Spain know all about this, for they have nothing left them but their name. The cities of Africa know it—and they no longer exist. The cities of Gaul know it, for they are laid waste, but not by all their officials. They still hold a tenuous existence in a very few corners of the land, because the honesty of a few has temporarily supported those provinces which the ravages of the many have made void.

UNJUST REMISSION OF TAXATION

Now who can speak eloquently about the following robbery and crime: because the Roman state, if not already dead or at least drawing its last breath where it still has a semblance of life, is dying, strangled by the chains of taxation as if by the hands of brigands, a great number of rich can be found whose taxes are borne by the poor; that is to say there is found a great number of rich whose taxes kill the poor. I say many can be found. I am afraid I should more truly say all. So few, if there are any at all, are free from this crime that we can find almost all the rich in the category in which I said there were many.

Consider the remedies recently given to some cities. What this accomplished was to make all the rich immune and pile more taxes on the wretched poor. The old taxes were remitted for the benefit of the rich and new taxes imposed on the poor. The cancellation of the least type of taxation enriched the wealthy; the increase of the heaviest has made the poor suffer. The rich have become richer by lessening the obligations which they bore lightly; the poor are dying from the multiplication of the burdens which they were already unable to bear. Thus, the great remedy most unjustly exalted the one and most unjustly killed the other; to one it was a most wicked reward, to the other a most wicked poison. Hence it is I make the observation that there is nothing more vicious than the rich who are destroying the poor by their remedies, and none more unfortunate than the poor whom those things kill which are given as a remedy to all.

ROMANS AND BARBARIANS COMPARED

[Those who assert nothing is seen by God] say that if God watches over human affairs, if He cares for and loves and rules, why does He permit us to be weaker and more wretched than all other peoples? Why does He allow us to be conquered by the barbarians? Why does He allow us to be subject to the law of the enemy? Very briefly, as I have said before, He allows us to bear these evils because we deserve to suffer them. * * *

Someone says, so be it! Certainly we are sinners and evil. What cannot be denied is that we are better than the barbarians. By this also it is clear that God does not watch over human affairs, because, although we are better, we are subject to those who are worse. We will now see whether we are better than the barbarians. Certainly, there is no doubt that we should be better. For this very reason we are worse, if we who should be better are not better. The more honorable the position, the more criminal the fault. If the person of the sinner is the more honorable, the odium of his sin is also greater. * * *

* * * Therefore, because some men think it is unbearable that we are judged worse, or not even much better than the barbarians, let us see how, and of which barbarians we are better. For there are two kinds of barbarians in every nation: heretics and pagans. I say we are incomparably better than all these, therefore, insofar as it pertains to divine Law. In what pertains to life and the acts of life, I sorrow and weep that we are worse * * *. It profits us nothing that the Law is good if our life and way of life are not good. That the Law is good is a gift of Christ, but that our life is bad is the product of our own sin. * * *

Having put aside the prerogative of the Law, which either helps us not at all or condemns us by a just condemnation, let us compare the pursuits, morals, and vices of the barbarians with ours. The barbarians are unjust, and so are we. The barbarians are avaricious, and so are we. The barbarians are unfaithful, and so are we. The barbarians are greedy, and so are we. The barbarians are lewd, and so are we. The barbarians have all manner of wickedness and impurities, and so do we. * * *

COMPARISON WITH PAGANS

And by this we understand, as I have said above, that we who have and spurn the Law of God are much more culpable than those who neither have it nor know it at all. Nobody despises things which are unknown to him. * * * But we are scorners as well as transgressors of the Law and, accordingly, are worse than the pagans, for they do not know the commandments of God and we do. They do not have them, but we do. They do not follow commands which are unknown to them, but we trample underfoot what we know. Therefore, ignorance among them is transgression among us, because it is being guilty of a lesser crime to be ignorant of the commandments of God than to spurn them. * * *

Questions

1. What does Salvian see as the chief problems in the late Roman Empire?

2. What is his explanation for these problems?

3. How does Salvian use his comments on the "barbarians" as a way to criticize his Roman contemporaries?

Gregory of Tours, On the Conversion of Clovis to Christianity (sixth century CE)

In many ways the most important legacy of the Roman Empire to medieval Europe was the Christian church, "the noblest Roman of them all." Indeed, in the centuries after the disintegration of the western half of the Roman Empire, Christianity made considerable progress in converting new peoples. Among these were the pagan Franks, a Germanic people who had lived on the northern frontier of the province of Gaul. In the fourth century CE imperial authorities allowed them to settle in what is today Belgium. In the fifth century one of their kings, Clovis (c. 466–511 CE), defeated rival Frankish kings and the last Romans exercising rule in northern Gaul. He fought a series of wars against other Germanic peoples, including the Alemanni, the Visigoths, the Thuringians, and the Saxons. By the time of his death he had made the Franks the dominant political power in western Europe. He converted to Christianity some time in the last decade of the fifth century or the first decade of the sixth. This description of his baptism comes from Gregory (538–594 CE), Bishop of Tours. Gregory's *History of the Franks* is one of the most important sources for the history of the earlier middle ages. Note that he is writing almost a century after the events he describes.

At this time [AD 486] the army of Clovis pillaged many churches, for he was still sunk in the errors of idolatry. The soldiers had borne away from a church, with all the other ornaments of the holy ministry, a vase of marvelous size and beauty. The bishop of this church sent messengers to the king, begging that if the church might not recover any other of the holy vessels, at least this one might be restored. The king, hearing these things, replied to the messenger: "Follow thou us to Soissons, for there all things that have been acquired are to be divided. If the lot shall give me this vase, I will do what the bishop desires."

When he had reached Soissons, and all the booty had been placed in the midst of the army, the king pointed to this vase, and said: "I ask you, O most valiant warriors, not to refuse to me the vase in addition to my rightful part." Those of discerning mind among his men answered, "O glorious king, all things which we see are thine, and we ourselves are subject to thy power; now do what seems pleasing to thee, for none is strong enough to resist thee." When they had thus spoken one of the soldiers, impetuous, envious, and vain, raised his battle-ax aloft and crushed the vase with it,

SOURCE: James Harvey Robinson, *Readings in European History* (Boston: Ginn, 1904), vol. 1, pp. 51–55.

crying, "Thou shalt receive nothing of this unless a just lot give it to thee." At this all were stupefied.

The king bore his injury with the calmness of patience, and when he had received the crushed vase he gave it to the bishop's messenger; but he cherished a hidden wound in his breast. When a year had passed he ordered the whole army to come fully equipped to the Campus Martius and show their arms in brilliant array. But when he had reviewed them all he came to the breaker of the vase, and said to him, "No one bears his arms so clumsily as thou; for neither thy spear, nor thy sword, nor thy ax is ready for use." And seizing his ax, he cast it on the ground. And when the soldier had bent a little to pick it up the king raised his hands and crushed his head with his own ax. "Thus," he said, "didst thou to the vase at Soissons."

[Clovis took to wife Clotilde, daughter of the king of the Burgundians. Now Clotilde was a Christian. When her first son was born] she wished to consecrate him by baptism, and begged her husband unceasingly, saying, "The gods whom thou honorest are nothing; they cannot help themselves nor others; for they are carved from stone, or from wood, or from some metal. The names which you have given them were of men, not of gods,—like Saturn, who is said to have escaped by flight, to avoid being deprived of his power by his son; and like Jupiter himself, foul perpetrator of all uncleanness. * * * What power have Mars and Mercury ever had? They are endowed with magical arts rather than divine power.

"The God who should be worshiped is he who by his word created from nothingness the heavens and the earth, the sea and all that in them is; he who made the sun to shine and adorned the sky with stars; who filled the waters with creeping things, the land with animals, the air with winged creatures; by whose bounty the earth is glad with crops, the trees with fruit, the vines with grapes; by whose hand the human race was created; whose bounty has ordained that all things should give homage and service to man, whom he created."

But when the queen had said these things, the mind of Clovis was not stirred to believe. He answered: "By the will of our gods all things are created and produced. Evidently your god can do nothing, and it is not even proved that he belongs to the race of gods."

Meantime the faithful queen presented her son for baptism. She had the church adorned with tapestry, seeking to attract by this splendor him whom her exhortations had not moved. But the child whom they called Ingomer, after he had been born again through baptism, died in his white baptismal robe. Then the king reproached the queen bitterly. "If the child had been consecrated in the name of my gods he would be alive still. But now, because he is baptized in the name of your god, he cannot live." * * *

After this another son was born to him, and called in baptism Clodomir. He fell very ill. Then the king said: "Because he, like his brother, was baptized in the name of Christ, he must soon die." But his mother prayed, and by God's will the child recovered.

The queen unceasingly urged the king to acknowledge the true God, and forsake idols. But he could not in any wise be brought to believe until a war broke out with the Alemanni. Then he was by necessity compelled to confess what he had before willfully denied.

It happened that the two armies were in battle, and there was great slaughter. Clovis' army was near to utter destruction. He saw the danger; his heart was stirred; he was moved to tears, and he raised his eyes to heaven, saying: "Jesus Christ, whom Clotilde declares to be the son of the living God, who it is said givest aid to the oppressed, and victory to those who put their hope in thee, I beseech the glory of thy aid. If thou shalt grant me victory over these enemies and I test that power which people consecrated to thy name say they have proved concerning thee, I will believe in thee and be baptized in thy name. For I have called upon my gods, but, as I have proved, they are far removed from my aid. So I believe that they have no power, for they do not succor those who serve them. Now I call upon thee, and I long to believe in thee—all the more that I may escape my enemies."

When he had said these things, the Alemanni turned their backs and began to flee. When they saw that their king was killed, they submitted to the sway of Clovis, saying: "We wish that no more people should perish. Now we are thine." When the king had forbidden further war, and praised his soldiers, he told the queen how he had won the victory by calling on the name of Christ.

Then the queen sent to the blessed Remigius, bishop of the city of Rheims, praying him to bring to the king the gospel of salvation. The priest, little by little and secretly, led him to believe in the true God, maker of heaven and earth, and to forsake idols, which could not help him nor anybody else.

But the king said: "Willingly will I hear thee, O father; but one thing is in the way—that the people who follow me are not content to leave their gods. I will go and speak to them according to thy word."

When he came among them, the power of God went before him, and before he had spoken all the people cried out together: "We cast off mortal gods, O righteous king, and we are ready to follow the God whom Remigius tells us is immortal."

These things were told to the bishop. He was filled with joy, and ordered the font to be prepared. The streets were shaded with embroidered hangings; the churches were adorned with white tapestries, the baptistery was set in order, the odor of balsam spread around, candles gleamed, and all the temple of the baptistery was filled with divine odor. * * * Then the king confessed the God omnipotent in the Trinity, and was baptized in the name of the Father, and of the Son, and of the Holy Ghost, and was anointed with the sacred chrism with the sign of the cross of Christ. Of his army there were baptized more than three thousand.

Questions

1. What is Clovis's conception of religion? What benefits does right belief bring; what evils result from wrong belief?

2. Who plays the principal role in converting Clovis to Christianity? What does this suggest about the conversion process in general?

3. Why do Clovis's followers decide to receive baptism?

Taming Frontier Deities in China
(third–tenth centuries CE)

These tales are typical of a large body of local legends from roughly the third- to tenth-century China, although in some frontier areas, they appear later. In all of them a powerful local deity faces off against a man of culture and virtue who comes in from outside, often an imperial official or candidate for office, but sometimes a Buddhist or Daoist clergyman. The local deity is sometimes represented as an aristocrat, sometimes as a monster, and sometimes as a dangerous natural force, such as a plague or a river subject to powerful floods. Sometimes he can assume all of these identities, and often, as in the second story here, he requires live sacrifices from the community. In fact, human sacrifice was very rare, though not nonexistent, in imperial China.

"The Magistrate and the Local Deity" is the older of these two tales, definitely already known in the period of disunion between the end of the Han (220 CE) and the beginning of the Sui (589 CE). "Yu guai lu" dates from some time during the Tang dynasty (618–907 CE). There was a famous official named Guo Yuanzhen during the Tang, but his biography doesn't match up well with this tale. In general, earlier tales, like the first one here, tend to end in the defeat of the outsider, and later ones in his victory. Many of the victorious heroes—though certainly not all of them—were later enshrined as local "city gods": deities specific to one county, with a temple in the county capital. They were generally represented as the supernatural counterpart of the imperial magistrate or other official based in that town. Spelling has been updated in the following excerpts to reflect modern orthography.

SOURCE: Hsien-yi Yang, *The Man Who Sold a Ghost: Chinese Tales of the 3rd–6th Centuries* (Peking: Foreign Language Press, 1958), pp. 100–101, and E. D. Edwards, *Chinese Prose Literature of the T'ang Period* A.D. *618–906.* (London: Arthur Probsthain, 1938), vol. 2, pp. 248–52.

The Magistrate and the Local Deity

Zhen Chong, a native of Zhongshan, was appointed magistrate of Yuntu. On his way to his post he was informed that the son of the local deity wished to call on him. Soon a young, handsome god arrived and they exchanged the usual courtesies.

"I am here at my father's behest," announced the young god. "He longs to be allied to your noble house, and hopes you will take my younger sister in marriage. I have come to bring you this message."

"I am past my prime and have one wife already." Zhen was taken aback. "How can I do such a thing?"

"My sister is young and remarkably beautiful. We must find a good match for her. How can you refuse?"

"I am old and have a wife. It would not be right."

They argued back and forth several times, but Zhen remained adamant. The young god looked put out.

"Then my father will come himself," he said. "I doubt if you can refuse him."

He left, followed on both banks of the river by a large retinue of attendants with caps and whips.

Soon the local deity arrived in person with an equipage like a baron's. His carriage had a dark-green canopy and red reins and was escorted by several chariots. His daughter rode in an open carriage with several dozen silk pennants and eight maids before it, all of them dressed in embroidered gowns more splendid than mortal eye has ever seen. They pitched a tent on the bank near Zhen and spread a carpet. Then the deity alighted and sat by a low table on a white woollen rug. He had a jade spittoon, a hat-box of tortoise-shell and a white fly-whisk. His daughter remained on the east bank, with eunuchs carrying whisks at her side and maids in front. The local deity ordered his assistant officers, some sixty of them, to sit down before him, and called for music. The instruments they used seemed to be of glass.

"I have a humble daughter dear to my heart," said the deity. "Since you come of a renowned and virtuous family, we are eager to be connected with you by marriage. That is why I sent my son with this request."

"I am old and my health is failing," replied Zhen Chong. "I already have a wife and my son is quite big. Much as I am tempted by this proffered honour, I must beg to decline."

"My daughter is twenty," continued the deity. "She is beautiful and gentle, and possesses all the virtues. As she is now on the bank, there is no need for any preparations. The wedding can take place at once."

Still Zhen Chong stood out stubbornly, and even called the deity an evil spirit. He drew his sword and laid it on his knees, determined to resist to the death, and refused to discuss the matter any further. The local deity flew into a passion. He summoned three leopards and two tigers, which opened wide their crimson mouths and shook the earth with their roars as they leaped at Zhen. They attacked several dozen times, but Zhen held them at bay till dawn when the deity withdrew, thwarted. He left behind one carriage and several dozen men to wait for Zhen, however. Then Zhen moved into the Huihuai County office. The waiting carriage and men followed him in, and a man in plain clothes and cap bowed to him and advised him to stay there and not go any further.

Zhen Chong did not dare leave for another ten days. Even then he was followed home by a man in a cap with a whip. And he had not been back many days before his wife contracted an illness and died.

Yu guai lu

In the early part of the 8th century [CE] Guo Yuanzhen returning home after failing in the official examination, was on the road from Qin to Fên one night when he lost his way. After wandering about for a long time, he saw a light in the distance. Thinking it must indicate some sort of human habitation he hastened forward and found himself before a lofty and imposing mansion. The rooms were brightly lighted and he could see a wedding-feast spread, but all was silent and deserted. He tethered his horse, and approached the main hall.

As he hesitated at the door, wondering where he was, he heard sounds of sobbing from a room somewhere on the east side of the house.

"Is it a human or a demon there?" he cried. "Why do you weep so bitterly?"

"I am being offered as a sacrifice," replied a tearful voice. "General Wu, who holds the fortunes of this village in his hands, demands a new bride every year and the people are forced to give him a beautiful maiden. Though I am ugly and stupid, my father, being in debt, has been obliged to let them make me the victim. This evening the wedding-feast was prepared and I was beguiled into this room, locked in, and left to await the general. Now that my parents have cast me out what is left but death? I am so frightened! If you have the courage to save me I will serve you with the faithfulness of a wife as long as I live."

Deeply moved, Guo asked when the general would arrive.

"At the second watch," replied the girl.

"I will play the man and save you!" he cried. "I would rather die than allow you to fall into the hands of this licentious demon."

Gradually the sobbing ceased. Guo sat on the western steps and ordered a man to lead his horse to the back of the house, and another to stand in front as if on duty. Before long General Wu appeared with his attendants, and after a preliminary exchange of courtesies he and Guo sat down to table, wine and laughter flowing freely. Guo had a dagger in his wallet but lacked an excuse to use it, so presently he inquired:

"Are you fond of dried venison, General?"

"One can never get it in this district," replied the other.

"I have a small portion which came from the imperial kitchen," Guo returned. "May I cut you a piece?"

The general was delighted. Guo took out the venison and the dagger, and cut several slices. These he laid upon a small dish, and the general, invited to help himself and suspecting nothing, stretched out his hand to take a piece. Seizing the moment when he was off his guard, Guo threw down the venison, gripped his wrist, and cut off his hand.

The general fled with a yell, and his terrified followers scattered in all directions. Wrapping the hand in his cloak, Guo dispatched a man to look for the general and his party, but they had all vanished. He then knocked and called to the maiden to come out and have something to eat.

"I have the general's hand here," he called, "and judging by the blood-tracks, he will soon die and you will be safe."

The maiden came out and Guo saw a pretty girl of about seventeen.

"I pledge myself to be your handmaid and obey your orders," she said bowing low to her rescuer.

As soon as it was light they opened the cloak, but inside, instead of a hand they found a pig's foot! Soon the sound of wailing announced the approach of the girl's relatives and the village elders bringing a coffin for her corpse. Seeing her alive they demanded an explanation. When Guo told the story they were furious with him for injuring their patron spirit.

"General Wu was the guardian of the village," they cried. "We have always sacrificed to him, and so long as we give him a bride once a year we are safe, but if we fail he will send tempests to destroy us. Shall a chance wayfarer be allowed to wound our patron and injure our people? We will not submit to it! Let the stranger be sacrificed to General Wu!"

Quickly they bound Guo, and were about to hale him before the magistrate when he began to cry out on them for their folly in serving a spirit who preferred evil to good.

"If he were a good spirit, would he have a pig's foot? And if he is only a licentious brute, was I not right to slay him? How do you know that I was not sent expressly to rid you of this vile beast? Listen to my words and let me destroy for ever this incubus which you maintain."

Perceiving the truth of these arguments the elders gathered several hundred men armed with bows and arrows, swords, spears, spades and bill-hooks, and set out to pursue the general. Guided by the blood-tracks they came at length to a cave, and having enlarged the opening, they gathered quantities of brushwood and set fire to it outside. Peering in, Guo could see a great boar with its left forefoot cut off and blood soaking the ground round about it. Driven out by the smoke, the beast rushed forth and was quickly dispatched. The villagers then wished to reward Guo, but he would accept nothing, nor would he allow them to entertain him.

"I am a righter of wrongs," he said, preparing to depart, "not a hunter to be hired."

The rescued maiden bade farewell to her relatives.

"But for this man," she told them, "I should not be alive to-day. You sacrificed me to a loathsome beast, and left me to die. To you therefore I am dead henceforth, and from this moment I begin to live for Guo. My one desire is to go with him and never more remember my native place."

With tears streaming from her eyes, and deaf to the kindly words with which he tried to dissuade her, she followed Guo. Yielding at last, he took her with him and she became his concubine, bearing him many sons. In after years he rose to high rank, and occupied the most exalted posts in the administration.

It is apparent that that which is fore-ordained must befall a man, however remote he may live, and demons notwithstanding.

Questions

1. Compare the deity in "The Magistrate" with the general in "Yu guai lu." How do the humans, Zhen Chong and Guo Yuanzhen respond to their respective supernatural encounter?

2. In both stories, the deity wants to arrange a marriage with a human. Why? What does this suggest in each case?

3. What kinds of social, political, and cultural change might these tales (which were especially common in parts of China subordinated to the empire relatively recently) represent?

Han Yu, Memorial on the Bone of the Buddha (819 CE)

Buddhism arrived in China (via central Asian merchants) during the first century CE, and initially spread slowly. But by the time that Sui Wendi (581–618 CE) reunified the Chinese Empire, Buddhism had become very popular, and the dynasty publicly supported Buddhist temples, clerics, and text-copying projects. The Tang dynasty (618–907 CE) extended this patronage; among other things, Buddhism provided a set of religious and cultural practices that the hybrid Chinese and central Asian elite of the Tang court could share. By contrast, the practices we call "Confucian" and "Daoist" had little resonance for central Asian society.

But the relative merits of different religious traditions were always controversial; so were the expensive gifts, tax exemptions, and other privileges given to Buddhist and Daoist establishments. After the An Lushan Rebellion (755–763 CE), started by a general of Turkish origin, some elites turned against what they considered excessive foreign influence, seeking alternative models in the Chinese past.

Han Yu (768–824 CE), a high-ranking official and leading intellectual, was probably the most important advocate of this "back to the classics" movement, promoting ancient models for prose writing, ritual, and political institutions. This essay, written in 819 CE to protest imperial celebration of the arrival of a Buddhist relic, got him sentenced to exile on the empire's southern frontier. But in 845 CE, another emperor greatly reduced state support for Buddhism; the succeeding Song dynasty (960–1279) gave Confucianism the central place in official culture, which it retained until the twentieth century. Subsequent generations of Chinese scholars generally celebrated Han Yu as a pioneer of this Confucian (or, as Westerners later called it, Neo-Confucian) revival.

Your servant begs leave to say that Buddhism is no more than a cult of the barbarian peoples, which spread to China in the time of the Latter Han. It did not exist here in ancient times. * * * When Emperor Gaozu [founder of the Tang] received the throne from the House of Sui, he deliberated upon the suppression of Buddhism. But at that time the various officials, being of small worth and knowledge, were unable fully to comprehend the ways of the ancient kings and the exigencies of past and present, and so could not

SOURCE: *Sources of Chinese Tradition*, 2nd ed., compiled by Wm. Theodore de Bary and Irene Bloom et al. (New York: Columbia University Press, 1999), vol. 1, pp. 583–85.

implement the wisdom of the emperor and rescue the age from corruption. Thus the matter came to naught, to your servant's constant regret.

Now Your Majesty, wise in the arts of peace and war, unparalleled in divine glory from countless ages past, upon your accession prohibited men and women from taking Buddhist orders and forbade the erection of temples and monasteries, and your servant believed that at Your Majesty's hand the will of Gaozu would be carried out. Even if the suppression of Buddhism should be as yet impossible, your servant hardly thought that Your Majesty would encourage it and, on the contrary, cause it to spread. Yet now your servant hears that Your Majesty has ordered the community of monks to go to Fengxiang to greet the bone of Buddha, that Your Majesty will ascend a tower to watch as it is brought into the palace, and that the various temples have been commanded to welcome and worship it in turn. Though your servant is abundantly ignorant, he understands that Your Majesty is not so misled by Buddhism as to honor it thus in hopes of receiving some blessing or reward, but only that, the year being one of plenty and the people joyful, Your Majesty would accord with the hearts of the multitude in setting forth for the officials and citizens of the capital some curious show and toy for their amusement. * * * But the common people are ignorant and dull, easily misled and hard to enlighten, and should they see their emperor do these things they might say that Your Majesty was serving Buddhism with a true heart. "The Son of Heaven is a Great Sage," they would cry, "and yet he reverences and believes with all his heart! How should we, the common people, then begrudge our bodies and our lives?" Then would they set about singeing their heads and scorching their fingers, binding together in groups of ten and a hundred, doffing their common clothes and scattering their money, from morning to evening urging each other on lest one be slow, until old and young alike had abandoned their occupations to follow [Buddhism]. * * * Then will our old ways be corrupted, our customs violated, and the tale will spread to make us the mockery of the world. This is no trifling matter!

Now Buddha was a man of the barbarians who did not speak the language of China and wore clothes of a different fashion. His say-

ings did not concern the ways of our ancient kings, nor did his manner of dress conform to their laws. He understood neither the duties
that bind sovereign and subject nor the affections of father and son.
If he were still alive today and came to our court by order of his ruler,
Your Majesty might condescend to receive him, but [it would amount
to no more than one audience in the Xuancheng Hall, a banquet by
the office for receiving guests, the presentation of a suit of clothes,
and] he would then be escorted to the borders of the state, dismissed,
and not allowed to delude the masses. How then, when he has long
been dead, could his rotten bones, the foul and unlucky remains of
his body, be rightly admitted to the palace? * * * Now without reason
Your Majesty has caused this loathsome thing to be brought in and
would personally go to view it. * * * The host of officials have not
spoken out against this wrong, and the censors have failed to note its
impropriety. Your servant is deeply shamed and begs that this bone
be given to the proper authorities to be cast into fire and water, that
this evil may be rooted out, the world freed from its error, and later
generations spared this delusion. Then may all men know how the
acts of their wise sovereign transcend the commonplace a thousand-
fold. Would this not be glorious? Would it not be joyful?

Should the Buddha indeed have supernatural power to send
down curses and calamities, may they fall only upon the person of
your servant, who calls upon high Heaven to witness that he does
not regret his words. With all gratitude and sincerity your servant
presents this memorial for consideration, being filled with respect
and awe.

Questions

1. What does Han Yu say about the effects of welcoming the Buddha bone?
   About the Buddha himself?

2. What sorts of precedents does Han Yu try to get the emperor to
   heed?

3. Why do you think Han Yu became such a great hero to later generations of non-Buddhist Chinese intellectuals?

Chapter 9

NEW EMPIRES AND COMMON CULTURES, 600–1000 CE

Quranic Comments on the Torah and the Gospels (early seventh century CE)

One of the chief issues that early Islam had to deal with was its relation to the preexisting monotheistic religions. Muhammad saw himself as the last in a line of prophets sent by God, which included the Jewish patriarchs and Jesus of Nazareth. This became particularly acute when Muslims began to rule over large populations of Jews, Christians, and Zoroastrians. In general, there have been two schools of thought in Islam about the other monotheistic religions. One line of interpretation held that Christians, Jews, and other "people of the book," despite having neglected and altered the messages they had received from their prophets, could achieve salvation in their own religions. Another held that Muhammad's revelation had superseded and abrogated previous revelations and that salvation was possible only in Islam. The source Muslims have for guidance on these issues is the Quran, which Muslims regard as the direct, unmediated word of God delivered to Muhammad. Islam holds that Allah revealed the Quran to Muhammad through the angel Jibrīl (Gabriel) starting around 610 CE and continuing until Muhammad's death in 632. The following passage is Sura (chapter) 5, verses 43–48.

---

43. But why should they make you a judge when the Torah is with them which contains the Law of God? Even then they turn away. They are those who will never believe.

[44.] We sent down the Torah which contains guidance and light, in accordance with which the prophets who were obedient (to God) gave instructions to the Jews, as did the rabbis and priests, for they were the custodians and witnesses of God's writ. So, therefore, do not fear men, fear Me, and barter not My messages away for a paltry gain. Those who do not judge by God's revelations are infidels indeed.

45. And there (in the Torah) We had ordained for them a life for a life, and an eye for an eye, and a nose for a nose, and an ear for an ear, and a tooth for a tooth, and for wounds retribution, though he who forgoes it out of charity, atones for his sins. And those who do not judge by God's revelations are unjust.

46. Later, in the train (of the prophets), We sent Jesus, son of Mary, confirming the Torah which had been (sent down) before him, and gave him the Gospel containing guidance and light, which corroborated the earlier Torah, a guidance and warning for those who preserve themselves from evil and follow the straight path.

47. Let the people of the Gospel judge by what has been revealed in it by God. And those who do not judge in accordance with what God has revealed are transgressors.

48. And to you We have revealed the Book containing the truth, confirming the earlier revelations, and preserving them (from change and corruption). So judge between them by what has been revealed by God, and do not follow their whims, side-stepping the truth that has reached you. To each of you We have given a law and a way and a pattern of life. If God had pleased He could surely have made you one people (professing one faith). But He wished to try and test you by that which He gave you. So try to excel in good deeds. To Him will you all return in the end, when He will tell you of what you were at variance.

SOURCE: *Al-Qurʾān: A Contemporary Translation*, translated by Ahmed Ali (Princeton: Princeton University Press, 1993), pp. 103–4.

Questions

1. What is the understanding of Christianity and Judaism that appears in this text?

2. How does this passage portray the relationship between Judaism and Christianity?

3. What is the relationship of Judaism and Christianity to Islam? Is it necessary for someone to become a Muslim to worship God correctly?

Ibn Ishaq, Biography of Messenger of God (eighth century CE)

After the death of the Prophet Muhammad in 632 CE, the members of the Muslim community maintained many traditions about his life. In the eighth century the Muslim scholar Muhammad ibn Ishaq ibn Yasār collected many of these and wrote the first biography of Muhammad, *The Life of God's Messenger*. The original of this work has been lost, but much of it is preserved in the abbreviated edition put together by Ibn Hisham (died 827 CE). The following passage describes how Muhammad, who had made a practice of retiring to a cave on Mount Ḥirā' near Mecca for reflection and contemplation, began receiving the divine revelation of the Quran.

When Muhammad the apostle of God reached the age of forty God sent him in compassion to mankind, "as an evangelist to all men." Now God had made a covenant with every prophet whom he had sent before him that he should believe in him, testify to his truth and help him against his adversaries, and he required of them that they should transmit that to everyone who believed in them, and they carried out their obligations in that respect. God said to

---

SOURCE: Ibn Ishaq, *The Life of Muhammad*, translated by A. Guillaume (Karachi: Oxford University Press, 1967), pp. 104–7.

Muhammad, "When God made a covenant with the prophets (He said) this is the scripture and wisdom which I have given you, afterwards an apostle will come confirming what you know that you may believe in him and help him." He said, "Do you accept this and take up my burden?" i.e. the burden of my agreement which I have laid upon you. They said, "We accept it." He answered, "Then bear witness and I am a witness with you." Thus God made a covenant with all the prophets that they should testify to his truth and help him against his adversaries and they transmitted that obligation to those who believed in them among the two monotheistic religions.

* * *

The apostle would pray in seclusion on Ḥirā' every year for a month to practise *taḥannuth* as was the custom of Quraysh in heathen days. *Taḥannuth* is religious devotion.

* * *

Wahb b. Kaisān told me that "Ubayd said to him: Every year during that month the apostle would pray in seclusion and give food to the poor that came to him. And when he completed the month and returned from his seclusion, first of all before entering his house he would go to the Ka'ba and walk round it seven times or as often as it pleased God; then he would go back to his house until in the year when God sent him, in the month of Ramaḍān in which God willed concerning him what He willed of His grace, the apostle set forth to Ḥirā' as was his wont, and his family with him. When it was the night on which God honoured him with his mission and showed mercy on His servants thereby, Gabriel brought him the command of God. "He came to me," said the apostle of God, "while I was asleep, with a coverlet of brocade whereon was some writing, and said, 'Read!' I said 'What shall I read?' He pressed me with it so tightly that I thought it was death; then he let me go and said, 'Read!' I said, 'What shall I read?' He pressed me with it again so that I thought it was death; then he let me go and said 'Read!' I said, 'What shall I read?' He pressed me with it the third time so that I thought it was death and said 'Read!' I said, 'What then shall I read?'—and this I said only to deliver myself from him, lest he should do the same to me again. He said:

'Read in the name of thy Lord who created,
Who created man of blood coagulated.
Read! Thy Lord is the most beneficent,
Who taught by the pen,
Taught that which they knew not unto men.'

"So I read it, and he departed from me. And I awoke from my sleep, and it was as though these words were written on my heart. (Ṭ. Now none of God's creatures was more hateful to me than an (ecstatic) poet or a man possessed: I could not even look at them. I thought, Woe is me poet or possessed—Never shall Quraysh say this of me! I will go to the top of the mountain and throw myself down that I may kill myself and gain rest. So I went forth to do so and then) when I was midway on the mountain, I heard a voice from heaven saying, 'O Muhammad! thou art the apostle of God and I am Gabriel.' I raised my head towards heaven to see (who was speaking), and lo, Gabriel in the form of a man with feet astride the horizon saying, 'O Muhammad! thou art the apostle of God and I am Gabriel.' I stood gazing at him, (Ṭ. and that turned me from my purpose) moving neither forward nor backward; then I began to turn my face away from him, but towards whatever region of the sky I looked, I saw him as before. And I continued standing there, neither advancing nor turning back until Khadīja sent her messengers in search of me and they gained the high ground above Mecca and returned to her while I was standing in the same place; then he parted from me and I from him, returning to my family. And I came to Khadīja and sat by her thigh and drew close to her. She said, 'O Abū'l-Qāsim, where hast thou been? By God, I sent my messengers in search of thee, and they reached the high ground above Mecca and returned to me.' (Ṭ. I said to her, 'Woe is me poet or possessed.' She said, 'I take refuge in God from that O Abūl-Qāsim. God would not treat you thus since he knows your truthfulness, your great trustworthiness, your fine character, and your kindness. This cannot be, my dear. Perhaps you did see something.' 'Yes, I did,' I said.) Then I told her of what I had seen; and she said, 'Rejoice, O son of my uncle, and be of good heart. Verily, by Him in whose hand is Khadīja's soul, I have hope that thou wilt be the prophet of this people.'" Then she rose and gathered her garments about her and set forth to her cousin Waraqa b. Naufal b. Asad b. ʿAbdu'l-ʿUzzā b. Quṣayy, who had become a Christian and read the scriptures and learned from those that follow the Torah and the Gospel. And when she related to him what the apostle of God told her he had seen and heard, Waraqa cried, "Holy! Holy! Verily by Him in whose hand is Waraqa's soul, if thou hast spoken to me the truth, O Khadīja, there hath come unto him the greatest Nāmūs (Ṭ. meaning Gabriel) who came to Moses afore-time, and lo, he is the prophet of this people. Bid him be of good heart." So Khadīja returned to the apostle of God and told him what Waraqa had said. (Ṭ. and that calmed his fears somewhat.) And when the apostle of God had finished his period of seclusion and returned (to Mecca), in the first place he performed the circum-ambulation of the Kaʿba, as was his wont. While he was doing it, Waraqa met him and said, "O son of my brother, tell me what thou hast seen and heard." The apostle told him, and Waraqa said, "Surely, by Him in whose hand is Waraqa's soul, thou art the prophet of this people. There hath come unto thee the greatest Nāmūs, who came unto Moses. Thou wilt be called a liar, and they will use thee despitefully and cast thee out and fight against thee. Verily, if I live to see that day, I will help God in such wise as He knoweth." Then he brought his head near to him and kissed his forehead; and the apostle went to his own house.

Questions

1. What convinces Muhammad that his visions are truly from God?

2. What is the importance of texts and literacy to Muhammad's mission?

3. How is Muhammad's relation to previous prophets portrayed?

Pact of Umar (ninth century CE)

In the years immediately after the death of the prophet Muhammad Muslims launched a series of military expeditions against the Byzantine and the Persian Sassanian empires. Whether these were intended as wars of conquest or merely raids is not clear. However, they were fabulously successful. By the mid-seventh century CE the Muslims had defeated the Byzantines and destroyed the Persian Empire. Muslim rule extended from Afghanistan to North Africa, with Iran, Iraq, Syria, and Egypt all under their control. Within a very short time a small number of Muslims had become masters of millions of Jews, Christians, and Zoroastrians. One of the major tasks the Muslim community faced was working out its relationship with these groups. Eventually the Muslims devised an arrangement by which these "people of the book" became *dhimmis.* In return for payment of a special tax known as *jizya*, they were allowed to practice their religions. Various restrictions were also imposed on them. The following document reflects this process. According to traditional Islamic historiography, it was an arrangement reached by the Caliph Umar II (c. 682 CE–720 CE) with his Christian subjects. Most Western historians believe it was actually composed at a later time, probably in the ninth century, by jurists who attributed it to Umar. Spelling has been updated in the following excerpt to reflect modern orthography.

In the name of God, the Merciful, the Compassionate!

This is a writing to Umar from the Christians of such and such a city. When you [Muslims] marched against us [Christians], we asked of you protection for ourselves, our posterity, our possessions, and our co-religionists; and we made this stipulation with you, that we will not erect in our city or the suburbs any new monastery, church, cell or hermitage; that we will not repair any of such buildings that may fall into ruins, or renew those that may be situated in the Muslim quarters of the town; that we will not refuse the Muslims entry into our churches either by night or by day; that we will open the

---

SOURCE: Jacob R. Marcus, *The Jew in the Medieval World: A Source Book, 315–1791* (Cincinnati: Sinai Press, 1938), pp. 13–15.

gates wide to passengers and travellers; that we will receive any Muslim traveller into our houses and give him food and lodging for three nights; that we will not harbor any spy in our churches or houses, or conceal any enemy of the Muslims.

•That we will not teach our children the Quran; that we will not make a show of the Christian religion nor invite any one to embrace it; that we will not prevent any of our kinsmen from embracing Islam, if they so desire. That we will honor the Muslims and rise up in our assemblies when they wish to take their seats; that we will not imitate them in our dress, either in the cap, turban, sandals, or parting of the hair; that we will not make use of their expressions of speech, nor adopt their surnames, that we will not ride on saddles, or gird on swords, or take to ourselves arms or wear them, or engrave Arabic inscriptions on our rings; that we will not sell wine; that we will shave the front of our heads; that we will keep to our own style of dress, wherever we may be; that we will wear girdles round our waists.

That we will not display the cross upon our churches or display our crosses or our sacred books in the streets of the Muslims, or in their market-places; that we will strike the clappers in our churches lightly; that we will not recite our services in a loud voice when a Muslim is present; that we will not carry palm-branches or our images in procession in the streets; that at the burial of our dead we will not chant loudly or carry lighted candles in the streets of the Muslims or their market-places; that we will not take any slaves that have already been in the possession of Muslims, nor spy into their houses; and that we will not strike any Muslim.

All this we promise to observe, on behalf of ourselves and our co-religionists, and receive protection from you in exchange; and if we violate any of the conditions of this agreement, then we forfeit your protection and you are at liberty to treat us as enemies and rebels.•

Questions

1. What privileges do the Muslims have vis-à-vis Christians?

2. What restrictions are put on Christians in the practice of their religion?

3. How likely do you think it is that Christians actually wrote this document?

Avicenna, The Life of Ibn Sina (early eleventh century CE)

Abu Ali Al-Husayn Ibn Sina (980–1037 CE) was one of the most famous and influential Islamic philosophers. He was born in Bukhara, in what is today Uzbekistan, and died in Isfahan in Iran. Known to the Arabs as *Al-Sheikh al-Rais*, the "Chief and Leader (of thinkers)" and in the West as Avicenna, he wrote between 100 and 200 works on various subjects including his autobiography, excerpted below. He was a follower of Neoplatonism, a philosophical school originated by Plotinus (205–270 CE), who combined Plato's philosophy with religious, Pythagorean, and other classical ideas. In Neoplatonism the universe is the eternal emanation of the Good, a transcendental and unknowable object of desire and worship. In the twelfth century Ibn Sina's work was translated into Latin and had immense influence on the medieval Latin Christian philosophical tradition known as Scholasticism. Spelling has been updated in the following excerpt to reflect modern orthography.

My father was a man of Balkh; he moved from there to Bukhārā in the days of Amīr Nūh ibn Mansūr, during whose reign he worked in the administration, being entrusted with the governing of a village in one of the royal estates of Bukhārā. [The village,] called Kharmaythan, was one of the most important villages in this territory. Near it is a village called Afshanah, where my father married my mother and where he took up residence and lived. I was born there, as was my brother, and then we moved to Bukhārā. A teacher of the Quran and a teacher of literature were provided for me, and when I reached the age of ten I had finished the Quran and many works of literature, so that people were greatly amazed at me.

My father was one of those who responded to the propagandist of the Egyptians and was reckoned among the Ismā'īliyya [a Shi'ite

SOURCE: *The Life of Ibn Sina*, edited by William E. Gohlman (Albany: State University of New York Press, 1974), pp. 17, 19, 21, 23, 25, 27.

sect]. From them, he, as well as my brother, heard the account of the soul and the intellect in the special manner in which they speak about it and know it. Sometimes they used to discuss this among themselves while I was listening to them and understanding what they were saying, but my soul would not accept it, and so they began appealing to me to do it [to accept the Ismāʿīlī doctrines]. And there was also talk of philosophy, geometry, and Indian calculation. Then he [my father] sent me to a vegetable seller who used Indian calculation and so I studied with him.

At that time Abū ʿAbd Allāh al-Nātilī, who claimed to know philosophy, arrived in Bukhārā; so my father had him stay in our house and he devoted himself to educating me. Before his arrival I had devoted myself to jurisprudence, with frequent visits to Ismāʿīl the Ascetic about it. I was a skillful questioner, having become acquainted with the methods of prosecution and the procedures of rebuttal in the manner which the practitioners of it [jurisprudence] follow. Then I began to read the *Isagoge* ["Introduction" to Aristotle's "Categories" by Porphyry of Tyre (234–c. 305 CE), a pagan Neoplatonist philosopher who lived much of his life in Athens, Rome, and Sicily] under al-Nātilī, and when he mentioned to me the definition of genus, as being that which is predicated of a number of things of different species in answer to the question "What is it?," I evoked his admiration by verifying this definition in a manner unlike any he had heard of. He was extremely amazed at me; whatever problem he posed I conceptualized better than he, so he advised my father against my taking up any occupation other than learning.

I continued until I had read the simple parts of logic under him; but as for its deeper intricacies, he had no knowledge of them. So I began to read the texts and study the commentaries by myself until I had mastered logic. As for Euclid, I read the first five or six figures under him; then I undertook the solution of the rest of the book in its entirety by myself. Then I moved on to the *Almagest*, and when I had finished its introductory sections and got to the geometrical figures, al-Nātilī said to me, "Take over reading and solving them by yourself, then show them to me, so that I can explain to you what is right with it and what is wrong." But the man did not attempt to deal with the text, so I deciphered it myself. And many a figure he did not grasp until I put it before him and made him understand it. Then al-Nātilī left me, going on to Gurgānj.

I devoted myself to studying the texts—the original and commentaries—in the natural sciences and metaphysics, and the gates of knowledge began opening for me. Next I sought to know medicine, and so I read the books written on it. Medicine is not one of the difficult sciences, and therefore I excelled in it in a very short time, to the point that distinguished physicians began to read the science of medicine under me. I cared for the sick and there opened to me some of the doors of medical treatment that are indescribable and can be learned only from practice. In addition I devoted myself to jurisprudence and used to engage in legal disputations, at that time being sixteen years old.

Then, for the next year and a half, I dedicated myself to learning and reading; I returned to reading logic and all the parts of philosophy. During this time I did not sleep completely through a single night nor devote myself to anything else by day.

Questions

1. How widely spread was philosophic and mathematical knowledge in tenth-century Bukhara?

2. How did Ibn Sina acquire his education?

3. From what regions was tenth- and eleventh-century Bukhara receiving cultural influences?

Abû Ûthmân al-Jâhiz, On the Zanj (c. 860 CE)

Abû Ûthmân al-Jâhiz (781–c. 869 CE) was born in Basra (then in the Abbasid caliphate). The grandson of a Zanj (East African) slave, he gained prominence as a scholar, writing prose and learned commentary on history, botany, zoology, politics, Islamic philosophy, and Arabic literature. He moved to Baghdad after the Abbasid caliphs founded the House of Wisdom, where he engaged with leading intellects and the caliph's family. It is said al-Jâhiz authored over 200 books, of which thirty survived to modern times. In this excerpt he defends peoples of sub-Saharan Africa. Long-standing trade relationships between the Persian Gulf and the East African coast intensified with the arrival of many East Africans in southern Iraq as slaves in the seventh and eighth centuries CE. As al-Jâhiz's life shows, some of their descendants married into local families.

In this passage, al-Jâhiz is countering the "curse of Ham," which claims that black-skinned people are descended from the disgraced Ham (one of Noah's sons) and bear the mark of God's displeasure. This myth was used by both Arab and European slave traders to justify enslaving Africans. This passage addresses social tensions, which later erupted as Zanj rebellions (869–883 CE) that happened near Basra.

Everybody agrees that there is no people on earth in whom generosity is as universally well developed as the Zanj. * * * These people have a natural talent for dancing to the rhythm of the tambourine, without needing to learn it. There are no better singers anywhere in the world, no people more polished and eloquent, and no people less given to insulting language. * * * No other nation can surpass them in bodily strength and physical toughness. One of them will lift huge blocks and carry heavy loads that would be beyond the strength of most Bedouins or members of other races. They are courageous, energetic and generous, which are the virtues of nobility, and also good-tempered and with little propensity to evil. They are always cheerful, smiling and devoid of malice, which is a sign of a noble character. * * *

The Zanj say to the Arabs: You are so ignorant that during the *jāhiliyya* you regarded us as your equals [when it came to marrying] Arab women, but with the advent of the justice of Islam you decided this practice was bad. Yet the desert is full of Negroes married to Arab wives, and they have been princes and kings and have safeguarded your rights and sheltered you against your enemies.

SOURCE: *The Life and Works of Jāḥiẓ*, translated by Charles Pellat and D. M. Hawke (London: Routledge & Kegan Paul, 1969).

* * *

[The Zanj] say that God did not make [them] black in order to disfigure [them]; rather it is our environment that has made [them] so. The best evidence of this is that there are black tribes among the Arabs, such as the Banū Sulaim b. Manṣūr, and that all the peoples settled in the Ḥarra besides the Banū Sulaim are black. These tribes take slaves from among the Ashbān to mind their flocks and for irrigation work, manual labour and domestic service, and their wives from among the Byzantines; and yet it takes less than three generations for the Ḥarra to give them all the complexion of the Banū Sulaim. This Ḥarra is such that the gazelles, ostriches, insects, wolves, foxes, sheep, asses, horses and birds that live there are all black. White and black are the results of environment, the natural properties of water and soil, distance from the sun and intensity of heat. There is no question of metamorphosis, or of punishment, disfigurement or favour meted out by [Allah]. Besides, the land of the Banū Sulaim has much in common with the land of the Turks, where the camels, beasts of burden and everything belonging to these people is similar in appearance: everything of theirs has a Turkish look.

Questions

1. How would you characterize al-Jâhiz's description of Africans? Which elements of the description are most believable, and which might be exaggerations?

2. Is al-Jâhiz in favor of marriage between Arabs and Zanj?

3. How do you interpret al-Jâhiz's claim that "everybody agrees" on the generosity and skills of people from Zanj, given that many Zanj familiar to peoples living along the Persian Gulf or between the Tigris and Euphrates rivers would have been slaves?

Ahmad Ibn Fadlan, Journey to Russia (920 CE)

In 920 CE a Slavic king in what is today Kazan (along the Volga River in Russia's Republic of Tatarstan) wrote to the Abbasid caliph, asking for assistance and instruction in the Islamic faith. Sensing a chance to spread the faith and perhaps win useful military allies, the caliph sent an expedition that departed the next year, traveling through the lands of various mostly Turkic pastoralists on the way, and later encountering both Russians and people trading with them who were probably Vikings. A scribe on that mission, Ahmad Ibn Fadlan, left behind a lengthy record of his experiences and impressions.

The selection below records Ibn Fadlan's impressions of the Oghuz Turks. As with many of these peoples—both Muslim and pagan—Ibn Fadlan considered their customs crude, their material living standards low, and their religious understanding very limited; he was, after all, coming from one of the world's great cities, and the contrast between Baghdad and nomadic life sometimes shocked him. At the same time, he found much to admire in at least some of these people—particularly their honesty, straightforwardness, and hospitality.

After we had crossed, we reached a Turkish tribe, which are called Oghuz. They are nomads and have houses of felt. They stay for a time in one place and then travel on. One sees their dwellings placed here and there according to nomad custom. Although they lead a hard existence they are like asses gone astray. They have no religious bonds with God, nor do they have recourse to reason. They never pray, rather do they call their headmen lords. When one of them takes counsel with his chief about something he says: "O lord, what shall I do in this or the other matter?" Their undertakings are based upon counsel solely among themselves; when they come to an agreement on a matter and have decided to put it through, there comes one of the lowest and basest of them and disrupts their decision.

I have heard how they enounce: "There is no God but Allah and Muhammad is the prophet of Allah," so as to get close to any Mus-

SOURCE: *Ibn Fadlan's Journey to Russia: A Tenth-Century Traveler from Baghdad to the Volga River*, translated by Richard N. Frye (Princeton: Markus Wiener Publishers, 2005), pp. 33–36.

lims who come to them by these words, but not because they believe them. When one of them has been dealt with unjustly, or something happens to him which he cannot endure, he looks up to the sky and says: "*bir tengri*," that is in Turkish, "By the one God," because *bir* means one in Turkish and *tengri* is in the speech of the Turks God. The Oghuz do not wash themselves either after defecation or urination, nor do they bathe after seminal pollution, or on other occasions. They have nothing whatever to do with water, especially in winter.

Their women do not veil themselves neither in the presence of their own men nor of others, nor does any woman cover any of her bodily parts in the presence of any person. One day we stopped off with one of them and were seated there. The man's wife was present. As we conversed, the woman uncovered her pudendum and scratched it, and we saw her doing it. Then we veiled our faces and said: "I beg God's pardon." Her husband laughed and said to the interpreter: "Tell them she uncovers it in your presence so that you may see it and be abashed, but it is not to be attained. This, however, is better than when you cover it up and yet it is reachable."

Adultery is unknown among them; but whomsoever they find by his conduct that he is an adulterer, they tear him in two. This comes about so: they bring together the branches of two trees, tie him to the branches and then let both trees go and so the man who was tied to the branches is torn in two.

One of them said he heard [my recitation] from the Quran and found that this recitation was beautiful; he approached addressing the interpreter: "Tell him do not stop." One day this man said to me through the interpreter: "Ask this Arab if our God, mighty and glorious, has a wife?" I felt this an enormity and uttered the formulas: "Praise God" and "I beg God's pardon." And he praised God and begged forgiveness, as I had done. This was the custom of the Turks: every time when a Turk hears a Muslim [pronounce these formulas] he repeats them after him.

Their marriage customs are as follows: one of them asks for the hand of a female of another's family, whether his daughter or his sister or any other one of those over whom he has power, against so and so many garments from Khwarazm. When he pays it he brings her home. The marriage price often consists of camels, pack animals, or other things; and no one can take a wife until he has fulfilled the obligation on which he has come to an understanding with those who have power over her in regard to him. If, however, he has met it, then he comes with any ado, enters the abode where she is, [and] takes her in the presence of her father, mother, and brothers; these do not prevent him. If a man dies who has a wife and children, then the eldest of his sons takes her to wife if she is not his mother.

None of the merchants or other Muslims may perform in their presence the ablution after seminal pollution, except in the night when they do not see it, for they get angry and say: "This man wishes to put a spell on us for he is immersing himself in water," and they compel him to pay a fine.

None of the Muslims can enter their country until one of them has become his host, with whom he stays and for whom he brings garments from the lands of Islam and for his wife a kerchief and some pepper, millet, raisins, and nuts. When the Muslim comes to his friend, the latter pitches a tent for him and brings him sheep in accordance with his [the Turk's] wealth, so that the Muslim himself may slaughter the sheep. * * *

Should any of the Muslims wish to travel further and aught happen to some of his camels and horses, or if he needs resources, he leaves those [incapacitated] with his Turkish friend, takes from him camels, pack animals, and provisions, as much as he needs, and travels further. When he returns from where he went, he pays him [the Turk] money, and gives back his camels and pack animals. And in the same way, when a man stops off with a Turk whom he does not know, and he says to the Turk: "I am thy guest and I will have some of thy camels, [thy] horses, and thy *dirhams*," he gives him what he wishes. If the merchant dies in that region and the caravan returns, the Turk goes to meet them and says: "Where is my guest?" If they say: "He has died," then he stops the caravan and goes to the most prominent merchant whom he sees among the Muslims, opens his bales while he is looking, and takes of his *dirhams*, just the amount that he had claim upon the [deceased] merchant, without taking a grain more. In the same way, he takes some of the pack animals and camels and he [the Turk] says, "That one [the deceased] was thy cousin; thou art chiefly obligated to pay his debts." And if the [first merchant] has fled, the Turk does the same thing and tells him: "He is a Muslim just as thou art. You take from him." If he does not encounter his Muslim guest on the caravan trail, then he asks another [or a third] one: "Where is he?" If he receives an indication, he sets out to find him, journeying for days until he reaches him, and takes away from him what he had of his property and also what he has presented to the [Muslim].

Questions

1. What do Oghuz attitudes toward Islam seem to be? How does Ibn Fadlan feel about this?

2. What most surprises Ibn Fadlan about Oghuz marriage practices, family life, and gender roles? Does he have an opinion about these practices? How can you tell?

3. The last part of this selection describes how the Oghuz lend provisions to traveling merchants, thus facilitating trade. How do lending and repayment work? What ideas of personal and collective responsibility seem to underlie these practices? Do you think these norms could be effectively enforced?

Ouyang Xiu, On the Eunuch Zhang Chengye (d. 922 CE)

Ouyang Xiu (1007–1072 CE) was a court historian who lived during the early Song dynasty. He was commissioned to write an official *New History of the Tang Dynasty*; but he also wrote an unofficial *Historical Record of the Five Dynasties*, chronicling the political and military fragmentation and rough transition from the Tang (618–907 CE) to the Song (960–1279 CE) in the tenth century. Ouyang Xiu's histories contained year-by-year annals as well as biographies of a range of people important for understanding those historical developments, including royal families, subjects, "martyrs to virtue," court performers, and eunuchs. Ouyang Xiu was a remarkably talented intellectual, and his histories blend both Confucian morality—with its emphasis on benevolence, proper ritual, and filial piety—and a conscious emulation of the revered Chinese historian Sima Qian, who had composed his own *Histories* more than a millennium before.

Eunuchs played a significant role in Tang governance, exerting a great deal of influence in the imperial household and the military, in particular. The excerpt here from Ouyang Xiu's *Historical Record of the Five Dynasties* recounts the biography of a particularly influential eunuch named Zhang Chengye. During the tumultuous period between the more stable Tang and Song dynasties, the eunuch Chengye primarily served Li Cunxu, who was Prince of Jin (908–923 CE) and became the Later Tang emperor Zhuangzong (r. 923–926 CE).

We lament. Since antiquity, the havoc wrought by eunuchs and women has been grave! The enlightened ruler knows to shun them long before problems arise. The muddled ruler stays smug even as peril approaches and expresses no regrets as tumult and extinction overtake him. All the same, I cannot fail to forewarn—the inspiration for these "Biographies of Eunuchs."

Zhang Chengye

Zhang Chengye [C.E. 845–921] was a eunuch of the Xizong era of Tang times, his courtesy name Jiyuan and original surname Kang. Castrated as a child, he was adopted as son to Zhang Tai, attendant for palace eunuchs. When troops of the Prince of Jin stormed Wang Xingyu, Chengye repeatedly shuttled between battling armies, and the Prince of Jin came to appreciate his character. Later, Emperor Zhaozong considered flight to Taiyuan under pressure from Li Maozhen and commissioned Chengye as emissary to Jin, conveying his intentions beforehand. Chengye thereby became military overseer for Hedong. Minister Cui Yin later conducted a mass execution of eunuchs: all those away from the capital were to be murdered at their local postings. The Prince of Jin pitied Chengye and could not coun-

---

SOURCE: Ouyang Xiu, *Historical Records of the Five Dynasties,* translated with an introduction by Richard L. Davis (New York: Columbia University Press, 2004), pp. 316–19.

tenance killing him, so Chengye was hidden at the Hulü temple. His release followed Zhaozong's death, resuscitation to military overseer ensuing.

As the Prince of Jin [Li Keyong] turned fatally ill, he entrusted the future Zhuangzong to Zhang Chengye, saying "I must place Yazi in your care." Zhuangzong tended to treat Chengye as an older brother. Through regular visits to his own mother's home, he developed enormous love and esteem for the eunuch. For more than ten years, as he battled Liang armies along the Yellow River from his base at Weizhou, Zhuangzong delegated all military affairs to Chengye, who proved thoroughly dedicated and never remiss. All of the gold and grains accumulated by the regime, all of the soldiers enlisted and horses procured for its armies, all of the foodstuffs produced and silk taxed to further the dynastic agenda—much of the merit for these belongs to Chengye. He consistently applied the rule of law of rein in everyone at the Jinyang [Taiyuan] court, from the Chaste and Austere Dowager, to the Virtuous Consort Han, to the Pure Consort Yin, to the royal sons. The rich and powerful all held back their hands in response to an intimidating Chengye.

Often returning home from Weizhou to visit family, Zhuangzong needed cash to gamble with and patronize his retinue of actors. Chengye presided over the treasury, however, making it impossible to obtain cash. At a banquet on treasury grounds, and inebriated Zhuangzong prodded son Jiji to rise in a dance for Chengye. The dance finished, Chengye provided from the treasury some precious sashes, silks, and steeds. Zhuangzong pointed to a pile of cash and employed Jiji's nickname in yelling out to Chengye, "The 'Amicable Brother' is short on cash and a pile of cash strings is available. Why bother with sashes and steeds?" Chengye declined, saying, "The monies of the empire cannot be tapped by Your Subject for private purposes." The words of Zhuangzong turned aggressive, and a defiant Chengye retorted, "Your Subject, as eunuch commissioner of long standing, does not act out of concern for my own posterity. Rather, I treasure the money, quite simply, because it will advance the Prince's mission of world dominance. If you really wish to spend it, why inquire of me? Once our wealth vanishes and soldiers scatter, I will scarcely face calamity alone!" Zhuangzong looked to Yuan Xingqin.

"Bring me my sword," he said. A weeping Chengye arose and gripped Zhuangzong's garment, adding, "Entrusted with the Former Prince's death wish to care for you, Your Subject swore to satisfy the vendetta of family and country. Should I die today because the Prince covets objects in the treasury, at least my death will bring no shame to the Former Prince!" Approaching from the side, Yan Bao tried to release the grip of Chengye and remove him, but an indignant Chengye clenched his fists to beat him to the floor, cursing him: "A hooligan under Zhu Wen of Liang, you, Yan Bao, have enjoyed the charity and beneficence of our Jin. Still, you present not a single word of loyal candor, only flatter to aggrandize yourself."

Once the Empress Dowager learned of the matter, she summoned Zhuangzong. Exceedingly filial by character, Zhuangzong was utterly petrified by news of the Dowager's summons. He thus poured two goblets of wine to apologize to Chengye, saying, "I have misbehaved under the influence of wine, even offended the Empress Dowager. I hope you will accept this drink and excuse my excesses." Chengye refused the drink, and Zhuangzong entered the palace. Dowager Cao hence had a messenger convey gratitude to Chengye, stating, "The youth, having been rude to you, was flogged with a light rod." On the next day, she accompanied Zhuangzong to Chengye's residence to console him further.

Lu Zhi was a man fond of drink and arrogantly dismissive, someone Zhuangzong loathed ever since Lu Zhi treated him and the other royal princes insolently. Chengye exploited the rift to request, "In his affinity for wine, Lu Zhi lacks decorum and Your Subject wishes to kill him, on the Prince's behalf." "I am in the throes of calling men of character and talent to the cause of dynasty," Zhuangzong responded. "How can your convictions be so extreme?" Chengye rose to congratulate him, adding, "If the Prince can abide by this principle, then not even pacification of the world will be enough!" Lu Zhi thereby escaped death.

By the eighteenth year of Tianyou [c.e. 921], Zhuangzong had secured his commanders' support to become emperor. Zhang Chengye lay bedridden with illness as the news arrived but insisted on traveling from Taiyuan to Weizhou by sedan chair to admonish him. "For thirty years, Your Eminence the Prince joined his father in fighting bloody battles against the Liang: our original intent was to satisfy the vendetta of family and country while restoring the ancestral altars of the Tang dynasty. If you hastily assume esteemed titles today, even as the primal monster [the Liang] remains unvanquished, you would contradict the original will of father and son and lose the world's respect—something wholly unacceptable!" An unpersuaded Zhuangzong insisted, "This represents the wish of the commanders." Chengye now enjoined, "They are wrong! The Liang is the erstwhile enemy of both Tang and Jin, loathed by the entire world as well. The Prince today should simply expel this horrific scourge on the world's behalf, reiterate its profound offense against your Sagacious Predecessor, then search for descendants of Tang royals to install. If heirs to the Tang are found alive, how can you presume to replace them? If no heirs are found, then who in the world would challenge the Prince's accession? Your Servant is merely an old slave of the Tang dynasty, who genuinely wishes to witness the success of our Eminent Prince. Then, I could retire to the countryside, with ranked officiary escorting me beyond Luoyang's eastern gates as sendoff, commoners along the road exclaiming as they pointed, 'He was the imperial commissioner for our dynasty and served as military overseer for the Former Prince.' This would be a common honor for ruler and subject alike." Zhuangzong failed to heed him, and Chengye reckoned further remonstrance to be futile, so, looking to the heavens, he wept aloud and declared, "My Prince will claim the title for himself and repudiate this old slave." Returning to Taiyuan by sedan chair, he starved himself to death at seventy-seven *sui*. In the inaugural year of Tongguang [C.E. 923], he received posthumous rank as generalissimo of the Left Martial Guard and the title "Forthright and Illustrious." * * * [A brief biography of the eunuch Zhang Juhan follows.]

* * *

We lament. Humans are predisposed toward self-contentment: except for the sagaciously wise, arrogant indifference is unavoidable as time passes. The havoc of eunuchs and women occurs not in a single day, for these must await arrogant indifference to sink in gradually. Hardly a diffident ruler, Mingzong perhaps succumbed owing to a relatively long reign. Most other rulers of the period began as military men whose successors faced fleeting reigns and short lives. Eunuchs thus had little time to do their deeds, so the wreaking of serious havoc is scarcely visible. The statements of Chengye emerge as singularly venerable and splendid, while Juhan spared a thousand persons by altering one word. When a superior man appraises others, he will recognize any good deed. For these two persons, I have chosen to cite the good while exposing the bad in the spirit of "rendering respect but acknowledging evil, harboring contempt but acknowledging good." This chapter further reveals how the calamities and defeats of others came about.

Questions

1. Compose a résumé for the eunuch Zhang Chengye. What positions does he hold in the Later Tang and under whose authority? What does such a career suggest about the role of eunuchs in governance?

2. What pieces of advice—about managing money and about seizing power—does Chengye offer to the Prince of Jin (also called Yazi, and later Zhuangzong) in the text? How would you rate the advice and the prince's response to it?

3. How would you describe the eunuch Chengye's character? The future emperor Zhuangzong's character? What events contribute to your estimation of their integrity? How do these characterizations offer an exploration of Confucian morality?

Njal's Saga, Kolskegg and Thrain: Icelanders on the Move (c. 1000 CE)

Iceland was settled by Vikings in the ninth century. By 930 CE, Icelanders had established farming communities that were joined together as a commonwealth that met yearly at a General Assembly to settle disputes, to transact other business, and even to be entertained by storytellers. One of many sagas that tell the stories of Vikings and Icelanders, *Njal's Saga*, reached its present form in the late thirteenth century and recounts an elaborate blood feud playing out between the Icelandic

farmer Njal, his sons, and their wider community in the final decades of
the tenth century. The saga is full of, and even driven by, fascinating
female characters—including Bergthora and Hallgerd—and includes an
oft-cited passage that describes the conversion of Icelanders to Christianity in 1000 CE. Yet what is perhaps most striking in the saga is the
range of individual Icelanders, their motivations, and their travels.
Complex social dynamics play out between husbands and wives,
parents and children, landowners and slaves, "heathens" and Christians,
and leaders and those who voluntarily give their allegiance. The
passage excerpted here is not central to the main narrative of *Njal's
Saga,* but it does focus on a recurring character (Thrain Sigfusson)
and offers a telling snapshot of life in Iceland and Scandanavia, circa
1000 CE.

81

Now the saga returns to Kolskegg. He reached Norway and
stayed the winter in Oslo Fjord. The following summer he went
south to Denmark, where he committed his allegiance to King Svein
Fork-Beard, and was held in high esteem.

One night he dreamt that a man came to him, radiant with
light, and roused him.

"Arise and follow me," he said.

"What do you want of me?" asked Kolskegg.

"I shall find you a bride, and you shall be my knight"

Kolskegg agreed—and with that he awoke. He went to see a sage
and told him the dream. This wise man interpreted it to mean that
Kolskegg was to journey to southern lands and become God's knight.

Kolskegg was baptized in Denmark. But he never found happiness
there, and moved on east to Russia, where he stayed for one winter.
From there he travelled to Constantinople, where he joined the
Emperor's army. The last that was heard of him was that he had mar-

SOURCE: *Njal's Saga,* translated with an introduction by Magnus
Magnusson and Hermann Pálsson (New York: Penguin Books, 1960),
pp. 176–79.

ried there and become a leader in the Varangian Guard. He stayed there for the rest of his life; and he is now out of this saga.

82

Now the saga returns to the time when Thrain Sigfusson went to Norway. He reached Halogaland in the north, and then continued south towards Trondheim and on to Lade. When Earl Hakon heard of the arrival, he sent messengers over to find out who the newcomers were; they came back and told the earl who they were. The earl then sent for Thrain.

Thrain came to the court, and the earl asked him about his kin. Thrain replied that he was a close kinsman of Gunnar of Hliderand.

"That will stand you in good stead," said the earl, "for I have met many Icelanders, and not one of them has been his equal."

"Will you permit me to stay at your court this winter, my lord?" asked Thrain.

The earl accepted him, and Thrain stayed the winter there in high favour.

A Viking named Kol, the son of Asmund Ash-Side of Smaland, lay in the Gotaelv, in Sweden, with five ships and a strong force of men. From there he made a raid on Norway; he landed at Fold and surprised Hallvard Soti in his sleeping-loft. Hallvard defended himself well, until they set fire to the house; then he surrendered, and they put him to death. They seized a lot of booty, and then sailed back to Lodose. When Earl Hakon heard of this, he declared Kol an outlaw throughout his kingdom and put a price on his head.

Some time later the earl said, "Gunnar of Hlidarend is too far away now; he would have killed this outlaw for me if he had been here. But now Gunnar himself will be killed by the Icelanders; it is a pity he never came back to me."

"I may not be Gunnar," said Thrain, "but I am Gunnar's kinsman, and I am willing to take on this task myself."

"Excellent," said the earl. "I shall equip you well for the expedition."

His son Eirik intervened. "You make many fine promises, father," he said, "but you tend to be less consistent in fulfilling them. The mission is a difficult one; this Viking is a ruthless and formidable opponent. You will have to be very particular in your choice of men and ships."

"I am still determined to go, even though the prospects are not good," said Thrain.

The earl gave him five ships, all well manned. Thrain was accompanied by Gunnar Lambason and Lambi Sigurdarson; Gunnar Lambason was Thrain's nephew and had lived with him from an early age, and they were very fond of each other.

Eirik Hakonarson helped them, inspecting the crews and their weapons and making any changes he thought fit. When they were ready to sail, he provided them with a pilot.

They sailed south along the coast, and wherever they landed they had the earl's permission to obtain whatever they needed. They set course east for Lodose. There they heard that Kol had gone south to Denmark, and so they followed him. When they came south to Helsingborg, they met some men in a boat, who told them that Kol was in the neighbourhood and was planning to stay there for a while.

It was a clear day and Kol saw their ships approaching. He said that he had dreamt about Earl Hakon the previous night, and that these must be the earl's men. He ordered his forces to arm themselves, and they made ready. There was long and indecisive fighting. Then Kol leapt on to Thrain's ship and scattered the crew, killing many of them. He was wearing a gilded helmet. Thrain realized that the moment was crucial; rallying his men, he himself led the attack on Kol. Kol swung at Thrain and split his shield in two; but then he was struck on the hand by a stone, and dropped his sword. Thrain struck at him, and cut off his leg. After that they killed him. Thrain cut off his head and kept it, but threw the body overboard.

They seized a lot of booty, and then headed north to Trondheim, where they went to see the earl. The earl welcomed Thrain warmly. Thrain showed him Kol's head, and the earl thanked him for what he had done. Eirik said that it was worth more than mere words; the earl agreed. He took them down to the yards, where some good ships were being built for him. One of them, though not designed like a longship, had a prow carved in the shape of a vulture's head and richly decorated.

The earl said, "You have a taste for the ornate, Thrain, just like your kinsman Gunnar of Hlidarend. I want to give you this ship as a gift. It is called the Vulture. With it goes my friendship, and I want you to stay with me as long as you wish."

Thrain thanked the earl for his kindness, and said that he had no desire to return to Iceland for the time being. The earl had a journey to make to his eastern boundaries to meet the king of Sweden. Thrain accompanied him that summer, commanding the Vulture, and sailed his ship with such verve that few could keep up with him; he was bitterly envied. But it was always obvious how highly the earl regarded Gunnar of Hlidarend, for he heavily rebuffed all those who tried to molest Thrain.

Thrain stayed with the earl throughout the winter. In the spring, the earl asked him whether he wanted to stay on, or go back to Iceland. Thrain replied that he had not yet made up his mind, and that he was waiting for news from Iceland first. The earl told him to do whatever he preferred, and Thrain remained with him.

Then word came from Iceland that Gunnar of Hlidarend was dead; many thought this news indeed. The earl now did not want Thrain to go back to Iceland, and so Thrain remained at court.

Questions

1. What is the geography across which this brief excerpt takes place? How far do Kolskegg and Thrain travel? What does this suggest about mobility of at least some medieval Icelanders?

2. How does the relationship between the Icelander Thrain Sigfusson and the Norwegian Earl Hakon work? How does the earl motivate and reward Thrain? What do those motivations and rewards suggest about the nature of leadership and power at this time in Iceland and Norway?

3. How is Thrain's pursuit of and fight with Kol described? What is the difference, if any, between the Icelander Thain and the Viking Kol? Why do you think the author offers so much detail of the pursuit and combat?

Chapter 10

BECOMING "THE WORLD," 1000–1300 CE

The Rise of Chinggis Khan (c. 1206)

Chinggis Khan (c. 1162–1227) was the founder of the Mongol Empire, which ultimately became the largest contiguous land empire ever known. The construction of this empire began in Chinggis's reign, with successful military campaigns in China, central Asia, and Persia. Despite these successes, Chinggis's early life was beset with troubles. Fatherless, deserted by his kinsmen, at times a fugitive from his enemies in the wilderness, he nevertheless managed by 1206 to make himself master of the peoples of the East Asia steppe. The first text below comes from *The Secret History of the Mongols*, probably composed sometime between 1228 and 1252. This is the best source we have for Chinggis's early life. The excerpt describes the capture and execution of one of Chinggis's greatest rivals, Jamukha, in 1206. Before he turned against Chinggis, Jamukha had been the Khan's blood brother (or "anda"). The second text comes from Rashid al-Din's *Jami' al-tawarikh* (Compendium of Chronicles), which he was commissioned to write by Ghazan Khan (1271–1304), the Mongol ruler of Persia. Rashid, a Jewish convert to Islam, and his sons were Ghazan Khan's most trusted advisers. However, he fell out with one of Ghazan's successors and was executed in 1318. Spelling has been updated in the following excerpts to reflect modern orthography.

The Secret History of the Mongols

When Chinggis Khan defeated the Naiman army
Jamugha had been with the Naiman
and in the battle all of his people were taken away.
He had escaped with only five followers
and become a bandit in the Tangnu Mountains.
One day he and his companions were lucky enough to kill a great
   mountain sheep,
and as they sat around the fire roasting the mutton

*   *   *

his five followers seized him,
and binding Jamukha they brought him to Chinggis Khan.
Because he'd been captured this way, Jamukha said:
"Tell my anda [or blood brother], the Khan,
'Black crows have captured a beautiful duck.
Peasants and slaves have laid hands on their lord.
My anda the Khan will see this and know what to do.
Brown vultures have captured a mandarin duck.
Slaves and servants have conspired against their lord.
Surely my holy anda will know how to respond to this.'"
When he heard Jamukha's words Chinggis Khan made a decree:
"How can we allow men who lay hands on their own lord to live?
Who could trust people like this?
Such people should be killed
along with all their descendants!"
He brought before Jamukha the men who had seized him,
these men who had betrayed their own lord,
and in their lord's presence their heads were cut off.
Then Chinggis Khan said:

SOURCE: "The Secret History of the Mongols," from *The Secret History of the Mongols*, translated by Francis Woodman Cleaves (Cambridge: Harvard University Press, 1982), and "A Maxim of Chinggis Khan," from Timothy May, *The Mongol Art of War: Chinggis Khan and the Mongol Military System* (Yardley, PA: Westholme, 2007), p. 77. [Editorial insertions appear in square brackets—*Ed.*]

"Tell Jamukha this.
'Now we two are together.
Let's be allies.
Once we moved together like the two shafts of a cart,
but you thought about separating from me and you left.
Now that we're together again in one place
let's each be the one to remind the other of what he forgot;
let's each be the one to awaken the other's judgment whenever it sleeps.
Though you left me you were always my anda.
On the day when we met on the battlefield
the thought of trying to kill me brought pain to your heart.'"

* * *

Jamukha answered him:
"Long ago when we were children in the Khorkhonagh Valley
I declared myself to be your anda.
Together we ate the food which is never digested
and spoke words to each other which are never forgotten,
and at night we shared one blanket to cover us both.
Then it was as if people came between us with knives,
slashing our legs and stabbing our sides,
and we were separated from each other.
I thought to myself,
'We've made solemn promises to each other'
and my face was so blackened by the winds of shame
that I couldn't bring myself to show my face,
this shameful windburned face,
before the warm face of my anda, the Khan.

* * *

And now my anda, the Khan wants to favor me,
and says to me, 'Let's be allies.'
When I should have been his ally I deserted him.
Now, my anda, you've pacified every nation;
you've united every tribe in the world.
The Great Khan's throne has given itself to you.
Now that the world is ready for you

what good would I be as your ally?
I'd only invade your dreams in the dark night
and trouble your thoughts in the day.
I'd be like a louse on your collar,
like a thorn under your shirt.

* * *

Having been born a great hero,
he has skillful young brothers.
Having many fine men by his side,
he's always been greater than I am.
As for me,
since I lost both my parents when I was young,
I have no younger brothers.
My wife is a babbling fool.
I can't trust the men at my side.
Because of all this
my anda, whose destiny is Heaven's will,
has surpassed me in everything.
My anda, if you want to favor me,
then let me die quickly and you'll be at peace with your heart.
When you have me killed, my anda,
see that it's done without shedding my blood.
Once I am dead and my bones have been buried high on a cliff
I will protect your seed and the seed of your seed.
I will become a prayer to protect you.

* * *

Hearing this Chinggis Khan spoke:
"Though my anda deserted me
and said many things against me,
I've never heard that he ever wanted me dead.
He's a man we all might learn from
but he's not willing to stay with us.
If I simply ordered him to be killed
there isn't a diviner in the world who could justify it.
If I harmed this man's life without good reason
it would bring a curse on us.

*   *   *

Now I say 'Let's be allies' but you refuse me.
When I try to spare your life you won't allow it.
So speak to Jamukha and tell him,
'Allow this man to kill you
according to your own wishes,
without shedding your blood.'"
And Chinggis Khan made a decree, saying:
"Execute Jamukha without shedding his blood
and bury his bones with all due honor."
He had Jamukha killed and his bones properly buried.

[A maxim of Chinggis Khan:] Just as *ortaqs* [merchants engaged in commerce with capital supplied by the imperial treasury] come with gold spun fabrics and are confident of making profits on those goods and textiles, military commanders should teach their sons archery, horsemanship, and wrestling well. They should test them in these arts and make them audacious and brave to the same degree that *ortaqs* are confident of their own skill.

Questions

1. How important is loyalty to one's master in *The Secret History?*

2. What is Chinggis Khan's opinion of merchants? What status does he ascribe to them?

3. How can you account for the differences in the description of Chinggis Khan between *The Secret History* and Rashid's text?

Yuan Cai, The Problems of Women (twelfth century)

Yuan Cai (c. 1140–1195) was an official and scholar best known for writing an advice book on how members of the scholar-gentry class should manage family matters. Such books had already appeared in China many centuries before, but with the boom in woodblock printing during the Song dynasty (960–1279 CE) and a marked increase in literacy rates, they became far more popular and influential. Increased social mobility also made such books more important, as successful people found themselves occupying roles that they had not had the opportunity to observe their parents handling.

The passages selected here deal with various aspects of the lives of women (though the presumed reader is a male household head). The Song dynasty was a period of major changes in the status of women, with most modern scholars concluding that the choices available to at least elite women narrowed considerably. (One formulation has it that in the Tang dynasty a young female aristocrat might be out horseback riding when her suitor came to call; by the Song dynasty she would not have learned to ride horses, would not have gone out on her own, and would not have seen her suitor prior to marriage.) But recent scholarship has suggested a more complex picture, with women losing ground in some areas but gaining in others.

Women Should Not Take Part in Affairs Outside the Home

Women do not take part in extrafamilial affairs. The reason is that worthy husbands and sons take care of everything for them, while unworthy ones can always find ways to hide their deeds from the women.

Many men today indulge in pleasure and gambling; some end up mortgaging their lands, and even go so far as to mortgage their houses without their wives' knowledge. Therefore, when husbands are bad, even if wives try to handle outside matters, it is of no use. Sons must have their mothers' signatures to mortgage their family properties, but there are sons who falsify papers and forge signatures, sometimes borrowing money at high interest from people who would not hesitate to bring their claim to court.

* * * Therefore, when sons are bad, it is useless for mothers to try to handle matters relating to the outside world.

SOURCE: *Chinese Civilization: A Sourcebook*, 2nd ed., edited by Patricia Buckley Ebrey (New York: The Free Press, 1993), pp. 166–68.

* * * If husbands and sons could only remember that their wives and mothers are helpless and suddenly repent, wouldn't that be best?

WOMEN'S SYMPATHIES SHOULD BE INDULGED

Without going overboard, people should marry their daughters with dowries appropriate to their family's wealth. Rich families should not consider their daughters outsiders but should give them a share of the property. Sometimes people have incapable sons and so have to entrust their affairs to their daughters' families; even after their deaths, their burials and sacrifices are performed by their daughters. So how can people say that daughters are not as good as sons?

Generally speaking, a woman's heart is very sympathetic. If her parents' family is wealthy and her husband's family is poor, she wants to take her parents' wealth to help her husband's family prosper. If her husband's family is wealthy but her parents' family is poor, then she wants to take from her husband's family to enable her parents to prosper. Her parents and husband should be sympathetic toward her feelings and indulge some of her wishes. When her own sons and daughters are grown and married, if either her son's family or her daughter's family is wealthy while the other is poor, she wishes to take from the wealthy one to give to the poor one. Her sons and daughters should understand her feelings and be somewhat indulgent. But taking from the poor to make the rich richer is unacceptable, and no one should ever go along with it.

ORPHANED GIRLS SHOULD HAVE THEIR MARRIAGES ARRANGED EARLY

When a widow remarries she sometimes has an orphaned daughter not yet engaged. In such cases she should try to get a respectable relative to arrange a marriage for her daughter. She should also seek to have her daughter reared in the house of her future in-laws, with the marriage to take place after the girl has grown up. If the girl were to go along with the mother to her stepfather's house, she would not be able to clear herself if she were subjected to any humiliations.

For Women Old Age Is Particularly Hard to Bear

* * * For women who live a long life, old age is especially hard to bear, because most women must rely on others for their existence. * * * For this reason women often enjoy comfort in their youth but find their old age difficult to endure. It would be well for their relatives to keep this in mind.

It Is Difficult for Widows to Entrust Their Financial Affairs to Others

Some wives with stupid husbands are able to manage the family's finances, calculating the outlays and receipts of money and grain, without being cheated by anyone. Of those with degenerate husbands, there are also some who are able to manage the finances with the help of their sons without ending in bankruptcy. Even among those whose husbands have died and whose sons are young, there are occasionally women able to raise and educate their sons, keep the affection of all their relatives, manage the family business, and even prosper. All of these are wise and worthy women. But the most remarkable are the women who manage a household after their husbands have died leaving them with young children. Such women could entrust their finances to their husbands' kinsmen or their own kinsmen, but not all relatives are honorable, and the honorable ones are not necessarily willing to look after other people's business.

When wives themselves can read and do arithmetic, and those they entrust with their affairs have some sense of fairness and duty with regard to food, clothing, and support, then things will usually work out all right. But in most of the rest of the cases, bankruptcy is what happens.

Before Buying a Servant Girl or Concubine, Make Sure of the Legality

When buying a female servant or concubine, inquire whether it is legal for her to be indentured or sold before closing the deal. If the girl is impoverished and has no one to rely on, then she should be brought before the authorities to give an account of her past.

After guarantors have been secured and an investigation conducted, the transaction can be completed. But if she is not able to give an account of her past, then the agent who offered her for sale should be questioned. Temporarily she may be hired on a salaried basis. If she is ever recognized by her relatives, she should be returned to them.

HIRED WOMEN SHOULD BE SENT BACK WHEN THEIR PERIOD OF SERVICE IS OVER

If you hire a man's wife or daughter as a servant, you should return her to her husband or father on completion of her period of service. If she comes from another district, you should send her back to it after her term is over. These practices are the most humane and are widely carried out by the gentry in the Southeast. Yet there are people who do not return their hired women to their husbands but wed them to others instead; others do not return them to their parents but marry them off themselves. Such actions are the source of many lawsuits.

How can one not have sympathy for those separated from their relatives, removed from their hometowns, who stay in service for their entire lives with neither husbands nor sons. Even in death these women's spirits are left to wander all alone. How pitiful they are!

Questions

1. Which kinds of women seem to have the most control over their lives? Which ones have the least? What circumstances create openings for women to make their own choices?

2. The Song dynasty was a period in which commercial activity increased rapidly. What role do markets and money play in these documents?

3. What differences does Yuan Cai see between men and women? What capacities do they share? What moral significance, if any, does he attach to the differences?

Two Views of the Fall of Jerusalem (1099 CE)

In 1095 the Byzantine emperor, hard-pressed by the Seljuk Turks, wrote to Pope Urban II to request military aid. What he got was the First Crusade. Urban's call for an armed pilgrimage, full of stories of Muslim atrocities against Christians and promises of remission of sins for those who took part, touched off a wave of enthusiasm in western Europe. In 1096 large numbers of nobles and crowds of enthusiastic peasants set off to liberate Jerusalem from Muslim control. The three-year journey to Jerusalem was frightful, accompanied by massacres of Jews and Muslims, starvation, cannibalism, and near defeat and destruction. On July 15, 1099, those crusaders who had survived the frightful three-year-long journey captured Jerusalem. They then proceeded to massacre the Muslim population of the city, an atrocity whose memory is still alive in Muslim consciousness. The following excerpts give two different perspectives on this event: one Christian, the other Muslim. The first is from the cleric Raymond d'Aguilers, who appears to have been a chaplain of Raymond, count of Toulouse, one of the leaders of the crusade. He was present at the siege and final storming of Jerusalem. The second is a lament for the destruction of Jerusalem written by the Arab poet Abu l-Muzaffar al-Abiwardi (1064–1113), who held important administrative positions in Baghdad under the Seljuks.

THE FIRST CRUSADE

When our efforts were ended and the machines completed, the princes held a council and announced: "Let all prepare themselves for a battle on Thursday; in the meantime, let us pray, fast, and give alms. Hand over your animals and your boys to the artisans and carpenters, that they may bring in beams, poles, stakes, and branches to make mantlets [movable shelters designed to protect

SOURCE: August C. Krey, *The First Crusade: The Accounts of Eye-Witnesses and Participants* (Princeton: Princeton University Press, 1921), pp. 258–61, and *Arab Historians of the Crusades*, translated from Arabic by Francesco Gabrieli, translated from Italian by E. J. Costello (Berkeley: University of California Press, 1969), p. 12.

soldiers assaulting a fortress]. Two knights should make one mantlet and one scaling ladder. Do not hesitate to work for the Lord, for your labors will soon be ended." This was willingly done by all. * * *

Meanwhile, the Saracens in the city, noting the great number of machines that we had constructed, strengthened the weaker parts of the wall, so that it seemed that they could be taken only by the most desperate efforts. Because the Saracens had made so many and such strong fortifications to oppose our machines, the * * * [leaders] spent the night before the day set for the attack moving their machines, mantlets, and platforms to that side of the city which is between the church of St. Stephen and the valley of Josaphat. You who read this must not think that this was a light undertaking, for the machines were carried in parts almost a mile to the place where they were to be set up. When morning came and the Saracens saw that all the machinery and tents had been moved during the night, they were amazed. Not only the Saracens were astonished, but our people as well, for they recognized that the hand of the Lord was with us. * * *

But why delay the story? The appointed day arrived and the attack began. However, I want to say this first, that, according to our estimate and that of many others, there were sixty thousand fighting men within the city. * * * At the most we did not have more than twelve thousand able to bear arms, for there were many poor people and many sick. There were twelve or thirteen hundred knights in our army, as I reckon it, not more. I say this that you may realize that nothing, whether great or small, which is undertaken in the name of the Lord can fail. * * *

Our men began to undermine the towers and walls. From every side stones were hurled from the *tormenti* and the *petrariae* [that is, catapults], and so many arrows that they fell like hail. The servants of God bore this patiently, sustained by the premises of their faith, whether they should be killed or should presently prevail over their enemies. The battle showed no indication of victory, but when the machines were drawn nearer to the walls, they hurled not only stones and arrows, but also burning wood and straw. * * * Thus the fight continued from the rising to the setting sun in such splendid fashion that it is difficult to believe anything more glorious was ever done.

Then we called on Almighty God, our Leader and Guide, confident in His mercy. Night brought fear to both sides. * * * [O]n both sides it was a night of watchfulness, labor, and sleepless caution: on one side, most certain hope, on the other doubtful fear. We gladly labored to capture the city for the glory of God, they less willingly strove to resist our efforts for the sake of the laws of Mohammed. * * *

When the morning came, our men eagerly rushed to the walls and dragged the machines forward, but the Saracens had constructed so many machines that for each one of ours they now had nine or ten. * * *

By noon our men were greatly discouraged. They were weary and at the end of their resources. There were still many of the enemy opposing each one of our men; the walls were very high and strong, and the great resources and skill that the enemy exhibited in repairing their defenses seemed too great for us to overcome. But, while we hesitated, irresolute, and the enemy exulted in our discomfiture, the healing mercy of God inspired us and turned our sorrow into joy, for the Lord did not forsake us. * * * [A] knight on the Mount of Olives began to wave his shield to those who were with the Count and others, signalling them to advance. Who this knight was we have been unable to find out. At this signal our men began to take heart, and some began to batter down the wall, while others began to ascend by means of scaling ladders and ropes. Our archers shot burning firebrands, and in this way checked the attack that the Saracens were making upon the wooden towers of the Duke and the two Counts. * * * This shower of fire drove the defenders from the walls. Then the Count quickly released the long drawbridge which had protected the side of the wooden tower next to the wall, and it swung down from the top, being fastened to the middle of the tower, making a bridge over which the men began to enter Jerusalem bravely and fearlessly. * * *

[N]ow that our men had possession of the walls and towers, wonderful sights were to be seen. Some of our men (and this was more merciful) cut off the heads of their enemies; others shot them with arrows, so that they fell from the towers; others tortured them longer by casting them into the flames. Piles of heads, hands, and feet were to be seen in the streets of the city. It was necessary to pick one's way over the bodies of men and horses. But these were small matters compared to what happened at the Temple of Solomon, a place where religious services are ordinarily chanted. What happened there? If I tell the truth, it will exceed your powers of belief. So let it suffice to say this much, at least, that in the Temple and porch of Solomon, men rode in blood up to their knees and bridle reins. Indeed, it was a just and splendid judgment of God that this place should be filled with the blood of the unbelievers, since it had suffered so long from their blasphemies. * * *

Now that the city was taken, it was well worth all our previous labors and hardships to see the devotion of the pilgrims at the Holy Sepulchre. How they rejoiced and exulted and sang a new song to the Lord! For their hearts offered prayers of praise to God, victorious and triumphant, which cannot be told in words. A new day, new joy, new and perpetual gladness, the consummation of our labor and devotion, drew forth from all new words and new songs. This day, I say, will be famous in all future ages, for it turned our labors and sorrows into joy and exultation; this day, I say, marks the justification of all Christianity, the humiliation of paganism, and the renewal of our faith. "This is the day which the Lord hath made, let us rejoice and be glad in it," for on this day the Lord revealed Himself to His people and blessed them.

Abu l-Muzaffar al-Abiwardi, [Destruction of Jerusalem]

We have mingled blood with flowing tears, and there is no room
    left in us for pity
To shed tears is a man's worst weapon when the swords stir up the
    embers of war.
Sons of Islām, behind you are battles in which heads rolled at your
    feet.
Dare you slumber in the blessed shade of safety, where life is as soft
    as an orchard flower?
How can the eye sleep between the lids at a time of disasters that
    would waken any sleeper?
While your Syrian brothers can only sleep on the backs of their
    chargers, or in vultures' bellies!

Must the foreigners feed on our ignominy, while you trail behind
   you the train of a pleasant life, like men whose world is at peace?
When blood has been spilt, when sweet girls must for shame hide
   their lovely faces in their hands!
When the white swords' points are red with blood, and the iron of
   the brown lances is stained with gore!
At the sound of sword hammering on lance young children's hair
   turns white.
This is war, and the man who shuns the whirlpool to save his life
   shall grind his teeth in penitence.
This is war, and the infidel's sword is naked in his hand, ready to
   be sheathed again in men's necks and skulls.
This is war, and he who lies in the tomb at Medina seems to raise
   his voice and cry: "O sons of Hashim [an ancestor of the
   prophet Muhammad]!
I see my people slow to raise the lance against the enemy: I see
   the Faith resting on feeble pillars.
For fear of death the Muslims are evading the fire of battle,
   refusing to believe that death will surely strike them."
Must the Arab champions then suffer with resignation, while the
   gallant Persians shut their eyes to their dishonour?

Questions

1. What is Raymond's attitude toward the massacre of the inhabitants of
   Jerusalem?

2. To what does Raymond attribute the success of the crusaders?

3. What is al-Abiwardi's purpose in writing his poem? How does he try to
   motivate his fellow Muslims to take action?

Joseph ben Abraham, Letter from Aden to Abraham Yijū (c. 1130)

Dispersed communities of merchants who shared language, religion, or
ethnic identity facilitated thriving long-distance trade in the twelfth
century. Many records of Jewish merchants working in Mediterranean

and Indian Ocean networks were preserved in the Cairo Geniza. According to Jewish custom, text inscribed with the name of God should not be destroyed. So writings—from small scraps to complex documents—were stored in a dedicated room in a synagogue. Since God's blessing was frequently invoked in letters and commercial contracts, many of these ordinary documents connecting individual merchants were preserved. The synagogue in old Cairo accumulated documents and fragments from about 800 CE through the nineteenth century, at which point scholars began to work with this unparalleled collection of medieval sources to investigate aspects of Jewish life and the thick web of connections that linked communities across great distances.

Partnerships, many of them life-long, cemented connections between ports and served to spread the risks of long-distance trade. Ongoing correspondence, the exchange of presents, and sometimes the exchange of slaves or dependents created bonds between traders who might never have met in person. The following letter is a glimpse into one such relationship between Joseph ben Abraham in Aden, on the Arabian Peninsula, and Abraham Yijū in Mangalore, in southwestern India.

A. LOSSES AND ARRIVALS

In (Your) name, O Merci(ful).

The letter of your excellency, the illustrious elder, my master, has arrived. It was the most pleasant letter that came and the most delightful message that reached me. I read and understood it, etc. (another three lines).

You, my master, may God make your honored position permanent, wrote that you kindly sold the silk and sent goods for its proceeds and that you sent them in the ships of *Rāshmit*. I learned, however, that *Rāshmit's* two ships were lost completely. May *the H(oly one, be) he b(lessed)*, compensate me and you. Do not ask me, my master, how much I was affected by the loss of the cargo belonging

SOURCE: *Letters of Medieval Jewish Traders*, translated by S. D. Goitein (Princeton: Princeton University Press, 1973), pp. 192–96.

to you. But the Creator will compensate you soon. In any case, there is no counsel against the decree of God.

All the "copper" (vessels, *nahās*), which you sent with Abū 'Alī, arrived, and the "table-bowl" also arrived. It was exactly as I wished— may God give you a good reward and undertake your recompensation (for only he is able to do it adequately).

B. EXCOMMUNICATION OF A TARDY DEBTOR

You, my master, mentioned that you approached the *kārdāl* gently in order to get something for us back from him. Perhaps you should threaten him that here in Aden we excommunicate anyone that owes us something and does not fulfill his commitments. Maybe he will be afraid of the excommunication. If he does not pay, we shall issue an official letter of excommunication and send it to him, so that he will become aware of his crime.

C. VARIOUS ORDERS, ESPECIALLY FOR BRONZE VESSELS

The re(d) betel-nuts arrived, as well as the two washbasins— may God give you a good reward. Please do not send me any more red betel-nuts, for they are not good. If there are any white, fresh betel-nuts to be had, it will be all right.

Please do not send me anything either betel-nuts or any other goods you acquire for me, in partnership with anyone, but specify each person and every item of merchandise.

I am sending you a broken ewer and a deep washbasin, weighing seven pounds less a quarter. Please make me a ewer of the same measure from its copper (or bronze, *sufr*) for it is good copper. The weight of the ewer should be five pounds exactly.

I am also sending 18¼ pounds of good yellow copper (*sufr asfar*, hardly "brass") in bars and five pounds of Qal'ī "lead" in a big mold and a piece of Egyptian "lead" (in the form of) a shell. Please put the bars, the "lead," and what remains from the manufacture of the ewer together and have two table-bowls for two dishes made for your servant, each table-bowl being of seventeen *fil(l)*, of the same form as the table-bowl you sent me; they should be of good workmanship.

D. DETAILED DESCRIPTION OF A LAMP ORDERED

Make me a nice lamp from the rest of all the copper (*ṣufr*). Its column should be octagonal and stout, its base should be in the form of a lampstand with strong feet. On its head there should be a copper (*naḥās*) lamp with two ends for two wicks, which should be set on the end of the column so that it could move up and down. The three parts, the column, the stand and the lamp, should be separate from one another. If they could make the feet in spirals, then let it be so; for this is more beautiful. The late *Abu 'l-Faraj al-Jubaylī* made a lamp of such a description. Perhaps this will be like it.

E. ADDITIONAL ORDERS

This year, I did not succeed in sending gold or silk. Instead, I am sending currency, 20 Malikī dinars, old dinars of good gold. Please pay with it the price of the labor of the coppersmith and for the rest buy me a quantity of "eggs" (a kind of cardamom) and cardamom, and if this is not to be had, anything else which God, be he praised, makes available. And, please, send everything with the first ship sailing.

Please buy me two washbasins of middle size, somewhat larger than those you previously sent me, and a large washbasin, which holds two waterskins of water, measuring two *siqāyas*.

F. PRESENTS SENT

I am sending you some things of no importance or value, namely two ruba'iyyas of white sugar; a bottle, in a tight basket, entirely filled with raisins; and in a *mazza* a pound of Maghrebi kohl, a pound of costus, a pound of vitriol, half a pound of litharge, three ounces of *'ilk* gum, and five sets of Egyptian paper; furthermore, in a little basket seven molds of "kosher" cheese; five packages altogether. Furthermore, all the copper (*naḥās*) sent by me is in a canvas. This makes six packages. I wrote on each: "*Abraham Yijū*, shipment of Joseph," and sent the whole together with the 20 dinars with the Sheikh *Aḥmad, the captain, son of Abu 'l-Faraj.*

Furthermore, in a bag there are two linen *fūṭas* for the children and two network veils dyed with carthamus. Please accept delivery and forward them to the Sheikh *Abu 'l-Surūr b. Khallūf al-Ṭalḥī,* as well as the letter destined for him. His name is on the bag.

My lord mentioned that there remained from last year copper to manufacture two bowls for drinking water. Kindly send them with the other copper.

Altogether there are seven packages with the bag of *Abu 'l-Surūr al-Ṭalḥī.*

May my master receive for his honored self the best greetings. And *upon you be peace!*

Questions

1. Which passages in this letter suggest to you that Joseph ben Abraham and Yijū have an ongoing business relationship? What can you infer about twelfth-century Indian Ocean trade from the specificity of Joseph ben Abraham's requests?

2. What kinds of trade goods are moving between Mangalore and Aden? How do these items compare to the trade goods mentioned in *The Periplus of the Erythraean Sea* (see Chapter 6)? What does this suggest to you about change or continuity in long-distance trade over centuries?

3. What does this letter tell us about production in Yijū's bronze factory? What does the letter tell us about the relationship between the value of the materials, the utility of the items produced, their workmanship, and aesthetics?

Francesco Pegolotti, Advice to Merchants Bound for Cathay (c. 1340)

The rise of the Mongol Empire in the thirteenth century greatly facilitated contacts across Eurasia. For a long time the Mongols were able to maintain good order along the Silk Route that ran from China to the Mediterranean. Indeed, under their rule a new branch of the Silk Road opened that ran north of the Caspian Sea to the Black Sea, where the

Italian cities of Genoa and Venice had trading colonies. European envoys visited the court of the Great Khan in Mongolia. Catholic missionaries reached China; for a time there was even a Franciscan archbishop in Beijing. Dominican missionaries were even allowed into Muslim Iran. Merchants, the most famous of whom were the Polos, traveled to China. The following document (c. 1340) comes from a commercial handbook titled the *Book of Descriptions of Countries and of Measures of Merchandise*, written by the Florentine merchant Francesco Balducci Pegolotti (c. 1310–c. 1340). Among other things it describes markets, trade goods, exchange rates, and customs duties from the Atlantic to China.

This book is called the Book of Descriptions of Countries and of measures employed in business, and of other things needful to be known by merchants of different parts of the world, and by all who have to do with merchandise and exchanges; showing also what relation the merchandise of one country or of one city bears to that of others; and how one kind of goods is better than another kind; and where the various wares come from, and how they may be kept as long as possible.

* * *

In the first place, you must let your beard grow long and not shave. And at Tana [at the mouth of the Don River on the Sea of Azov in modern Russia] you should furnish yourself with a dragoman [translator]. And you must not try to save money in the matter of dragomen by taking a bad one instead of a good one. For the additional wages of the good one will not cost you so much as you will save by having him. And besides the dragoman it will be well to take at least two good menservants, who are acquainted with the Cumanian tongue. And if the merchant likes to take a woman with him from Tana, he can do so; if he does not like to take one there is no obligation, only if he does take one he will be kept much more comfortably than if he

---

SOURCE: *Cathay and the Way Thither*, translated and edited by H. Yule, 2nd ed. revised by H. Cordier (London: Hakluyt Society, 1916).

does not take one. Howbeit, if he do take one, it will be well that she be acquainted with the Cumanian tongue as well as the men.

And from Tana travelling to Gittarchan [Astrakhan on the Caspian Sea] you should take with you twenty-five days' provisions, that is to say, flour and salt fish, for as to meat you will find enough of it at all the places along the road. And so also at all the chief stations noted in going from one country to another in the route, according to the number of days set down above, you should furnish yourself with flour and salt fish; other things you will find in sufficiency, and especially meat.

The road you travel from Tana to Cathay is perfectly safe, whether by day or by night, according to what the merchants say who have used it. Only if the merchant, in going or coming, should die upon the road, everything belonging to him will become the perquisite of the lord of the country in which he dies, and the officers of the lord will take possession of all. And in like manner if he die in Cathay. But if his brother be with him, or an intimate friend and comrade calling himself his brother, then to such an one they will surrender the property of the deceased, and so it will be rescued.

And there is another danger: this is when the lord of the country dies, and before the new lord who is to have the lordship is proclaimed; during such intervals there have sometimes been irregularities practised on the Franks, and other foreigners. (They call "Franks" all the Christians of these parts from Romania [the Byzantine empire] westward.) And neither will the roads be safe to travel until the other lord be proclaimed who is to reign in room of him who is deceased.

Cathay is a province which contains a multitude of cities and towns. Among others there is one in particular, that is to say the capital city, to which is great resort of merchants, and in which there is a vast amount of trade; and this city is called Cambalec [Beijing]. And the said city hath a circuit of one hundred miles, and is all full of people and houses and of dwellers in the said city.

You may calculate that a merchant with a dragoman, and with two menservants, and with goods to the value of twenty-five thousand golden florins, should spend on his way to Cathay from sixty to eighty sommi of silver, and not more if he manage well; and for all the road back again from Cathay to Tana, including the expenses of living and the pay of servants, and all other charges, the cost will be about five sommi per head of pack animals, or something less. And you may reckon the sommo to be worth five golden florins. You may reckon also that each ox-waggon will require one ox, and will carry ten cantars Genoese weight; and the camel-waggon will require three camels, and will carry thirty cantars Genoese weight; and the horse-waggon will require one horse, and will commonly carry six and a half cantars of silk, at two hundred and fifty Genoese pounds to the cantar. And a bale of silk may be reckoned at between one hundred and ten and one hundred and fifteen Genoese pounds.

You may reckon also that from Tana to Sara[i] the road is less safe than on any other part of the journey; and yet even when this part of the road is at its worst, if you are some sixty men in the company you will go as safely as if you were in your own house.

Anyone from Genoa or from Venice, wishing to go to the places above-named, and to make the journey to Cathay, should carry linens with him, and if he visit Organci [Urgench in modern Turkmenistan] he will dispose of these well. In Organci he should purchase sommi of silver, and with these he should proceed without making any further investment, unless it be some bales of the very finest stuffs which go in small bulk, and cost no more for carriage than coarser stuffs would do.

Merchants who travel this road can ride on horseback or on asses, or mounted in any way that they list to be mounted.

Whatever silver the merchants may carry with them as far as Cathay the lord of Cathay will take from them and put into his treasury. And to merchants who thus bring silver they give that paper money of theirs in exchange. This is of yellow paper, stamped with the seal of the lord aforesaid. And this money is called balishi; and with this money you can readily buy silk and all other merchandise that you have a desire to buy. And all the people of the country are bound to receive it. And yet you shall not pay a higher price for your goods because your money is of paper. And of the said paper money there are three kinds, one being worth more than another, according to the value which has been established for each by that lord.

And you may reckon that you can buy for one sommo of silver nineteen or twenty pounds of Cathay silk, when reduced to Genoese weight, and that the sommo should weigh eight and a half ounces of Genoa, and should be of the alloy of eleven ounces and seventeen deniers to the pound.

You may reckon also that in Cathay you should get three or three and a half pieces of damasked silk for a sommo; and from three and a half to five pieces of nacchetti [cloths] of silk and gold, likewise for a sommo of silver.

Questions

1. What does Pegolotti see as the chief dangers for merchants traveling to China?

2. What role does the city of Urgench play in the flow of trade across Eurasia as it is described by Pegolotti?

3. How well informed does Pegolotti seem to be about mercantile affairs in the lands he discusses?

Chihab Al-'Umari, The Pilgrimage of Mansa Musa (1342–1349)

The following account of Mansa Musa's 1324 visit to Cairo has circulated widely since the fourteenth century. The author, Chihab Al-'Umari (1300–1384), was born in Damascus and visited Cairo shortly after Mansa Musa's highly visible stay. Mansa Musa, king of Mali, traveled with a large, well-supplied caravan to perform the *hajj*—the pilgrimage to Mecca incumbent upon all Muslims who can afford the journey. When Al-'Umari arrived in Cairo, people were still talking about the extraordinary visit of a monarch who brought so much wealth that his spending and alms-giving undermined the price of gold in Egypt for the next decade. The following selections provide descriptions of the Malian kingdom, the tribute system that provided abundant gold for the Malian king, Mansa Musa's piety, and the effect of his retinue's presence on the Cairene economy. As you read, remember that Al-'Umari, writing at least two decades later, relied on what people who met Mansa Musa had to say. The fact that he was not a direct witness does not make his account unreliable, but it does raise questions about how information was relayed from one person to the next in the fourteenth century.

[S]ultan Mūsā the king of [Mali] * * * came to Egypt on the Pilgrimage. He was staying in [the] Qarāfa [district of Cairo] and Ibn Amīr Ḥājib was governor of Old Cairo and Qarāfa at that time. A friendship grew up between them and this sultan Mūsā told him a great deal about himself and his country and the people of the Sūdān who were his neighbours. One of the things which he told him was that his country was very extensive and contiguous with the Ocean. By his sword and his armies he had conquered 24 cities each with its surrounding district with villages and estates. * * * He has a truce with the gold-plant people, who pay him tribute.

Ibn Amīr Ḥājib said that he asked him about the gold-plant, and he said: "It is found in two forms. One is found in the spring and blossoms after the rains in open country. It has leaves like grass and its roots are gold. The other kind is found all the year round at known sites on the banks of the Nīl and is dug up. There are holes there and roots of gold are found like stones or gravel and gathered up." * * * Sultan Mūsā told Ibn Amīr Ḥājib that gold was his prerogative and he collected the crop as a tribute except for what the people of that country took by theft.

But * * * in fact he is given only a part of it as a present by way of gaining his favour, and he makes a profit on the sale of it, for they have none in their country. * * *

[I]t is a custom of his people that if one of them should have reared a beautiful daughter he offers her to the king as a concubine and he possesses her without a marriage ceremony as slaves are possessed, and this in spite of the fact that Islam has triumphed among

---

SOURCE: *Corpus of Early Arabic Sources for West African History,* translated by J. F. P. Hopkins, edited by N. Levtzion and J. F. P. Hopkins (Cambridge: Cambridge University Press, 1981), pp. 267–71.

them and that * * * this sultan Mūsā was pious and assiduous in prayer, [Quran] reading, and mentioning God.

"I said to him (said Ibn Amīr Ḥājib) that this was not permissible for a Muslim, whether in law or reason and he said: 'Not even for kings?' and I replied: 'No! Not even for kings! Ask the scholars!' He said: 'By God, I did not know that. I hereby leave it and abandon it utterly!'

"I saw that this sultan Mūsā loved virtue and people of virtue. He left his kingdom and appointed as his deputy there his son Muḥammad and emigrated to God and His Messenger. He accomplished the obligations of the Pilgrimage, visited [the tomb of] the Prophet [at Medina] (God's blessing and peace be upon him!) and returned to his country with the intention of handing over his sovereignty to his son and abandoning it entirely to him and returning to Mecca the Venerated to remain there as a dweller near the sanctuary; but death overtook him, may God (who is great) have mercy upon him."

* * *

"This sultan Mūsā, during his stay in Egypt both before and after his journey to the Noble Ḥijāz, maintained a uniform attitude of worship and turning towards God. It was as though he were standing before Him because of His continual presence in his mind. He and all those with him behaved in the same manner and were well-dressed, grave, and dignified. He was noble and generous and performed many acts of charity and kindness. He had left his country with 100 loads of gold which he spent during his Pilgrimage on the tribes who lay along his route from his country to Egypt, while he was in Egypt, and again from Egypt to the Noble Ḥijāz and back. As a consequence he needed to borrow money in Egypt and pledged his credit with the merchants at a very high rate of gain so that they made 700 dinars profit on 300. Later he paid them back amply. He sent to me 500 mithqals of gold by way of honorarium.

* * *

"This man flooded Cairo with his benefactions. He left no court emir nor holder of a royal office without the gift of a load of gold.

The Cairenes made incalculable profits out of him and his suite in buying and selling and giving and taking. They exchanged gold until they depressed its value in Egypt and caused its price to fall."

* * *

[W]hen he made the Pilgrimage * * * the sultan was very open-handed towards the pilgrims and the inhabitants of the Holy Places. He and his companions maintained great pomp and dressed magnificently during the journey. He gave away much wealth in alms. * * *

Gold was at a high price in Egypt until they came in that year. The mithqal did not go below 25 *dirhams* and was generally above, but from that time its value fell and it cheapened in price and has remained cheap till now. The mithqal does not exceed 22 *dirhams* or less. This has been the state of affairs for about twelve years until this day by reason of the large amount of gold which they brought into Egypt and spent there.

Questions

1. How does Al-'Umari choose to document Mansa Musa's piety?

2. What is Al-'Umari's attitude toward Mansa Musa's incredible wealth?

3. Al-'Umari's retelling of a conversation between Mansa Musa and the governor of Cairo suggests that gold was the product of plants. Does this fanciful description undermine the reliability of other aspects of this account? Why or why not?

Casebook

Mobilizing for War in the Age of the Mongols

Although military technology did not differ dramatically across Afro-Eurasia in the eleventh through the fourteenth centuries, there were significant differences in the ways armies were conscripted, organized, and fielded. Moreover, armies related to their societies differently. For example, in settled societies military training is a distraction from the pursuit of other forms of economic productivity, but in a nomadic society, a horseman is more integral to general social and economic pursuits, so there can be less differentiation between martial and other goals. In most societies, the elites saw themselves as participants in military culture, and many hunted and rode horses as leisure—Chinese elites were a notable exception. Nevertheless, China wanted a skilled cavalry and at times recruited horsemen from central Asia.

Regardless of differences, all societies had to find ways of feeding and equipping the military, and motivating and disciplining the troops. As you will see from the following documents, various societies found different approaches to these problems. Another commonality across most of Afro-Eurasia was the influence of the Mongols. The painting of Sir Geoffrey Luttrell is the only source in this group that comes from the period after the Mongol threat had been eclipsed. The other sources are all either about Mongols or people who were worried about central Asian nomads.

These documents show multiple adaptations to shared sets of problems. As you read, pay attention both to questions of military effectiveness as well as to the material and cultural consequences of mobilization on society at large.

Images of Mongol Horsemen and a Medieval European Knight (fourteenth and fifteenth centuries)

The two images below show different ways of depicting, and perhaps conceptualizing, warriors in the fourteenth century. The first comes from the Luttrell Psalter (a psalter is a book containing psalms from the Old Testament). This was commissioned by an English knight, Sir Geoffrey Luttrell, and produced sometime between 1320 and 1340. The image shows Sir Geoffrey mounted on his war horse with his wife handing him his great helm and lance, while his daughter-in-law holds his shield. Both the shield and the horse's trapper (the cloth placed over the horse) bear the Luttrell family's coat of arms, a diagonal silver line between six silver swifts. The second image is from a fifteenth-century manuscript copy of the *Jami' al-tawarikh* (Compendium of Chronicles) by Rashid al-Din (1247–1318). He was commissioned to write this by Ghazan Khan (1271–1304), the Mongol ruler of Persia (see The Rise of Chinggis Khan, in this chapter). It shows dismounted Mongol warriors with their recurved bows fighting mounted opponents with small round shields.

Sir Geoffrey Luttrell on his war horse and in armor

SOURCE: Luttrell Psalter, in the collection of the British Library. HIP/Art Resource, NY.

Mongolian warriors

Questions

1. Compare the equipment shown in the Luttrell Psalter illustration with that in the illustration from the *Jami' al-tawarikh*. What differences or similarities do you see?

2. Which of these warriors would have cost more to equip? Which could move faster? Which would have an advantage in close-range fighting?

SOURCE: Rashid al-Din, *Jami' al-tawarikh*. AKG Images.

3. What makes Luttrell more identifiable as an individual than the Mongol soldiers? How does this reflect different ideas about warfare in medieval Afro-Eurasia?

'Ala-ad-Din 'Ata-Malik Juvaini, Genghis Khan: The History of the World Conqueror (mid-thirteenth century)

The Mongol army that carried out the great conquests of the thirteenth century was organized very differently from those of the settled peoples of Afro-Eurasia. In Afro-Eurasia armies were recruited in a great variety of ways. Some men served for pay; some received land in return for military service; and in some Muslim countries slaves were used as soldiers. When these armies assembled, their members often differed greatly in armament, training, and organization. Discipline, both on and off the battlefield, was often not very good. The following description of the Mongol military is from 'Ala-ad-Din 'Ata-Malik Juvaini's *History of the World Conqueror*. Juvaini (1226–1283) was a Persian historian and administrator. In the 1240s and 1250s he made two trips to Mongolia, where he began writing his history. In 1256 he entered the service of the Mongol Hülügü and accompanied him on the conquests of Persia and Iraq, which culminated with the destruction of Baghdad and the death of the last Abbasid caliph in 1258. Thereafter he became a provincial governor for the Mongols.

What army in the whole world can equal the Mongol army? In time of action, when attacking and assaulting, they are like trained wild beasts out after game, and in the days of peace and security they are like sheep, yielding milk, and wool, and many other useful things. In misfortune and adversity they are free from dissension and opposition. It is an army after the fashion of a peasantry, being

SOURCE: 'Ala-ad-Din 'Ata-Malik Juvaini, *Genghis Khan: The History of the World Conqueror,* translated from the text of Mizra Muhammad Qazvini by J. A. Boyle (Seattle: University of Washington Press, 1997), pp. 30–32.

liable to all manner of contributions (*mu'an*) and rendering without complaint whatever is enjoined upon it, whether *qupchur*, occasional taxes ('*avārizāt*), the maintenance (*ikhrājāt*) of travellers or the upkeep of post stations (*yam*) with the provision of mounts (*ulagh*) and food ('*ulūfāt*) therefor. It is also a peasantry in the guise of an army, all of them, great and small, noble and base, in time of battle becoming swordsmen, archers and lancers and advancing in whatever manner the occasion requires. Whenever the slaying of foes and the attacking of rebels is purposed, they specify all that will be of service for that business, from the various arms and implements down to banners, needles, ropes, mounts and pack animals such as donkeys and camels; and every man must provide his share according to his ten or hundred. On the day of review, also, they display their equipment, and if only a little be missing, those responsible are severely punished. Even when they are actually engaged in fighting, there is exacted from them as much of the various taxes as is expedient, while any service which they used to perform when present devolves upon their wives and those of them that remain behind. Thus if work be afoot in which a man has his share of forced labour (*bīgār*), and if the man himself be absent, his wife goes forth in person and performs that duty in his stead.

The reviewing and mustering of the army has been so arranged that they have abolished the registry of inspection (*daftar-i-'arz*) and dismissed the officials and clerks. For they have divided all the people into companies of ten, appointing one of the ten to be the commander of the nine others; while from among each ten commanders one has been given the title of "commander of the hundred," all the hundred having been placed under his command. And so it is with each thousand men and so also with each ten thousand, over whom they have appointed a commander whom they call "commander of the *tümen*." In accordance with this arrangement, if in an emergency any man or thing be required, they apply to the commanders of *tümen*; who in turn apply to the commanders of thousands, and so on down to the commanders of tens. There is a true equality in this; each man toils as much as the next, and no difference is made between them, no attention being paid to wealth or power. If there is a sudden call for soldiers an order is issued that so many thousand men must present themselves in such and such a place at such and such an hour of that day or night. *"They shall not retard it* (their appointed time) *an hour; and they shall not advance it."* And they arrive not a twinkling of an eye before or after the appointed hour. Their obedience and submissiveness is such that if there be a commander of a hundred thousand between whom and the Khan there is a distance of sunrise and sunset, and if he but commit some fault, the Khan dispatches a single horseman to punish him after the manner prescribed: if his head has been demanded, he cuts it off, and if gold be required, he takes it from him.

How different it is with other kings who must speak cautiously to their own slave, bought with their own money, as soon as he has ten horses in his stable, to say nothing of when they place an army under his command and he attains to wealth and power; then they cannot displace him, and more often than not he actually rises in rebellion and insurrection! Whenever these kings prepare to attack an enemy or are themselves attacked by an enemy, months and years are required to equip an army and it takes a brimful treasury to meet the expense of salaries and allotments of land. When they draw their pay and allowances the soldiers' numbers increase by hundreds and thousands, but on the day of combat their ranks are everywhere vague and uncertain, and none presents himself on the battle-field. A shepherd was once called to render an account of his office. Said the accountant: "How many sheep remain?" "Where?" asked the shepherd. "In the register." "That," replied the shepherd, "is why I asked: there are none in the flock." This is a parable to be applied to their armies; wherein each commander, in order to increase the appropriation for his men's pay, declares, "I have so and so many men," and at the time of inspection they impersonate one another in order to make up their full strength.

Another *yasa* is that no man may depart to another unit than the hundred, thousand or ten to which he has been assigned, nor may he seek refuge elsewhere. And if this order be transgressed the man who transferred is executed in the presence of the troops, while he that received him is severely punished. For this reason no man can give refuge to another; if (for example) the commander be a prince, he does not permit the meanest person to take refuge in his company and so avoids a breach of the *yasa*. Therefore no man can take liberties with his commander or leader, nor can another commander entice him away.

Questions

1. What strikes Juvaini as most remarkable about the Mongol army?

2. What does he mean by the comments that "it is an army after the fashion of a peasantry" and "a peasantry in the guise of an army"?

3. How does Juvaini compare the Mongol military organization to those he was familiar with in Persia and Iraq?

Ouyang Xiu and Fan Zhen, Conscription and Professional Soldiers in Song China (960–1127 CE)

The northern Song dynasty (960–1127 CE) was the largest empire on earth, and also the richest; its army often had well over 1 million men—far more than any other state of that era. But most of the time it was on the defensive against nomadic invaders from the north, to whom it succumbed in 1127.

The Song could not raise enough high-quality horses themselves, and had to import them from central Asian pastoralists. The large infantry forces they could raise were not fast enough to contend with nomadic cavalry, and were prohibitively expensive to feed if stationed along the semi-arid northern frontier. Moreover, after a mutiny had nearly destroyed the previous (Tang) dynasty, the Song had strengthened civilian control of its armies—but at the cost of weakening them. Defense and defense costs were central issues in debates that ran throughout the dynasty's life.

The two brief texts excerpted here come from high-ranking, reform-minded civilian politicians who favored reducing reliance on professional soldiers and relying more on conscription. There had been a universal draft in the Qin and early Han dynasties, and various modified draft systems in other periods. Although farmers could quickly learn the skills needed for local self-defense tasks, or serve the army as porters, learning the sophisticated horsemanship and archery needed on the northern frontiers would have required a long, very burdensome service period. The professional army, however, attracted many of the "wrong" people, and cost a great deal even during peacetime. Spelling has been updated in the following excerpts to reflect modern orthography.

FROM A MEMORIAL BY OUYANG XIU, C. 1040

The weakness of our forces has been exposed recently by the defeat sustained on the western frontier by our troops under Qi Zongju. If only the troops were hardy and efficient it might be considered justifiable to expend the resources of the farming class upon their maintenance. But what reason have we for maintaining the mere pretence of an army, composed as it is of such proud, lazy, and useless men?

The ancient practice was to give the strong and robust fellows of the farming class military drill and instruction in the intervals between the agricultural seasons, keeping them free for their farming work at other times. But this practice no longer obtains. The recruiting officers go out in times of dearth, measuring the height of the men, testing their strength, and enrolling them in the standing army. Those of better physique are drafted into the Imperial Army, while those of inferior standard are allocated to the Provincial Corps. The recruiting officers are rewarded according to the number of recruits they enroll. In times of dearth and poverty it is only natural that there should be competition to enter the army. So it has come about that after every period of famine, the strong and robust have been found in the army, while the older and feebler folk have been left on the fields.

I am not unaware of the criticism that if such men were not received into the army at such times they might turn to banditry for a living. But the pity is that while such critics are conscious of

---

SOURCE: H. R. Williamson, *Wang An-Shih: A Chinese Statesman and Educationalist of the Song Dynasty* (London: Arthur Probsthain, 1935), vol. 1, pp. 187, 189–90.

the danger that these men might become robbers for a short period, they seem completely to overlook the fact that once they are enrolled in the regular army they become robbers for practically the whole of their lives.

FROM A MEMORIAL BY FAN ZHEN, C. 1260

Though taxation is heavy the revenue remains insufficient. The chief cause for this is to be found in the size of our standing army. It is said that this is essential to our frontier policy, as we must be prepared for the Qitans. But, as a matter of fact, the Qitans have made no incursion southwards for over fifty years. Why? Because it is much more to their advantage to go on receiving our handsome tribute gifts of money and silk, and to maintain the peace. But supposing they were to decide to launch an attack. In that case I venture to predict that the only defenders of our cities north of the Yellow River would be found to be composed of women and girls. For the soldiery who are stationed in the districts, and who engage in no farming or other productive work, would be found quite useless.

And yet we continue to maintain them at the expense of the people. The policy of creating and maintaining a standing army leads to a great decrease in the numbers of those engaged in agriculture. This, of course, means that great areas of arable land lie fallow. This in its turn involves the people in heavier taxation and an increase of the burden of public services. So the loyalty of the people gets strained, and cannot be relied upon.

On the contrary, the policy of raising Militia or People's Corps, making soldiers of them while they continue their work of farming, tends to eliminate these evils. The number engaged in farming operations is not decreased, more land gets tilled, taxation is lighter, and the loyalty of the people remains staunch and true.

It is surely preferable to prepare to meet the Qitans by a policy which ensures the loyalty of the people than by pressing a policy which tends to deprive the State of such an asset. I am convinced that if we pursue our present policy our resources both in money and men will be exhausted before the enemy appears. Whereas our revenue will be sufficient and our military strength more than adequate, if we adopt a policy of making soldier-farmers of our people.

Questions

1. What do each of these officials object to about the professional standing army?

2. What advantages do they see in training and mobilizing farmer-soldiers?

3. What assumptions do these writers make about how people think and act? What assumptions are made about the sources of their state's strength and weakness?

Ziya' al-Din Barani, The Challenges of Raising an Army (1357)

Alauddin Khilji (ruled 1296–1316), part of the second Muslim dynasty to rule the Delhi Sultanate, is best remembered for his attack on Chittor. Legend has it that Alauddin seized the city in order to possess the beautiful queen Rani Padmini, a story recounted in the epic poem *Padmavat*—though more recent scholarship emphasizes the strategic importance of the city. The sultanate was always vulnerable to attacks from central Asia, and the Khilji dynasty was engaged in territorial conquest of the south, so the military was an important part of the dynasty's success.

The following passage makes explicit some of the challenges of maintaining political power in a turbulent era. Like the Mongols and the Song, Alauddin had to worry about the caliber of his soldiers. Also like the Song, the sultanate faced real financial constraints to support the large army necessary to protect itself from the threat of Mongol invasion.

Ziya' al-Din Barani (1285–1357) was a Muslim political thinker from an aristocratic family that served the Delhi Sultanate. He wrote a history of thirteenth- and early fourteenth-century India and an important tract on Muslim social hierarchies in South Asia. Spelling has been updated in the following excerpt to reflect modern orthography.

After Sultan Alauddin had taken care to make these preparations against another inroad of the Mongols, he used to have discussions with his councillors both by day and night as to the means of effectually resisting and annihilating these marauders. * * *

The Sultan then took counsel with his advisers, everyone of whom was unequalled and eminently distinguished, saying: "To maintain an immense picked and chosen force well mounted, so that they may be fully equipped and efficient at all times, is impossible, without the expenditure of vast treasures; for one must give regularly every year whatever sum is fixed upon at first; and if I settle a high rate of pay upon the soldiery, and continue to disburse money to them at that rate annually, at the end of a few years, not withstanding all the treasure I possess, nothing will be left, and without treasure it is of course impossible to govern or deliberate.

"I am accordingly desirous of having a large force, well mounted, of picked and chosen men, expert archers, and well armed that will remain embodied for years; and I will give 234 *tankahs* to a *Murat-tab* and 78 *tankahs* to a *Du-aspah*; from the former of whom I shall require two horses with their corresponding equipments, and from the latter one with its usual gear. Consider now and inform me how this idea that has entered into my mind about raising a large force, and maintaining it permanently, may be carried into execution."

The councillors, endowed with abilities like those of Āśaf, exercised their brilliant intellects, and after some reflection unanimously expressed the following opinion before the throne: "As it has entered into your Majesty's heart, and become implanted there, to raise a large force and permanently maintained on small allowances such can never be accomplished unless horses, arms and all the equipments of a soldier, as well as subsistence for his wife and family, become excessively cheap, and are reduced to the price of water; for if your Majesty can succeed in lowering the price of pro-

SOURCE: Ziya' al-Din Barani, *The Reign of Alauddin Khilji*, translated by A. R. Fuller and A. Khallaque (Calcutta: Pilgrim Publishers, 1967), pp. 100–103, 128–29.

visions beyond measure, a large force can be raised and permanently maintained according to the idea that has entered your august mind; and by the aid of this vast force all fear of danger from the Mongols will be averted."

The Sultan then consulted with his trusty and experienced councillors and ministers, as to what he should do, in order that the means of livelihood might be made exceedingly cheap and moderate, without introducing capital punishment, torture, or severe [coercion]. The Sultan's ministers and advisers represented, that until fixed rules were established, and permanent regulations introduced for lowering prices, the means of livelihood would never get exceedingly cheap. First then, for the cheapening of grain, the benefit of which is common to all, they proposed certain measures, and by the adoption of these measures, grain became cheap, and remained so for years.

* * *

As soon then the cheapness of all necessaries of life had been secured, and a large standing army could be entertained, the Mongols were defeated each time they invaded Delhi or the Delhi territory, and were slain, or captured, and the standard of Islam obtained one signal victory after the other over them. Several thousand Mongols with ropes on their necks were brought to Delhi and trampled to death by elephants. Of their heads, they formed a large platform or made turrets of the Mongol skulls, and the stench in the city of the dead bodies of such as had been killed in battle or had been executed in Delhi, was very great. The army of Islam gained in fact such victories over the Mongols that a *Duaspah* would bring in ten Mongols with ropes on their necks, or a single Muslim trooper would drive one hundred Mongols before himself.

Questions

1. What was Alauddin's biggest constraint in fielding an army adequate to defend against the Mongols?

2. What strategy did Alauddin and his advisers pursue to address this

challenge? Whom else would this policy have benefited? Who might have opposed it?

3. What differences do you note between the concerns of Mongol, Chinese, and Indian rulers in this period? What can account for the similarities and the differences you note?

Chapter 11

CRISES AND RECOVERY IN AFRO-EURASIA, 1300s—1500s

Giovanni Boccaccio, The Decameron (1353)

The establishment of the Mongol Empire in the thirteenth century greatly promoted trade across Afro-Eurasia. The Black Death, known to the Europeans who lived through it as the Great Pestilence, was transmitted westward from the empire into Afro-Eurasia. It entered Sicily in September 1347. In the next five years it spread across Europe. The most common estimates are that it killed one-third to one-half of the population of Europe, a demographic catastrophe without parallel in European history. One of the most vivid descriptions of it was written by Giovanni Boccaccio (1313–1375) as an introduction to his *Decameron*, a collection of one hundred short stories which he portrays as being told by ten people who have fled the city of Florence to the countryside to escape the plague.

[In 1348] when in the illustrious city of Florence, there made its appearance that deadly pestilence, which, whether disseminated by the influence of the celestial bodies, or sent upon us mortals by God in His just wrath by way of retribution for our iniquities, had had its origin some years before in the East. * * *

SOURCE: Giovanni Boccaccio, *The Decameron*, translated by J. M. Rigg (London, 1903), pp. 5–11.

In Florence, despite all that human wisdom and forethought could devise to avert it, as the cleansing of the city from many impurities by officials appointed for the purpose, the refusal of entrance to all sick folk, and the adoption of many precautions for the preservation of health; despite also humble supplications addressed to God, and often repeated both in public procession and otherwise, by the devout; towards the beginning of the spring of the said year the doleful effects of the pestilence began to be horribly apparent by symptoms that [showed] as if miraculous.

* * * [I]n men and women alike it first betrayed itself by the emergence of certain tumours in the groin or the armpits, some of which grew as large as a common apple, others as an egg, some more, some less, which the common folk called gavoccioli. From the two said parts of the body this deadly gavocciolo soon began to propagate and spread itself in all directions indifferently; after which the form of the malady began to change, black spots or livid making their appearance in many cases on the arm or the thigh or elsewhere, now few and large, now minute and numerous. And as the gavocciolo had been and still was an infallible token of approaching death, such also were these spots on whomsoever they [showed] themselves. * * * [N]ot merely were those that recovered few, but almost all within three days from the appearance of the said symptoms, sooner or later, died, and in most cases without any fever or other attendant malady.

Moreover, * * * not merely by speech or association with the sick was the malady communicated to the healthy with consequent peril of common death; but any that touched the clothes of the sick or aught else that had been touched or used by them, seemed thereby to contract the disease.

* * *

In which circumstances, * * * divers[e] apprehensions and imaginations were engendered in the minds of such as were left alive, inclining almost all of them to the same harsh resolution, to wit, to shun and abhor all contact with the sick and all that belonged to them, thinking thereby to make each his own health secure. Among whom there were those who thought that to live temperately and avoid all excess would count for much as a preservative against seizures of this kind. Wherefore they banded together, and, dissociating themselves from all others, formed communities in houses where there were no sick, and lived a separate and secluded life, which they regulated with the utmost care, avoiding every kind of luxury, but eating and drinking very moderately of the most delicate viands and the finest wines, holding converse with none but one another, lest tidings of sickness or death should reach them, and diverting their minds with music and such other delights as they could devise. Others, the bias of whose minds was in the opposite direction, maintained, that to drink freely, frequent places of public resort, and take their pleasure with song and revel, sparing to satisfy no appetite, and to laugh and mock at no event, was the sovereign remedy for so great an evil: and that which they affirmed they also put in practice, so far as they were able, resorting day and night, now to this tavern, now to that, drinking with an entire disregard of rule or measure, and by preference making the houses of others, as it were, their inns, if they but saw in them aught that was particularly to their taste or liking. * * * Thus, adhering ever to their inhuman determination to shun the sick, as far as possible, they ordered their life. In this extremity of our city's suffering and tribulation the venerable authority of laws, human and divine, was abased and all but totally dissolved, for lack of those who should have administered and enforced them, most of whom, like the rest of the citizens, were either dead or sick, or so hard bested for servants that they were unable to execute any office; whereby every man was free to do what was right in his own eyes.

Not a few there were who belonged to neither of the two said parties, but kept a middle course between them, neither laying the same restraint upon their diet as the former, nor allowing themselves the same license in drinking and other dissipations as the latter, but living with a degree of freedom sufficient to satisfy their appetites, and not as recluses. They therefore walked abroad, carrying in their hands flowers or fragrant herbs or divers[e] sorts of spices, which they frequently raised to their noses * * * because the air seemed to be everywhere laden and reeking with the stench emitted by the dead and the dying. * * *

Some again, the most sound, perhaps, in judgment, as they were also the most harsh in temper, of all, affirmed that there was no medicine for the disease superior or equal in efficacy to flight; following which prescription a multitude of men and women, negligent of all but themselves, deserted their city, their houses, their estates, their kinsfolk, their goods, and went into voluntary exile, or migrated to the country parts, as if God in visiting men with this pestilence in requital of their iniquities would not pursue them with His wrath wherever they might be, but intended the destruction of such alone as remained within the circuit of the walls of the city; or deeming, perchance, that it was now time for all to flee from it, and that its last hour was come.

* * * Tedious were it to recount, how citizen avoided citizen, how among neighbours was scarce found any that [showed] fellow-feeling for another, how kinsfolk held aloof, and never met, or but rarely; enough that this sore affliction entered so deep into the minds of men and women, that in the horror thereof brother was forsaken by brother, nephew by uncle, brother by sister, and oftentimes husband by wife; nay, what is more, and scarcely to be believed, fathers and mothers were found to abandon their own children, untended, unvisited, to their fate, as if they had been strangers. Wherefore the sick of both sexes, whose number could not be estimated, were left without resource but in the charity of friends (and few such there were), or the interest of servants. * * *

It had been, as to-day it still is, the custom for the women that were neighbours and of kin to the deceased to gather in his house with the women that were most closely connected with him, to wail with them in common, while on the other hand his male kins-folk and neighbours, with not a few of the other citizens, and a due proportion of the clergy according to his quality, assembled without, in front of the house, to receive the corpse; and so the dead man was borne on the shoulders of his peers, with funeral pomp of taper and dirge, to the church selected by him before his death. Which rites, as the pestilence waxed in fury, were either in whole or in great part disused, and gave way to others of a novel order. For not only did no crowd of women surround the bed of the dying, but many passed from this life unregarded, and few indeed were they to whom were accorded the lamentations and bitter tears of sorrowing relations; nay, for the most part, their place was taken by the laugh, the jest, the festal gathering; observances which the women, domestic piety in large measure set aside, had adopted with very great advantage to their health. Few also there were whose bodies were attended to the church by more than ten or twelve of their neighbours, and those not the honourable and respected citizens; but a sort of corpse-carriers drawn from the baser ranks, who called themselves becchini and performed such offices for hire, would shoulder the bier, and with hurried steps carry it, not to the church of the dead man's choice, but to that which was nearest at hand, with four or six priests in front and a candle or two, or, perhaps, none; nor did the priests distress themselves with too long and solemn an office, but with the aid of the becchini hastily consigned the corpse to the first tomb which they found untenanted. The condition of the lower, and, perhaps, in great measure of the middle ranks, of the people [showed] even worse and more deplorable; for, deluded by hope or constrained by poverty, they stayed in their quarters, in their houses, where they sickened by thousands a day, and, being without service or help of any kind, were, so to speak, irredeemably devoted to the death which overtook them. Many died daily or nightly in the public streets; of many others, who died at home, the departure was hardly observed by their neighbours, until the stench of their putrefying bodies carried the tidings; and what with their corpses and the corpses of others who died on every hand the whole place was a sepulchre.

It was the common practice of most of the neighbours, moved no less by fear of contamination by the putrefying bodies than by charity towards the deceased, to drag the corpses out of the houses with their own hands, aided, perhaps, by a porter, if a porter was to be had, and to lay them in front of the doors, where any one who made the round might have seen, especially in the morning, more of them than he could count; afterwards they would have biers brought up, or, in default, planks, whereon they laid them. * * * And times without number it happened, that, as two priests, bearing the cross, were on their way to perform the last office for some one, three or four biers were brought up by the porters in rear of them, so that, whereas the priests supposed that they had but one corpse to bury, they discovered that there were six or eight, or sometimes more. Nor, for all their number, were their obsequies honoured by either tears or lights or crowds of mourners; rather, it was come to this, that a dead man was then of no more account than a dead goat would be to-day.

Questions

1. What are the physical symptoms of the plague as described by Boccaccio? What possible causes does he give for its outbreak?

2. How do the people of Florence try to deal with the outbreak in their city? How effective are their efforts?

3. What is the impact of the plague on the behavior of the people of Florence?

The Ordinance of Laborers (1349)

In England, the bubonic plague killed more than 60 percent of the population. With such a high death toll, there was a scarcity of workers of all kinds; wages roughly doubled, and prices rose as well. In response, King Edward III issued the Ordinance of Laborers in June 1349, and Parliament passed more specific legislation soon thereafter, in February 1351. The legislation sought to control wages, to keep them at pre-plague levels and protect the social order. It forced people without independent means to work, with the length of service and the terms regulated by the courts. Refusal could result in imprisonment.

Although the legislation appears to have depressed wages for a few years, it was not consistently enforced and proved ineffective. Employers and workers found ways to avoid the measures. By the early 1350s, wages resumed their increase, which continued for the better part of the next century.

The king to the sheriff of Kent, greeting. Because a great part of the people, and especially of workmen and servants, late died of the pestilence, many seeing the necessity of masters, and great scarcity of servants, will not serve unless they may receive excessive wages,

SOURCE: Albert Beebe White and Wallace Notestein, eds. *Source Problems in English History* (New York: Harper and Brothers, 1915).

and some rather willing to beg in idleness, than by labor to get their living; we, considering the grievous incommodities, which of the lack especially of ploughmen and such laborers may hereafter come, have upon deliberation and treaty with the prelates and the nobles, and learned men assisting us, of their mutual counsel ordained:

That every man and woman of our realm of England, of what condition he be, free or bond, able in body, and within the age of threescore years, not living in merchandise, nor exercising any craft, nor having of his own whereof he may live, nor proper land, about whose tillage he may himself occupy, and not serving any other, if he in convenient service, his estate considered, be required to serve, he shall be bounden to serve him which so shall him require; and take only the wages, livery, meed, or salary, which were accustomed to be given in the places where he oweth to serve, the twentieth year of our reign of England, or five or six other common years next before. Provided always, that the lords be preferred before other in their bondmen or their land tenants, so in their service to be retained; so that nevertheless the said lords shall retain no more than be necessary for them; and if any such man or woman, being so required to serve, will not the same do, that proved by two true men before the sheriff or the constables of the town where the same shall happen to be done, he shall anon be taken by them or any of them, and committed to the next gaol, there to remain under strait keeping, till he find surety to serve in the form aforesaid.

Item, if any reaper, mower, or other workman or servant, of what estate or condition that he be, retained in any man's service, do depart from the said service without reasonable cause or license, before the term agreed, he shall have pain of imprisonment. And that none under the same pain presume to receive or to retain any such in his service.

Item, that no man pay, or promise to pay, any servant any more wages, liveries, meed, or salary than was wont, as afore is said; nor that any in other manner shall demand or receive the same, upon pain of doubling of that, that so shall be paid, promised, required, or received, to him which thereof shall feel himself grieved, pursuing for the same; and if none such will pursue, then the same to be applied to any of the people that will pursue; and such pursuit shall be in the court of the lord of the place where such case shall happen.

Item, if the lords of the towns or manors presume in any point to come against this present ordinance either by them, or by their servants, then pursuit shall be made against them in the counties, wapentakes, tithings, or such other courts, for the treble pain paid or promised by them or their servants in the form aforesaid; and if any before this present ordinance hath covenanted with any so to serve for more wages, he shall not be bound by reason of the same covenant, to pay more than at any other time was wont to be paid to such person; nor upon the said pain shall presume any more to pay.

Item, that saddlers, skinners, white-tawers, cordwainers, tailors, smiths, carpenters, masons, tilers, [shipwrights], carters, and all other artificers and workmen, shall not take for their labor and workmanship above the same that was wont to be paid to such persons the said twentieth year, and other common years next before, as afore is said, in the place where they shall happen to work; and if any man take more, he shall be committed to the next gaol, in manner as afore is said.

Item, that butchers, fishmongers, hostelers, breweres, bakers, puters, and all other sellers of all manner of victual, shall be bound to sell the same victual for a reasonable price, having respect to the price that such victual be sold at in the places adjoining, so that the same sellers have moderate gains, and not excessive, reasonably to be required according to the distance of the place from whence the said victuals be carried; and if any sell such victuals in any other manner, and thereof be convict in the manner and form aforesaid, he shall pay the double of the same that he so received, to the party damnified, or, in default of him, to any other that will pursue in this behalf: and the mayors and bailiffs of cities, boroughs, merchant-towns, and others, and of the ports and places of the sea, shall have power to inquire of all and singular which shall in any thing offend the same, and to levy the said pain to the use of them at whose suit such offenders shall be convict; and in case that the same mayors or bailiffs be negligent in doing execution of the premises, and thereof be convict before our justices, by us to be assigned, then the same mayors and bailiffs shall be compelled by the same justices to pay the treble of the thing so sold to the party damnified, or to any other in default of him that will pursue; and nevertheless toward us they shall be grievously punished.

Item, because that many valiant beggars, as long as they may live of begging, do refuse to labor, giving themselves to idleness and vice, and sometime to theft and other abominations; none upon the said pain of imprisonment shall, under the color of pity or alms, give any thing to such, which may labor, or presume to favor them toward their desires, so that thereby they may be compelled to labor for their necessary living.

We command you, firmly enjoining, that all and singular the premises in the cities, boroughs, market towns, seaports, and other places in your bailiwick, where you shall think expedient, as well within liberties as without, you do cause to be publicly proclaimed, and to be observed and duly put in execution aforesaid; and this by no means omit, as you regard us and the common weal of our realm, and would save yourself harmless. Witness the king at Westminster, the 18th day of June. By the king himself and the whole council.

Like writs are directed to the sheriffs throughout England.

The king to the reverend father in Christ W. by the same grace bishop of Winchester, greeting. "Because a great part of the people," as before, until "for their necessary living," and then thus: And therefore we entreat you that the premises in every of the churches, and other places of your diocese, which you shall think expedient, you do cause to be published; directing the parsons, vicars, ministers of such churches, and others under you, to exhort and invite their parishioners by salutary admonitions, to labor, and to observe the ordinances aforesaid, as the present necessity requireth: and that you do likewise moderate the stipendiary chaplains of your said diocese, who, as it is said, do now in like manner refuse to serve without an excessive salary; and compel them to serve for the accustomed salary, as it behooveth them, under the pain of suspension and interdict. And this by no means omit, as you regard us and the common weal of our said realm. Witness, etc. as above. By the king himself and the whole council.

Like letters of request are directed to the serveral bishops of England, and to the keeper of the spiritualities of the archbishopric of Canterbury, during the vacancy of the see, under the same date.

Questions

1. Identify to whom the king issued this ordinance. How was it to be enforced, by whom, with whose support?

2. What is the significance of this legislation for beggars?

3. Identify the legal categories this document establishes. What are the major groups, and how do they relate to one another?

Ibn Battuta, Visit to Mombasa and Kilwa, Rhila (c. 1358)

Ibn Battuta (1304–c. 1368) was born in Tangier, Morocco. He studied Islamic law and in 1325 embarked on his first *hajj* to Mecca. The pilgrimage should have taken about a year and half—but Ibn Battuta traveled for twenty-four years, moving through the extensive *Dar-al-Islam* (areas ruled by Muslims) including Africa, Southwest Asia, central Asia, and India. His travels took him to places as diverse as Constantinople, Baghdad, and the Maldive Islands. He supported himself as a *qadi* (jurist) and so found work in numerous places. When he finally returned to Morocco, the sultan asked him to dictate his adventures. Whether due to the faulty memories of an aging man or deliberate fabrication, some segments of the *Rhila* (travels) do not correlate with other sources. Nevertheless, the work as a whole sheds light on the extensive world of educated, urbane elites connected through a shared belief in Islam. The following selections describe Ibn Battuta's visit to the Swahili coastal towns of East Africa.

———————————

   Manbasā [Mombasa] is a large island with two days' journey by sea between it and the land of the *Sawāḥil*. It has no mainland. Its trees are the banana, the lemon, and the citron. They have fruit which they call the *jammūn*, which is similar to the olive and its

———————————

SOURCE: Said Hamdun and Noël King, *Ibn Battuta in Black Africa* (Princeton, N.J.: Markus Wiener, 1975), pp. 21–22, 24–25.

stone is like its stone except that it is extremely sweet. There is no cultivation of grain among the people of this island: food is brought to them from the *Sawāhil*. The greater part of their food is bananas and fish. They are Shāfi'ī [a practice within Sunni Islam] by rite, they are a religious people, trustworthy and righteous. Their mosques are made of wood, expertly built. At every door of the mosques there are one or two wells. The depth of their wells is a cubit or two. They take water from them in a wooden container into which a thin stick of a cubit's length has been fixed. The ground around the well and the mosque is level. He who wants to enter the mosque washes his feet and enters. There is at its gate a piece of thick matting upon which he rubs his two feet. He who wants to make the ablution holds the pot between his thighs and pours water upon his hands and carries out the ablutions. All the people walk barefoot. We spent the night on this island and travelled by sea to the city of Kulwā [Kilwa]. [Kilwa is] a great coastal city. Most of its people are Zunūj, extremely black. They have cuttings on their faces like those on the faces of the Līmiyyīn of Janāda. * * * The city of Kulwā is amongst the most beautiful of cities and most elegantly built. All of it is of wood, and the ceiling of its houses are of *al-dīs* [reeds]. The rains there are great. They are a people devoted to the Holy War because they are on one continuous mainland with unbelieving Zunūj. Their uppermost virtue is religion and righteousness and they are Shāfi'ī in rite.

* * *

DESCRIPTION OF THE SULTAN OF KULWĀ

Its sultan at the time of my entry into Kulwā was Abū al-Muzaffar Ḥasan whose *kunya* [honorific title] was Abū al-Mawāhib [father of gifts] because of his many gifts and deeds of generosity. He was much given to razzias upon the land of the Zunūj; he raided them and captured booty. He used to set aside one fifth of it, which he spent in the ways indicated in the book of God the Exalted. He put the share of the kindred [of the prophet, the *sharīfs*] in a treasury by itself. When the *sharīfs* came to him he gave it to them. The *sharīfs* used to come to him from 'Irāq and Ḥijāz and other places. * * *

This sultan is a very humble man. He sits with the poor people [*faqīrs*] and eats with them, and gives respect to people of religion and of prophetic descent.

A STORY CONCERNING THE SULTAN OF KULWĀ'S DEEDS OF GENEROSITY

I was present with him on a Friday when he came out from the prayer and was returning to his house. He was confronted on the road by one of the Yemeni *faqīrs*. He said to him, "O father of gifts." He replied, "At your service, O *faqīr*, what is your need?" He said, "Give me these clothes which you are wearing." He replied, "Yes, I will give them to you." He said to him, "This very moment." He said, "Yes, this very moment." He went back to the mosque and went into the house of the preacher [*khatīb*]. He put on other clothes and took off those clothes. He said to the *faqīr*, "Enter and take them." So the *faqīr* went in, tied them in a piece of cloth and put them on his head and went away. The gratitude of the people to the sultan increased at the evidence of his humility and graciousness. His son and heir-apparent took that suit of clothes from the *faqīr* and compensated him for it with ten slaves. When the news reached the sultan of the gratitude of the people to him for that deed he ordered the *faqīr* to be given in addition ten head of fine slaves and two loads of ivory. (The greater part of their gifts are ivory and seldom do they give gold.) When this honourable and generous sultan was gathered to God (may God have mercy on him), his brother Dā'ūd succeeded him. He was the opposite from him. When a beggar came to him he said to him, "He who used to give has died, and he did not leave anything after him to be given."

Questions

1. This description of the sultan of Kilwa presents a ruler both belligerent and generous. How does Ibn Battuta reconcile these two different facets of a ruler?

2. As in many other passages of the book, Ibn Battuta's description of Mombasa is disjointed, with little apparent connection between the elements he chooses to mention. What captures his attention in Mom-

basa? Why might Ibn Battuta want to tell readers about these features of Mombasa and emphasize different things about Kilwa?

3. What social and religious values does this passage emphasize?

The Voyages of Zheng He (1405–1433)

The Ming dynasty in China (1368–1644) kept voluminous records, called the Ming Shi-lu (明實錄). They contain considerable information on the seven massive, state-funded naval ventures from 1405 to 1433, led by the explorer Zheng He. Ming officials sent dozens, perhaps hundreds of ships to the ports of what today are known as Southeast Asia, India, and as far away as East Africa. The records were compiled after the death of successive emperors by a history office established by the Grand Secretariat—that is, by court elites. They therefore present the mindset and views, the priorities and prejudices, of those within the imperial government, and they draw on official government records.

The following document addresses Zheng He's fifth and longest voyage (1417–1419). The emperor ordered a voyage to explore Hormuz and the African coast from Somalia to Zanzibar. The expedition provided a return trip to seventeen heads of state from South Asia who had all made their way to China after Zheng He's initial visits to their homelands, to present tribute to the Ming Court. It ventured from Aden to Mogadishu, Brawa (in today's Somalia), and Malindi (in today's Kenya) and returned with ambassadors from those countries as well as considerable tribute.

YONG-LE: YEAR 14, MONTH 12, DAY 10 (28 DEC 1416)

As the envoys from the various countries of Calicut, Java, Melaka, Champa, Sri Lanka, Mogadishu, Liu-shan, Nan-bo-li, Bu-la-wa, Aden, Samudera, Ma-lin, La-sa, Hormuz, Cochin, Nan-wu-li,

SOURCE: Geoff Wade, trans., *Southeast Asia in the Ming Shi-lu: An Open Access Resource* (Singapore: Asia Research Institute and the Singapore E-Press, National University of Singapore, 2005).

Sha-li-wan-ni and Pahang, as well as from the Old Port Pacification Superintendency, were departing to return home, suits of clothing made from patterned fine silks were conferred upon all of them. The eunuch Zheng He and others were sent with Imperial orders as well as embroidered fine silks, silk gauzes, variegated thin silks and other goods to confer upon the kings of these countries, to confer a seal upon Ke-yi-li, the king of the country of Cochin, and to enfeoff a mountain in his country as the "Mountain Which Protects the Country." The Emperor personally composed and conferred an inscription for the tablet, as follows: "The civilizing influences and Heaven and Earth intermingle. Everything which is covered and contained has been placed in the charge of the Moulder, who manifests the benevolence of the Creator. The world does not have two ultimate principles and people do not have two hearts. They are sorrowful or happy in the same way and have the same feelings and desires. How can they be divided into the near and the distant! One who is outstanding in ruling the people should do his best to treat the people as his children. The Book of Odes says: 'The Imperial domain stretches for thousands of li, and there the people have settled, while the borders reach to the four seas.' The Book of Documents says: 'To the East, extending to the sea, to the West reaching to the shifting sands and stretching to the limits of North and South, culture and civilizing influences reach to the four seas.' I rule all under Heaven and soothe and govern the Chinese and the *yi*. I look on all equally and do not differentiate between one and the other. I promote the ways of the ancient Sagely Emperors and Perspicacious Kings, so as to accord with the will of Heaven and Earth. I wish all of the distant lands and foreign regions to have their proper places. Those who respond to the influences and move towards culture are not singular. The country of Cochin is far away in the South-west, on the shore of the vast ocean, further distant than the other *fan* countries. It has long inclined towards Chinese culture and been accepting of civilizing influences. When the Imperial orders arrived, the people there went down on their hands and knees and were greatly excited. They loyally came to allegiance and then, looking to Heaven, they bowed and all said: 'How fortunate we are that the civilizing influences of the Chinese sages should reach us. For the last several years, the country has had fertile soil, and the people have had houses in which to live, enough fish and turtles to eat, and enough cloth and silk to make clothes. Parents have looked after their children and the young have respected their elders. Everything has been prosperous and pleasing. There has been no oppression or contention. In the mountains no savage beasts have appeared and in the streams no noxious fishes have been seen. The sea has brought forth treasures and the forests have produced excellent woods. Everything has been in bountiful supply, several times more bountiful than in ordinary times. There have been no destructive winds, and damaging rains have not occurred. Confusion has been eliminated and there is no evil to be found. This is all indeed the result of the civilizing influences of the Sage.' I possess but slight virtuous power. How could I have been capable of this! Is it not the elders and people who brought this about? I am now enfeoffing Ke-yi-li as king of the country and conferring upon him a seal so that he can govern the people. I am also enfeoffing the mountain in the country as 'Mountain Which Protects the Country.' An engraved tablet is to be erected on this mountain to record these facts forever. It will also be engraved as follows: The high peak which rules the land, guards this ocean state, It spits fire and fumes, bringing great prosperity to the country below, It brings rain and sunshine in a timely way, and soothes away troubles, It brings fertile soil and drives off evil vapours, It shelters the people, and eliminates calamities and disharmony, Families are joyful together, and people have plenty throughout the year, The mountain's height is as the ocean's depths! This poem is inscribed to record all for prosperity."

Questions

1. Identify the nature of the relationship between the Chinese empire and the peoples they encountered, as presented here. How does the author present those relationships? What kinds of terms does he use?

2. Analyze the document's use of the term *equality*. Does the author use the term consistently?

3. What does the author mean by "civilization"?

Leo Africanus, On Timbuktu (1526)

Leo Africanus (c. 1494–c. 1554) was born al-Hasan ibn Muhammad al-Wazzan al-Fasi in Granada. Given the difficulties for Muslims in Spain after the expulsion of the Moors, his family joined relatives in Fez, where al-Hasan grew up and studied at the university. As a young man he traveled with his uncle throughout the Maghreb, going as far south as Timbuktu, then part of the Songhai Empire. He later performed the *hajj* to Mecca, and traveled across the Mediterranean to Istanbul. In 1518 his ship was captured by pirates; he was eventually taken to Rome and presented to Pope Leo X. As a man of letters with extensive diplomatic knowledge, he was welcomed at the papal court. He was baptized as Leo Africanus in 1520.

The historical geography of Africa is Africanus's best known scholarly work. It was quickly translated from Italian and had several printings in the sixteenth century. Although he was well-traveled, it is unlikely that Africanus visited all the places he described. Like other early modern writers, he probably relied on relayed oral descriptions from other travelers. When Leo Africanus visited Timbuktu, it was a vibrant commercial city famous for its wealth and learning.

This name was in our times (as some think) imposed upon this kingdom from the name of a certain town, so called, which (they say) king Mansa Suleiman founded in the year of the Hegira 610 [1213 CE] and it is situated within twelve miles of a certain branch of the Niger. All the houses are now changed into cottages built of chalk, and covered with thatch. Howbeit there is a most stately temple [mosque] to be seen, the walls whereof are made of stone and lime; and a princely palace also built by a most excellent workman of Granada. Here are many shops of artificers [craftspersons], and merchants, and especially of such as weave linen and cotton cloth.

SOURCE: Leo Africanus, *The History and Description of Africa and of the Notable Things Therein Contained*, translated by Robert Brown (London: Hakluyt Society, 1896), vol. 3, pp. 824–26. Text modernized by Norton authors for this edition.

And hither do the Barbary [North African] merchants bring cloth of Europe.

All women of this region go with their faces covered, except maid-servants who sell all necessary victuals. The inhabitants and especially strangers there residing, are exceedingly rich, insomuch as the king that now is, married both his daughters to two rich merchants. Here are many wells containing most sweet water; and so often as the river Niger overflows, they convey the water thereof by certain sluices into the town. Grain, cattle, milk, and butter this region yields in great abundance, but salt is very scarce here. It is brought hither by land from Taghaza [also in modern-day Mali], which is five hundred miles distant. When I myself was here, I saw one camel load of salt sold for 80 ducats.

The rich king of Timbuktu has many plates and scepters of gold, some whereof weigh 1300 pounds. He keeps a magnificent and well furnished court. When he travels he rides upon a camel which is led by some of his noblemen. He does likewise when he goes to war, and all his soldiers ride upon horses. Whosoever will speak to this king must first fall down before his feet, and then taking up earth must sprinkle it upon his own head and shoulders. This custom is ordinarily observed by them that never saluted the king before, or come as ambassadors from other princes. He always has three thousand horsemen, and a great number of footmen that shoot poisoned arrows, attending on him. They often have skirmishes with those that refuse to pay tribute, and so many [prisoners] as they take they sell to the merchants of Timbuktu.

Very few horses are bred here. The merchants and courtiers keep certain little nags which they use to travel upon, but their best horses are brought out of Barbary. As soon as the king hears that any merchants are come to town with horses, he commands a certain number to be brought before him. Choosing the best for himself, he pays a most liberal price for them.

He so deadly hates all Jews that he will not admit any into his city. Any merchants he understands have dealings with Jews, he presently causes their goods to be confiscated.

Here are a great store of doctors, judges, priests, and other learned men that are bountifully maintained by the king's cost and charge.

And hither are brought diverse manuscripts or written books out of Barbary; they are sold for more money than any other merchandise.

The coin of Timbuktu is of gold without any stamps or superscription. In matters of small value they use certain shells brought out of Persia, four hundred of which shells are worth a ducat. Six pieces of their golden coin with two thirds parts weigh an ounce.

The inhabitants are people of a gentle and cheerful disposition, and spend a great part of the night in singing and dancing through all the streets of the city. They keep a great store of men and women slaves. Their town is in much danger of fire; at my second visit, half the town was almost burned in five hours time. Without the suburbs there are no gardens or orchards at all.

Questions

1. What features of a sophisticated economy are evident in this description of Timbuktu?

2. What connection did Timbuktu have to other regions?

3. Both Leo Africanus and Ibn Battuta (see Ibn Battuta, Visit to Mombasa and Kilwa, in this chapter) left records of their visits to Muslim cities in Africa. Compare their descriptions. What explains the similarities and differences in their accounts?

Bernal Díaz, A Spanish view of Tenochtitlán (1567)

Generally recognized by historians as the most important Spanish chronicler of the conquest, Bernal Díaz wrote *The True History of the Conquest of New Spain* at the end of his life. He completed it around 1567; it was sent to Spain in 1575 but not published until 1632, long

SOURCE: Bernal Díaz, *The True History of the Conquest of New Spain*, ed. A. P. Maudslay (London: Hakluy & Society, 1908) reprinted in Stuart Schwartz, ed., *Victors and Vanquished: Spanish and Nahua Views of the Conquest of Mexico* (Boston: Bedford / St Martins, 2000), pp. 133, 149–150.

after the author's death. Díaz opposed his *True History* to earlier works, written by intellectuals, men who had not experienced the conquest firsthand. Born in Spain, Díaz had been to Mexico twice before the Cortés expedition. He wrote his book to set the record straight about the role of colonists and common soldiers like himself.

Early next day we left Iztapalapa with a large escort of those great Caciques whom I have already mentioned. We proceeded along the Causeway which is here eight paces in width and runs so straight to the City of Mexico that it does not seem to me to turn either much or little, but, broad as it is, it was so crowded with people that there was hardly room for them all, some of them going to and others returning from Mexico, besides those who had come out to see us, so that we were hardly able to pass by the crowds of them that came; and the towers and cues were full of people as well as the canoes from all parts of the lake. It was not to be wondered at, for they had never before seen horses or men such as we are.

Gazing on such wonderful sights, we did not know what to say, or whether what appeared before us was real, for on one side, on the land, there were great cities, and in the lake ever so many more, and the lake itself was crowded with canoes, and in the Causeway were many bridges at intervals, and in front of us stood the great City of Mexico, and we—we did not even number four hundred soldiers! And we well remembered the words and warnings given us by the people of Huexotzingo and Tlaxcala and Tlamanalco, and the many other warnings that had been given that we should beware of entering Mexico, where they would kill us, as soon as they had us inside.

* * *

Now let us leave the great market place, and not look at it again, and arrive at the great courts and walls where the great Cue stands. Before reaching the great Cue there is a great enclosure of courts, it seems to me larger than the plaza of Salamanca, with two walls of masonry surrounding it and the court itself all paved with very smooth great white flagstones. And where there were not these stones it was cemented and burnished and all very clean, so that one could not find any dust or a straw in the whole place. . .

When we arrived there Moctezuma came out of an oratory where his cursed idols were, at the summit of the great Cue, and two priests came with him, and after paying great reverence to Cortés and to all of us he said: "You must be tired, Señor Malinche, from ascending this our great Cue," and Cortés replied through our interpreters who were with us that he and his companions were never tired by anything. Then Moctezuma took him by the hand and told him to look at his great city and all the other cities that were standing in the water, and the many other towns on the land round the lake, and that if he had not seen the great market place well, that from where they were they could see it better.

So we stood looking about us, for that huge and cursed temple stood so high that from it one could see over everything very well, and we saw the three causeways which led into Mexico, that is the causeway of Iztapalapa by which we had entered four days before, and that of Tacuba, along which later on we fled on the night of our great defeat, when Cuitlahuac the new prince drove us out of the city, as I shall tell later on, and that of Tepeaquilla, and we saw the fresh water that comes from Chapultepec which supplies the city, and we saw the bridges on the three causeways which were built at certain distances apart through which the water of the lake flowed in and out from one side to the other, and we beheld on that great lake a great multitude of canoes, some coming with supplies of food and others returning loaded with cargoes of merchandise; and we saw that from every house of that great city and of all the other cities that were built in the water it was impossible to pass from house to house, except by drawbridges which were made of wood or in canoes; and we saw in those cities Cues and oratories like towers and fortresses and all gleaming white, and it was a wonderful thing to behold; then the houses with flat roofs, and on the causeways other small towers and oratories which were like fortresses.

After having examined and considered all that we had seen we turned to look at the great market place and the crowds of people that were in it, some buying and others selling, so that the murmur and hum of their voices and words that they used could be heard more than a league off. Some of the soldiers among us who had been in many parts of the world, in Constantinople, and all over Italy, and in Rome, said that so large a market place and so full of people, and so well regulated and arranged, they had never beheld before.

Questions

1. What are some signs of Díaz's respect and wonder at Mexican civilization?

2. What are some signs of disgust and prejudice in this passage?

3. How does Díaz portray Moctezuma?

Galileo Galilei, Letter to Madame Cristina di Lorena, Grand Duchess of Tuscany (1615)

Galileo Galilei (1564–1642) was born to a relatively poor noble family. Sent to the University of Pisa to study medicine, he instead became interested in physics and mathematics. He became a professor of mathematics at Padua in 1592. He made important discoveries about falling objects that called Aristotelian physics into question, about the motion of the pendulum, and in several other areas. He also developed an improved water pump and other practical implements. He is best known, however, for inventing a telescope. The observations he made with it in 1610 confirmed the arguments of Copernicus (1473–1543) that the sun is the center of the solar system, and the earth and other planets move around it.

This position conflicted with the doctrine of the Catholic Church; Galileo was denounced in 1614, tried by the Inquisition in 1616, and warned against publicly advocating Copernicanism. Still, he persisted. Various powerful people, including the Pope, tried to arrange a compromise in which Galileo would be protected so long as he was relatively quiet in his support of heliocentrism; Galileo, however, continued to publish. In 1632 he was tried and convicted of heresy, and spent the rest of his life under house arrest.

In the letter excerpted below, Galileo addresses Cristina di Lorena (1565–1636), Grand Duchess of Tuscany—a descendant of French royalty who married into the Medici family, which had patronized Galileo.

Although Galileo had not yet been condemned by the Inquisition, and this letter was not made public until much later, it represents a forceful statement of views on the relationship between science and religious authority that the Catholic Church of his time was unwilling to accept. The Catholic Church stopped prohibiting books advocating heliocentrism in 1758, but it did not formally absolve Galileo until 1992.

Some years ago, as your Serene Highness well knows, I discovered many things in the heavens that had remained unseen until our own era. Perhaps because of their novelty, perhaps because of certain consequences which followed from them, these discoveries conflicted with certain propositions concerning nature which were commonly accepted by the philosophical schools. Hence no small number of professors became stirred up against me—almost as though I, with my own hand, had placed these things in heaven in order to disturb and obscure nature and the sciences. Displaying greater affection for their own opinions than for true ones, and, at the same time, forgetting that the multitude of truths contribute to inquiry by augmenting and establishing science, and not by diminishing and destroying it, these professors set about trying to deny and abolish these new discoveries. Although their very senses, had they seen fit to heed them attentively, would have rendered these things as certain, they nonetheless alleged various things and published various writings full of empty reasoning and containing—a still graver error— scattered testimonies from Holy Scripture. The latter were not only cited out of context, but had little to do with the matter at hand. * * *

Thus it is that these men persist in their primary objective, which is to try, by every means imaginable, to destroy me and all that is mine. They know that, in my astronomical and philosophical studies concerning the structure of the world, I maintain that the Sun, with-

SOURCE: *Introduction to Contemporary Civilization in the West*, 2nd ed., edited by the Contemporary Civilization Staff of Columbia College, Columbia University (New York: Columbia University Press, 1954), vol. 1, pp. 724–27.

out moving, remains stationary in the center of the revolution of celestial orbs; and that the Earth, turning about its own axis, revolves around the Sun as well. They are aware, moreover, that I proceed to confirm the above hypothesis (*posizione*), not simply by condemning the account of Ptolemy and Aristotle, but by bringing forward much conflicting evidence—in particular, certain natural effects, the causes of which cannot be explained in any other manner, and certain celestial effects, determined by the concordance of many new astronomical discoveries, which clearly confute the Ptolemaic system, and which admirably agree with and support the other hypothesis. Now, perhaps they are confused by the fact that certain other propositions, contrary to common opinion but affirmed by me, have been recognized as true. And thus unsure of their defenses on the battlefield of philosophy, they have sought to make a shield for their fallacious arguments out of the mantle of simulated piety and the authority of Scripture, applied by them with little intelligence to combat arguments which they have neither thought about nor understood. * * *

But who could with all certainty insist that the Scripture has chosen rigorously to confine itself to the strict and literal meaning of words when it speaks incidentally of the Earth, water, the Sun, and other creatures? And above all when it asserts something about these creatures which in no way touches upon the primary purpose of Holy Writ, which has to do with the service of God, the salvation of souls, and things far removed indeed from vulgar apprehension? Considering this, then, it seems to me that, when discussing natural problems, we ought to begin with sensory experience and logical demonstrations, and not with the authority of passages in Scripture. For both Nature and the Holy Scripture proceed alike from the Word of God, the latter being the dictate of the Holy Spirit, and the former being the utterly obedient executrix of Divine Law. Now, it is the case that Scripture finds it convenient, in order to accommodate itself to the understanding of everyone, to say many things which, from the bare meaning of the words it employs, differ in aspect from the absolute truth. But in just the opposite way, Nature is inexorable and immutable, never transcending the limits imposed upon her by law; and it is as though she feels no concern whether her deep reasons and hidden modes of operation shall ever be revealed to the understanding of humankind or not. From this it would seem that natural effects, either those which sensory experience sets before our eyes or those which are established by logical demonstration, ought never on any account to be called into question, much less condemned, on the basis of Scriptural passages whose words may appear to support a conflicting opinion. For not every Scriptural dictum is connected to conditions as severe as those which hold with respect to effects of Nature; nor does God reveal Himself less excellently to us in the effects of Nature than He does in the sacred utterances of Scripture. It is this, perchance, that Tertullian meant when he wrote: *We conclude that God is first cognized in Nature, then recognized in Doctrine: in Nature through His works; in Doctrine through His word preached.* * * *

I should judge that the authority of Scripture was intended principally to persuade men of certain articles and propositions which transcend the powers of human reason, and which could be made credible by no other science and by no means other than the very voice of the Holy Spirit. * * * But I do not feel it necessary to believe that God, Who gave us senses, reason, and intellect, should have wished us to postpone using these gifts; that He has somehow given us, by other means, the information which we can obtain with our own senses, reason, and intellect; nor that He should want us to deny the senses and reason when sensory experience and logical demonstration have revealed something to our eyes and minds! And above all I do not feel it necessary to believe this where a science [like astronomy] is concerned, only a tiny part of which is written about (and then in contradictory ways) in Scripture. * * *

Experience plainly indicated that, concerning the rest and motion of Sun and Earth, it was necessary for Scripture to assert what it did, in order that the popular capacity [for understanding] should be satisfied. For even in our own day, individuals far less rude still persist in the same opinion for reasons which, if they were well weighed and examined, would be found to be completely specious, and which experiment would show to be wholly false or altogether beside the point. Nor can we attempt to remove their ignorance, for they are incapable of grasping the contrary reasons, which depend upon the most delicate observations and the most subtle demonstrations, involving abstractions the comprehension of which demands a more vigorous imagination than they possess. And though the stability of the Sun and the motion of the Earth are more than certain and demonstrated to the wise, it is nonetheless necessary, in order to maintain belief amongst the innumerable vulgar, to assert the contrary. If a thousand ordinary men were interrogated on this matter, perhaps not a single one would be found who would not respond by saying that he thinks, and firmly believes, that the Sun moves and the Earth stands still. But such common popular assent must in no way be taken as an argument for the truth of what is being affirmed. For if we were to question the same men about the causes and motives which provide the basis for their belief, and then to contrast what they say with the experiments and reasons which lead a few to believe otherwise, we would find the former to have been persuaded by simple appearances and the shallowest and silliest objections, and the latter to have been persuaded by the most substantial reasons. It is obvious, then, how necessary it was [for Scripture] to attribute motion to the Sun and stability to the Earth. It was necessary in order not to confuse the limited understanding of the vulgar, and in order not to render them obstinate and antagonistic, and in order that they should have faith in the principal doctrines which have altogether to do with Faith. And if this had to be done, it is not at all to be wondered at that it was done with such consummate wisdom in divine Scripture.

Questions

1. How does Galileo think people should read the Bible? What should they do when it appears to conflict with evidence observed in nature?

2. Does Galileo believe that his position is consistent with Christian faith and church authority? Why or why not?

3. What do you think Galileo was trying to accomplish with this letter?

TEXT PERMISSIONS

ABÛ ÛTHMÂN AL- JÂHIZ: From *The Life and Works of Jāḥiẓ: Translations of Selected Texts* by Charles Pellat, translated from the French by D. M. Hawke. Copyright © 1969 Routledge & Kegan Paul. Reproduced by permission of Taylor & Francis Books UK.

AHMED ALI: The excerpt from *Al-Qur'ān: A Contemporary Translation* by Ahmed Ali (Princeton University Press, 1993) is reprinted by kind permission of Orooj Ahmed Ali.

ARRIAN: Reprinted by permission of the publishers and the Trustees of the Loeb Classical Library from *Arrian: Vol. II*, translated by E. Iliff Robson, B. D., Loeb Classical Library Volume 269, pp. 213–221 (odd), Cambridge, Mass.: Harvard University Press, First printed 1933. Loeb Classical Library ® is a registered trademark of the President and Fellows of Harvard College.

AVICENNA: From *The Life of Ibn Sina*, translated and edited by William E. Gohlman (Albany: State University of New York Press, 1974). Copyright © 1974 State University of New York. Reprinted by permission of the publisher.

WILLIAM THEODORE DE BARY AND IRENE BLOOM (EDS.): Excerpts from "Debate on Salt and Iron" and "Memorial on the Bone of the Buddha" from *Sources of Chinese Tradition* 2nd Ed., Vol. 1, compiled by William Theodore de Bary and Irene Bloom. Copyright © 1999 Columbia University Press. Reprinted with permission of the publisher.

BIBLE. CONTEMPORARY ENGLISH VERSION: Ezra 1:1–8 from the Contemporary English Version. Copyright © 1991, 1992, 1995 by American Bible Society. Used by Permission.

BIBLE. REVISED STANDARD VERSION: Genesis 6:9-8:22, 2 Kings 18–19 (excerpted), and 1 Maccabees 1:7-2:28 from the Revised Standard Version of the Bible, copyright 1952 [2nd edition, 1971] by the Division of Christian Education of the National Council of the Churches of Christ in the United States of America. Used by permission. All rights reserved.

FRANCIS WOODMAN CLEAVES (TRANS.): From *The Secret History of the Mongols*, translated by Francis Woodman Cleaves. Copyright © 1982 by the Harvard-Yenching Institute. Reprinted by permission.

CONFUCIUS: Excerpts from "Analects" from *Sources of Chinese Tradition*, Vol. 1, compiled by William Theodore de Bary, Wing-tsit Chan, Burton Watson. Copyright © 1960 Columbia University Press. Reprinted with permission of the publisher.

JERROLD S. COOPER: From *The Curse of Agade* by Jerrold S. Cooper, pp. 57, 59, 61, 63. Copyright © 1983 The Johns Hopkins University Press. Reprinted with permission of Johns Hopkins University Press.

RAFE DE CRESPIGNY (TRANS.): From *Emperor Huan & Emperor Ling* Vol. 1, translated by Rafe de Crespigny (Canberra, Australia: Faculty of Asian Studies,

321

Australian National University, 1989). Reprinted by permission of Australian National University.

DIODORUS SICULUS: Reprinted by permission of the publishers and the Trustees of the Loeb Classical Library from *Diodorus Siculus*: Vol. XII, translated by Francis R. Walton, Loeb Classical Library Volume 423, pp. 57–71 (odd), Cambridge, Mass.: Harvard University Press, Copyright © 1967 by the President and Fellows of Harvard College. Loeb Classical Library® is a registered trademark of the President and Fellows of Harvard College.

E. D. EDWARDS (ED.): From *Chinese Prose Literature of the T'ang Period A.D. 618–906*, Vol. 2, by E. D. Edwards (London: Arthur Probasthain, 1938), pp. 248–252.

ELECTRONIC TEXT CORPUS OF SUMERIAN LITERATURE: "Lament for Ur" from The Electronic Text Corpus of Sumerian Literature (http://etcsl.orinst.ox.ac.uk/), Oxford 1998–2006. Copyright © J. A. Black, G. Cunningham, E. Robson, and G. Zólyomi 1998, 1999, 2000; J. A. Black, G. Cunningham, E. Flückiger-Hawker, E. Robson, J. Taylor, and G. Zólyomi 2001; J. A. Black, G. Cunningham, J. Ebeling, E. Robson, J. Taylor, and G. Zólyomi 2002, 2003, 2004, 2005; G. Cunningham, J. Ebeling, E. Robson, and G. Zólyomi 2006. The authors have asserted their moral rights. Reprinted by permission of Faculty of Oriental Studies, University of Oxford.

AINSLIE T. EMBREE (ED.): "Rig-Veda," "Duties of the King," and "Three Edicts" from *Sources of Indian Tradition* 2nd Ed., Vol. 1 edited by Ainslie T. Embree. Copyright © 1988 Columbia University Press. Reprinted with permission of the publisher.

ROBERT O. FINK (TRANS.): From *Roman Military Records on Papyrus* edited by Robert O. Fink, pp. 248–249. Copyright 1971 by the Society for Classical Studies, founded in 1869 as the American Philological Association.

TIM FRIEND: "Fossil Find Confounds Human Family Tree," by Tim Friend. From *USA Today*, July 11, 2002. © 2002 Gannett. All rights reserved. Used by permission and protected by the Copyright Laws of the United States. The printing, copying, redistribution, or retransmission of this Content without express written permission is prohibited.

FRANCESCO GABRIELI (TRANS.): From *Arab Historians of the Crusades*, translated from Arabic by Francesco Gabrieli, translated from Italian by E. J. Costello. Translation copyright © 1969 by Routledge & Kegan Paul Ltd. Reprinted by permission of the publishers, University of California Press and Taylor and Francis Books UK.

GALILEO GALILEI: "Letter to Madame Cristina di Lorena, Grand Duchess of Tuscany," from *Introduction to Contemporary Civilization in the West* 2nd Ed., Vol. 1, edited by the Contemporary Civilization Staff at Columbia University. Copyright © 1946, 1954, 1961 Columbia University Press. Reprinted with permission of the publisher.

CLIVE GAMBLE: "The changes in behavior between Ancients and Moderns" and "Technological changes in hunting weapons" from *Timewalkers: The Prehistory of Global Colonization* by Clive Gamble (Penguin Books, 1994), pp. 160–161. Copyright © Clive Gamble, 1994. Reproduced by permission of Penguin Books Ltd.

S. D. GOITEIN (TRANS.): Excerpts republished with permission of Princeton University Press from *Letters of Medieval Jewish Traders*, translated by S. D. Goitein. Copyright © 1973 Princeton University Press; renewed 2001 Princeton University Press; permission conveyed through Copyright Clearance Center, Inc.

RACHAEL MOELLER GORMAN: "Cooking up Bigger Brains," by Rachael Moeller Gorman, *Scientific American,* January 2008, pp. 102–105. Reproduced with permission. Copyright © 2008 Scientific American, a division of Nature America, Inc. All rights reserved.

from *Southeast Asia in the Ming Shi-lu: An Open Access Resource* translated by Geoff Wade (Singapore: Asia Research Institute and the Singapore E-Press, National University of Singapore). The reproduction of the text is copyright © Geoff Wade, 2005 and is used by permission.

M. L. WEST (TRANS.): Excerpts republished with permission of I. B. Tauris & Co. Ltd. from *Hymns of Zoroaster: A New Translation of the Most Ancient Sacred Texts of Iran,* edited and translated by M. L. West. © 2010 M. L. West; permission conveyed through Copyright Clearance Center, Inc.

H. R. WILLIAMSON (ED.): From *Wang An-Shih: A Chinese Statesman and Educationalist of the Sung Dynasty,* Vol. 1, by H. R. Williamson (London: Arthur Probasthain, 1935), pp. 187, 189–190.

YANG HSIEN-YI: "The Magistrate and the Local Deity" from *The Man Who Sold a Ghost: Chinese Tales of the 3rd–6th Centuries,* translated by Yang Hsien-yi and Gladys Yang (Peking: Foreign Language Press, 1958). Reprinted by permission of Foreign Language Press.

YUAN CAI: "The Problems of Women" is reprinted with the permission of The Free Press, a division of Simon & Schuster, Inc. from *Chinese Civilization: A Sourcebook,* 2nd ed., edited by Patricia Buckley Ebrey. Copyright © 1981 by The Free Press, a Division of Simon & Schuster, Inc. Copyright © 1993 by Patricia Buckley Ebrey. All rights reserved.